Amazing Gifts

Amazing Gifts

Stories of Faith,
Disability,
and Inclusion

Mark I. Pinsky

 | ALBAN

Herndon, Virginia
www.alban.org

The Alban Institute
2121 Cooperative Way, Suite 100
Herndon, VA 20171

Cover design by Signal Hill

Library of Congress Cataloging-in-Publication Data

Pinsky, Mark I., 1947-
  Amazing gifts : stories of faith, disability, and inclusion / Mark I. Pinsky.
      p. cm.
  Includes index.
  ISBN 978-1-56699-421-7
  1. Church work with people with disabilities. 2. People with disabilities–Religious life. I. Title.
  BV4460.P56 2011
  259'.44–dc23
                          2011045516

11   12   13   14   15   VP   5   4   3   2   1

In memory of Reynolds Price

This book was made possible by generous donations from

The David and Lura Lovell Foundation
The Alice W. Dorr Foundation
The Clinton H. and Wilma T. Shattuck Foundation
David and Karen Miller
The HCS Foundation

We are deeply grateful for their support.

Contents

Foreword by Ginny Thornburgh   xi
Introduction   xix

Part 1
Empowering People and Congregations
1

1	A Spirit of Hospitality / Sue Montgomery	5
2	Building Bridges / Bill Gaventa	10
3	When Faith and Disability Collide / Jacob Pratt	16
4	Access to Faith / Robin Gray	19
5	Interpreting God's Word / David Kay	22
6	A Celebration of Faith / Jim Schwier	27
7	A Place for Everybody / Hartmut and Susan Kramer-Mills	31
8	Gathering Karma / Vidya Bhushan Gupta	38
9	Telling the Story / Cindy Merten	42
10	The Joy of Giving / Dennis Schurter	45
11	Circles of Support / Barb Eiler and Ben Smith	49
12	Finding Acceptance / Lucas McCarty	53
13	Getting Involved / Rejoicing Spirits	56
14	Reunited with the Past / Isadore Rosen	62
15	The Gift of Friendship / Deb	66
16	Intending to Include / Kelsey Johnson	69

17 Elevators to Inclusion / Bill Zalot   70
18 Welcoming Whosoever Walks In / Liz Lang   73
    and Raymond
19 A Safe Venue / Military Veterans   76
20 Looking for "That of God" / Kevin Camp   81
21 Feeling Part of a Community / Ezra Freedman-Harvey   87
22 Sharing Space / The Cleggs Lane Men's Group   92
23 A New Way to Share God's Grace / Steve Schoon   96
24 A Mass for Everyone / Rosita Kardashian   101

Part 2
Ministry by People with Disabilities
107

25 Thrust into Untried Territory / JoAnn Misail   110
26 Life over Adversity / Jim Hukill   116
27 Civil Rights Begin at Home / Lynne Landsberg   119
28 Open to Real Experiences / Chris Maxwell   125
29 Purpose in the Pain / Lisa Copen   131
30 The Advantages of Disadvantages / Thomas H. Graves   136
31 Called to Community / Mark Johnson   142
32 Everyone Has Some Challenges / Al Mead   149
33 Nourishing Vocation / Jamie Dennis   152
34 Facing the Abyss without Flinching / Christine Guth   157
35 Contributing Our Talents / Terry Chaney and Marcie   163
    Brink-Chaney
36 God's Great and Fiery Compassion / Claire Wimbush   165
37 Letting Go of Victim Vanity / John Alex Lowell   172
38 The Gift of Hope / Susan Gregg-Schroeder   175
39 Breaking the Silence / Mary Heron Dyer   179
40 Rolling Back into Ministry / Joe Kovitch   183
41 Listening for Justice / Nancy Eiesland   185
42 Off the Pillow of Self-Pity / Angela Victoria Lundy   188
43 Serving Communion / Jo D'Archangelis   191
44 Realizing a Dream / Elsie Vander Weit   195
45 Mental Health Matters / Barbara Meyers   201

Part 3
Family Members in Ministry
205

46	Traveling from Grief to Joy / Kathleen Deyer Bolduc	209
47	God's Plan / Linda Starnes	214
48	Daughter of the Commandments / Hannah Ruth Greenblatt Eppinette	221
49	The Greatest Is Love / Karen and David Miller	226
50	The Gospel in Action / Stephanie Hubach	230
51	A Mother's Letter / Amy Julia Becker	237
52	Invited In / Fran Jarratt	242
53	Completing the Community / Karen Jackson	246
54	The Right to Kindness and Charity / Laila	252
55	Links of Love / Courtney Smith	256
56	Experiencing a L'Arche Community / Caroline McGraw	262
57	Overcoming Awkwardness / Nancy Guthrie	267
58	Traveling Together / Monica and Mark Masiko	271
59	Practicing What You Preach / Tom and Irene Powell	275
60	The Worth of an Individual Soul / Christopher Phillips	280
61	A Bitter Cup / Sue and Fred Odena	284
62	A Right to Faith / Safiyyah Amina Muhammad	288
63	Take a Break / Tim and Marie Kuck	292
64	Standing Some Disorder / Stanley Hauerwas	295
	Conclusion	299
	Resources	307

Foreword

You hold in your hand a collection of sixty-four amazing stories—real-life stories of people with disabilities, their family members, and their congregations. These are everyday people like those in your parish, church, synagogue, temple, or mosque who have taken actions, often simple actions, to make their congregations more inclusive of children and adults with all types of disabilities. These people are not necessarily heroes or heroines, although what they have done and continue to do will inspire you, the reader, to feel, think, and act in new ways.

These are stories of people who understand the uniqueness of every human being, the pain of isolation and exclusion, and the healing power of inclusion within communities of faith. Some of the stories come from the experiences of lay and ordained leaders who happen to have a disability or have children with disabilities. Others come from people with no personal disability connection who have chosen to value, enjoy, and support congregational members and visitors with disabilities.

All of the stories reflect the vitality that results from understanding that there is a place for everyone in God's house and that excluding anyone diminishes everyone. The motivations for action within the congregations represented in *Amazing Gifts* differ widely. Some are motivated by a personal challenge, others from community concern, and still others out of a call for justice.

Reading these stories will move congregational members to the next level of comfort, the next level of understanding, and the next level of responsibility. Readers will see that any steps forward—stumbles and all—are worthy. Readers will come to realize, "This is something I can do. This is something our congregation can do."

More than fifty million Americans live with physical, sensory, psychiatric, and intellectual disability. But when one is at worship and looks around, there appear to be few people present who have disabilities. While wheelchairs, scooters, walkers, white canes, guide and companion dogs, or sign language interpreters alert congregations that someone with a disability is present, many disabilities are not apparent. Disabilities such as lupus, chronic pain, kidney failure, HIV/AIDS, psychiatric disability, learning disability, traumatic brain injury (TBI), epilepsy, arthritis, cancer, heart disease, diabetes, narcolepsy, asthma, environmental illness, fibromyalgia and chronic fatigue syndrome, covered under the Americans with Disabilities Act (ADA), may not be revealed within a congregation unless it offers true affirmation and acceptance.

The idea of a book of stories of people with apparent and not apparent disabilities from many faiths grew out of conversations in 2004 with Dan Hotchkiss, a senior consultant at the Alban Institute. He suggested that in my decades of work on behalf of people with disabilities I had heard many stories that would move a reader's heart to action. Dan's affirmation of stories confirmed my experience that stories of everyday people with disabilities do more than entertain. They instruct. And they provide motivation for needed change.

Dan introduced me to others at the Alban Institute. Together, we developed a grant proposal for this book and secured the necessary funds. The funders who stepped forward understood that our goal was to publish a book of stories that will empower and motivate congregations and their leaders to include and fully welcome children and adults with disabilities. It is with immense gratitude that I name these generous funders: The David and Lura Lovell Foundation, the Alice W. Dorr Foundation, The

Clinton H. and Wilma T. Shattuck Foundation, David and Karen Miller, and the HCS Foundation. I am also deeply grateful that Mark I. Pinsky agreed to collect the stories and tell them with such mastery. Both his skill and his compassion are evident on every page. My son Peter, a man of faith who has both intellectual and physical disability, fueled my passion for the book and reminded me of the blessing that an affirming congregation can provide in a person's life.

My disability advocacy began in 1963, the year I met and married Dick Thornburgh, a kind, smart, and witty lawyer from Pittsburgh. Dick was a single parent to his three sons—John, six, David, five, and Peter, three. His beloved first wife, Ginny Hooton Thornburgh, had been killed on July 1, 1960, in an automobile accident in which Peter, then four months old, was seriously brain injured. Following the accident, Peter was a patient in Mercy Hospital in Pittsburgh for six months and endured many brain surgeries. When Dick would visit, he would almost always find Peter, tubes running in and out of his small body, in the arms of one of the Sisters of Mercy while she filled out charts or met in clinical discussions. During this critical period of Peter's development, the Sisters of Mercy encircled him with love and compassionate care, allowing Dick to spend more of his nonworking time with Peter's two brothers.

Little did I know on our wedding day, October 12, 1963, what lay ahead when I married this dear family. Although I had been a third-grade teacher, the challenges and joys of motherhood were a complete surprise. Luckily I was young, energetic, and in love. And as my new sons moved from calling me "Ginny" to calling me "Mom," my heart grew a mile.

When I became Peter's mother, he was not talking, walking, or toilet trained. Although functionally delayed, Peter started the morning with a smile on his face, which continued most of the day, and he won the hearts of everyone he met. Soon Dick and I enrolled him in a preschool day program at The Children's Institute in Pittsburgh (then called The Home for Crippled Children), the first child with brain injury accepted in this exceptionally fine program. How significant it was 46 years later when on November 24, 2010, Peter, using his walker and wearing a navy blue Joseph Banks suit, striped shirt, and red tie, delivered brief halting remarks at the dedication ceremony of the Peter Thornburgh Patient Care Services Suite at The Children's Institute.

During the first years of our marriage, Dick and I got a sitter for Peter when we took John and David to Sunday school and church. Now, as a disability advocate, I wonder with shame what Peter must have thought on Sunday mornings. His parents and his older brothers would leave home for several hours and return with stories, art projects, and delicious snacks. It just never occurred to me that our church could accept Peter in the same way our neighbors, friends, and relatives had accepted him.

In a strange way, it was the birth of our fourth son, Bill, in 1966 that jump-started my career in religion and disability. Although the members of our church knew I had a son with disability named Peter, when Bill was born, a woman came up to me and said: "We have new mattresses in the church's nursery. When are you bringing that sweet new baby to church?" I was hurt and angry. What about Peter? Why don't they ask about Peter? All of a sudden it hit me. The church had skipped over Peter and I had allowed it to happen. I went into "Mother Bear" mode and met with the pastor and the director of Christian education. Within a month or so, a room had been assigned and a woman with a special-education background had volunteered to teach the class.

With the class in place, it became my responsibility to recruit children with disabilities. We put a notice in the church bulletin and placed an ad in the local paper. Finally the first Sunday arrived and I snuck out of the church service during the second hymn to see how many children had joined Peter in the class. There was only one child present—Peter. My feelings about this disappointment were summarized in an article about Peter in the October 1993 issue of *Guideposts* magazine: "I felt humiliated. What was all our hard work for? Did other parents of children with intellectual disabilities feel so alone? Were they so accustomed to being excluded that they couldn't even imagine a welcoming church?" With Dick's encouragement, I approached The Children's Institute, and several children who were residents there joined the class. This was my baptism into religion and disability work, work that remains central to my life forty-five years later. I can close my eyes now and can see Peter, his three brothers, and Dick and me leaving for church together, Sunday after Sunday. Now we were worshiping as a family, not as only part of a family.

Through the local Allegheny County Chapter of the Pennsylvania Association for Retarded Citizens (now called ACHIEVA, a chapter of The Arc), I began to work with other volunteers to secure educational rights for children with disabilities and investigate care delivered in Pennsylvania state institutions. To our dismay, the conditions we found were wretched. Again I quote from the October 1993 *Guideposts* article: "At one of the state's oldest institutions, we discovered residents deemed unmanageable being kept in cages. One adolescent boy was cramped in a metal box so small he couldn't stretch his legs. The investigation that followed our visit in 1973 resulted in the firing of the institution's superintendent, the banning of cages, and state funding for upgrading facilities and retraining staff."

It was this work and The Arc training that taught me to learn the law, to pick and choose my battles, and to become an advocate, not just for Peter, but for anyone with disability whose rights have been denied. Later, my service on the President's Committee on Mental Retardation (now called the President's Committe for People with Intellectual Disabilities) gave me a national perspective and an opportunity to meet disability professionals and volunteer leaders from across the nation. Although much of this work was secular, it drew upon my strong sense of justice, nurtured by my faith.

In 1989, I founded the Religion and Disability Program at the National Organization on Disability (NOD). Our president and founder, Alan Reich, had been encouraged by the Rev. Harold Wilke to start an interfaith program, and somehow these men

gave me the confidence to move forward. I felt comfortable working in the disability community having just completed a job as
disability coordinator at Harvard University. But stepping into the
interfaith world was serious business. What if I said the wrong
thing to someone of a different faith than my own? Even though
I had majored in philosophy and religion at Wheaton College in
Norton, Massachusetts, nothing prepared me for the responsibility of talking about and writing about the rights of children and
adults with disabilities to be welcomed in the House of God of
their choice.

I will forever be grateful to a small group of people who did
disability advocacy within their denominations and faith groups
and who helped me articulate an interfaith disability message.
As I talked with people and listened to their stories, it became
clear that the message needed in an Orthodox synagogue is the
same message needed in a Catholic parish or in a Friends meeting
house: that people with disabilities, like all people, deserve to be
treated with dignity and respect; that barriers of attitude are more
difficult to identify and remove than barriers of architecture and
communications; that congregational disability work is about justice, not about pity; and that enormous gifts and talents will come
to congregations, no matter what the faith, once people with disabilities are included, enjoyed, and encouraged to be active and
full participants.

Peter's church, the Chestnut Grove United Methodist Church in
Harrisburg, Pennsylvania, is a medium-sized congregation that intentionally welcomes children and adults with disabilities. During
a renovation, a ramp to the chancel area was constructed. On May
30, 2004, this allowed Peter to walk with his walker to the lectern
when he was confirmed. This confirmation was preceded by Peter
meeting one-on-one with his pastor, who gave him an opportunity
to talk about his faith and what it meant to be a church member. In the presence of his parents, Peter read his Statement of
Faith that day with a strong confident voice: "My name is Peter
Thornburgh. I am happy in my church. I am happy to have Jesus

in my heart." The minister told me later that he wished all members of his congregation were "happy" in their church.

What makes this United Methodist church a model? Those connected to the congregation understand that the most important accommodation offered to someone with disability is the sacred gift of friendship. Leaders and members know Peter's name and they greet him by name. They know that he volunteers in the Central Pennsylvania Food Bank and they ask him about his work. They know that his brothers live in Pittsburgh and Philadelphia and that his parents live in Washington, D.C. And they ask Peter about his family. He is not just accommodated in his congregation, he is valued and enjoyed.

Which brings me to a concluding story about Peter. Once when our family was gathered for dinner, I asked Peter, "What is God like for you, Peter?" I hesitated as Peter took another bite of spaghetti. I rephrased my question: "When you think of God, Peter, what words come to your mind?" With that, Peter put down his fork, took a deep breath, and looked me straight in the eye. His unusual but eloquent reply was "Nice." Yes, that's right—"Nice." Through his church and through his family and friends, Peter had come to learn of a loving, caring God.

And so, with Peter on my heart, I ask you, the reader, about your parish, church, synagogue, temple or mosque.

Is it a place where someone like Peter Thornburgh could come to understand God as "nice"?

A place where someone who uses a wheelchair, scooter, walker, or cane can easily enter, make friends, worship, and go to the rest room?

A place where pain, difficulties, and weakness can be revealed?

A place where someone with a long-term mental illness or psychiatric disability is honored and welcomed?

A place where an older adult is comfortable suggesting ways to improve lighting and sound systems?

A place where no one is ignored and no one is treated as a nuisance or troublemaker?

A place where children and adults, with and without disabilities, are included, affirmed, valued, and enjoyed?

It is in my role as director of the Interfaith Initiative of the American Association of People with Disabilities that I write this foreword. Our mission is to support people with disabilities and their families as they seek spiritual and religious access and to bring the powerful and prophetic voice of the faith community to the twenty-first-century disability agenda. By opening yourself to the stories in this book, you will be equipped to listen, learn, and act in new ways in your own congregation and community, and you will be blessed in amazing ways.

Or to paraphrase anthropologist Margaret Mead: "Never doubt that a small group of thoughtful, committed members can change a congregation. Indeed it is the only thing that ever has."

Ginny Thornburgh
Director, Interfaith Initiative
American Association of People with Disabilities

Introduction

The television commercials were disturbing. Images showed congregants at traditional-looking churches barring or even physically ejecting members of racial and ethnic minorities, gay couples, and people with disabilities. One tag line read, "Jesus didn't turn people away. Neither do we." This national ad campaign, which aired in 2004, was sponsored by the United Church of Christ and was designed to attract new members. "We included people with physical disabilities in these commercials—in a wheelchair or with a walker—as an extension of the call and hope that churches would be intentionally inclusive of 'all the people,'" said the Reverend Gregg Brekke, a spokesman for the denomination.

Instead, the imagery provoked grumbling from some denominations because of its implied criticism of other faith traditions. Yet the criticism held more than a grain of truth. Churches, synagogues, mosques, and temples are places where people with disabilities might not expect to feel excluded, isolated, or patronized, but that has often been the norm. For years congregations have effectively excluded people with disabilities from worship—whether by steps and narrow doorways or by straitened attitudes—or segregated them in "special" services.

The U.S. Census in 2000 counted 54 million persons with disabilities—one in six Americans—and that number is growing. Wounded Iraq and Afghanistan war veterans, including men and women with amputations, traumatic brain injuries, and post-traumatic stress disorder, are swelling this population. Thanks to dramatic technological advances and improvements in neonatal care, formerly at-risk infants with severe and multiple disabilities now survive into adulthood. With the aid of breathing and feeding technologies and adaptive devices such as electronically operated prosthetics and speech-synthesizing computers, they are able to navigate and communicate. And the huge baby boom generation will soon be aging into infirmity, with attendant challenges of disabilities in hearing, vision, mobility, and cognition.

Members of all these groups want to pray at houses of worship. Yet a 2010 survey by the Kessler Foundation and the National Organization on Disability found that people with disabilities are less likely to attend religious services at least once a month than are people without disabilities, by a 50 percent to 57 percent margin. The greater the disability, the less likely a person is to participate.

People with disabilities "can attend school, hold down jobs, and turn the key in the door of their own apartments," wrote Erin R. DuBois in *The Mennonite* magazine. "They have won the legal battle for inclusion, but by the time they land in the pew at church, they may be too exhausted to fight for something more precious than their rights. Friendship is a gift the law can never guarantee to people with developmental disabilities. Churches across the United States, however, are reaping the rewards of building genuine relationships with those in their midst who are epitomized not by their disabilities but by their rare abilities to deepen the congregation's spiritual life."

Joe Landis, executive director of Peaceful Living, a Mennonite Health Services Alliance member organization based in Harleysville, Pennsylvania, agrees. Landis's interfaith program provides community-based services to people with developmental disabilities. People with disabilities "have their rights and laws and they can sue. They can fight all week, but they come to a service and don't want to have to put themselves forward in the faith community," Landis told *The Mennonite*. Friendship is what makes people flourish, and interfaith programs like his help local faith communities, including two synagogues and a Hindu temple, establish the mutual give and take of friendship with people with disabilities. Sometimes the starting point is as simple as canvassing the neighborhood and learning where excluded and ignored people live in any particular community.

In addition, people with disabilities and their families are often burdened by poverty. Some people with disabilities are unable to work, and many who are able to do so cannot find jobs, especially jobs with adequate benefits. Add to this the high cost of medication, treatment, and rehabilitation, and would-be worshipers "may feel socially stigmatized by their inability to provide financial support for their congregations," said Rabbi Lynne F. Landsberg, senior adviser on disability issues at the Washington-based Religious Action Center, the social justice organization of Reform Judaism. As a result of their embarrassment, they may not attend services even when places of worship are accessible and transportation is provided.

The prophets, great thinkers, and scriptures of most faiths mandate, at least in spirit, the inclusion of everyone. "Allah does not judge according to your bodies and appearances," wrote the Prophet Muhammad, "but he scans your hearts and looks into your deeds." India's Mahatma Gandhi asked, "What barrier is there that love cannot break?" In the book of Leviticus (19:14 NIV), the Lord says, "Do not curse the deaf or put a stumbling block in front of the blind," and Isaiah 56:7 NRSV admonishes, "For my house shall be called a house of prayer for all peoples." In the Gospel of Luke (14:13 NIV), early Christians are urged to invite to their gatherings "the poor, the crippled, the lame, the blind."

When, in the book of Exodus (4:10–14 NIV), the Lord orders Moses to speak to Pharaoh on behalf of the enslaved Hebrews, the prophet begs off, citing a speech impediment: "'O Lord, I have never been eloquent . . . I am slow of speech and tongue.' The LORD said to him, 'Who gave man his mouth? Who makes him deaf or mute? Who gives him sight or makes him blind? Is it not I, the Lord?'" With his brother Aaron's help, Moses was able to become a great religious leader.

Few people get to have a dialogue with the divine. For the rest of us, practices of faith can play a significant role in enriching the lives of people with disabilities and their families, friends, caregivers, and faith communities. But how far can—or should—modern religious congregations go to accommodate people with physical or intellectual disabilities?

Even congregations with the best of intentions can face challenges to fully embracing accessibility and inclusion. Seniors and people with disabilities can remind others uncomfortably of life's fragility and of death. People with emotional and intellectual disabilities can distract other worshipers during solemn moments. Religious people generally want to be sincere, welcoming, and open, but like everyone else, they often lack the experience to respond in the right way. Yet as Mother Teresa, founder of the Missionaries of Charity, put it, "We can do no great things; only small things with great love."

To be sure, money is an issue, especially for small, cash-poor congregations. More than half the religious congregations in North America, many of them in small towns and rural areas, have fewer than one hundred members, which limits their ability to adapt their buildings for handicapped accessibility. Building a ramp out of plywood is one thing; installing an elevator is quite another.

"When it comes to spending for architectural accessibility, there is sometimes reluctance on the part of finance committees," said Rabbi Landsberg, who herself suffered traumatic brain injury as the result of a traffic accident. Yet changing people's attitudes, implementing programs, and making modest accommodations—as opposed to major changes in architecture and additions of paid staff—can be relatively inexpensive, even for smaller congregations.

Nationally, many denominations—and more recently, nondenominational evangelical groups, who view this as a mission—now have ministries and task forces that offer advice and educational curriculums for people with disabilities, as does the Interfaith Initiative of the American Association of People with Disabilities

(AAPD). These programs are often offered for free online or at a small cost for materials and are designed for volunteer leaders, teachers, and ordained clergy.

Potential benefits—often unintended and unforeseen—await congregations that are willing to invest in architecture and attitudes in order to become more accessible and welcoming. Mainline congregations with declining memberships, for example, have much to gain by making their sanctuaries, social halls, meeting rooms, and rest rooms accessible to all people with disabilities. Elevators and ramps benefit, among others, mothers with strollers and seniors who use canes, walkers, or wheelchairs and long to participate and contribute. More families with disabled members would attend religious services, experts say, if congregations made efforts to open their buildings and programs to them. Older people are more likely to attend services than the young, and they are faithful donors. Communities that adapt to the world of disability are more likely to survive and grow; those that do not will lose out.

Market share notwithstanding, what else is gained when we value the gifts of people with disabilities and include them in our congregations? Collectively, the stories told in this book— stories of people with disabilities and the congregations in which they have found welcome—begin to answer this question. Some of the gains people described as I talked to them were policies, programs, and, yes, changes in architecture. But mostly the gains lay in attitude and commitment.

Bill Gaventa, the outstanding advocate and activist who is director of Community and Congregational Supports at the Elizabeth M. Boggs Center on Developmental Disabilities of the Robert Wood Johnson Medical School in New Brunswick, New Jersey, put his finger on the value of stories: "If you ask a family with a disabled child or member, or an adult with a disability, to 'tell me your church stories,' and if you are trusted, the response is rarely lukewarm. Some will talk about how important their faith or congregation has been to them. Others will tell you how painful and wounding their experience was. That's why trust is important, because responding truthfully about an issue around which there are powerful feelings, beliefs, and experiences is not an easy thing to do. You may be walking on holy or hellish ground."

Gaventa pinpointed the benefit of inclusiveness for congregations in their faith, worship, and theology: "In listening to those stories in the past few years, I think we are at a new point in the development of inclusive congregational and religious supports. This is a time when families, people with disabilities, and leaders in congregations are beginning to interpret their experience through the sacred scriptures, symbols, and traditions of their respective faiths. That's a crucial step, for it means that people who are advocating and working for more inclusive congregations can understand their experience as living out ancient understandings of faith. Including, accepting, and celebrating the gifts of everyone and the diversity of humankind is thus not something new but rather a response that represents the best of religious traditions and beliefs and illustrates the heart of key theological issues."

To write this book, I asked members of the disability community around the country to share their stories with me, and they did. I have tried to honor their personal accounts by preserving both their words and their perspectives. I have also tried to focus at least as much on people who cope as on people who conquer their disabilities—those whom some in the disability community refer to as "overcomers"—as inspiring as the latter may be. I have included as many disabilities, both physical and intellectual, from as many faith traditions as I could, though not all are represented.

The resulting tapestry of stories is intended to illustrate what can be done to integrate people with disabilities into faith communities, in the belief that the house of God should welcome everyone. The stories offer examples and ideas that can transform any congregation into one that includes, values, and enjoys people with disabilities. The emphasis is on "best practices" across the faith spectrum, particularly on actions that require no large financial commitment or expenditure. Embracing people with disabilities in our congregations is not primarily a matter of money and architecture—although commitments to those things can help. For communities of faith everywhere, what is in people's hearts matters more than what is in their budgets.

The good news is that some churches, synagogues, mosques, and temples are already welcoming people with disabilities and getting ready for the coming influx of wounded vets and creaky boomers. They are tapping technology and simple thoughtfulness to reach out in creative ways to this faith-hungry community:

- At Blessed Sacrament Catholic Church in Norfolk, Virginia, priest Joe Metzger instructs an eleven-year-old autistic girl in an empty sanctuary, wearing his vestments, so she'll feel at ease when she makes her first Communion.
- At Bet Shalom Congregation in Minnetonka, Minnesota, no sanctuary steps lead to the pulpit. Congregants approach it using a long ramp, symbolizing that all people come to the Torah equally. Similarly, when Temple Adath Israel in Lawrenceville, New Jersey, left its old building, the congregation built a new, accessible synagogue with a curved sanctuary and ramps on either side of the bimah—the platform from which the scriptures are read—which look like embracing arms.
- At St. John's Episcopal Church in Charlotte, North Carolina, and at St. Paul's Evangelical Lutheran Church in Exton, Pennsylvania, adult members with Down syndrome serve as altar servers, greeters, and Sunday morning ushers.

As these examples suggest, it takes more than just automatic door openers, large-print Bibles, and improved signage to make a congregation disability friendly. In recent years, many Christian and Jewish denominations have also established—sometimes under pressure— national outreach networks, which often are online resource centers, to make their congregations accessible. Through groups such as Joni Eareckson Tada's Joni and Friends Disability Center, evangelical churches have become increasingly involved in such efforts.

Although pastoral leadership can be critical, making faith communities welcoming and accessible to people with disabilities should not be a mission that falls mainly on the shoulders of clergy or other advocates. It is largely a matter of attitude on the part of lay people in the pews, on folding chairs, and kneeling on the carpet. This book is for you, and the message is: Making your congregation welcoming and accessible *can* be done because it *has* been done—somewhere, as you will see, by people just like you. I hope that after reading these stories you can replicate what has been successful, avoid what has failed, and, most important, generate creative programs of your own.

"Of all the barriers to full participation and inclusion, the barrier of unexamined attitudes is the most difficult to address," said Ginny Thornburgh, director of the AAPD Interfaith Initiative. The initiative's goal, she said, is "to bring the powerful and prophetic voice of the faith community to the twenty-first-century disability agenda" and to involve all religious communities. "There are no barriers to God's love," she said. "There should be no barriers in God's house."

Faith is a powerful thing, and children and adults with disabilities—regardless of how profound—benefit from expressing it and being part of a community of family, friends, and fellow believers who share it in worship.

Empowering People and Congregations

Part 1 of *Amazing Gifts* introduces people who have dared to *do* something to make their congregations inclusive of people with disabilities—not always the perfect thing, but *something*. It's a cliché, perhaps, but many hands do lighten the load when it comes to including people with disabilities. And frequently, there are unintended beneficiaries. For example, when congregations begin to practice inclusion, older adults—although they may not be comfortable with the word *disability*—benefit. Many people find railings, improved lighting and sound systems, and transportation helpful, and everyone deserves to be treated with dignity and respect. As stories from New Jersey to Indiana, from Texas to Manchester, England, demonstrate, opening the sanctuary and social hall doors to people with disabilities can revive dwindling congregations.

The house of God should welcome everyone. The goal of the stories in this section is to provide examples, ideas, and inspiration that can help transform any congregation into one that includes, values, and enjoys people with disabilities. The goal is to move you to action by highlighting things that you and members of your faith community can do—many of them relatively simple things.

Faith is enlivened by action, according to the New Testament's Epistle of James (2:14–26), and most other faiths share the concept in one form or another. In addition, all the world's great religions subscribe to a notion of hospitality that enjoins believers to welcome the stranger, sharing everything one has, as if the stranger were one's brother or sister. People with disabilities often feel like strangers.

As the following stories reveal, three main barriers exist to the full participation of people with disabilities in faith congregations:

- *Barriers of architecture.* Architectural barriers include features such as steps leading up to building entrances, interior stairways, and doorways too narrow to accommodate wheelchairs. Often, these are more easily removed than other barriers; congregations can, for example, build ramps and remodel doorways. Building renovations do cost money, though. People with disabilities are the expert consultants on projects to remove architectural barriers. They are problem solvers and often can suggest practical, less expensive solutions than those suggested by architects.
- *Barriers of communication.* A barrier of communication might be print in a hymnal or a bulletin that is too small to be read by people with poor vision, or it might be a lack of sound amplification that prevents people who are hard of hearing from listening to a worship service. Communication barriers can also exist when someone with labored speech is ignored or when worship services are not designed to engage people with intellectual disabilities. To overcome such barriers, congregations can embrace new technologies available in the secular world—for example, wiring their sanctuaries to broadcast FM signals to people with hearing aids, and installing screens on which to display sermon points and Scripture verses in large type.
- *Barriers of attitude.* Attitudinal barriers are the most difficult to identify and remove. They are evidenced in prejudice, unexamined ideas, unwillingness to learn new information

that goes against the grain, inaccurate judgments of what a person with a disability can do or might prefer to do, and feelings of insecurity in new situations with new people. To overcome such barriers, congregations might publish articles about members with disabilities in bulletins and newsletters, and they might devote service messages to the subject of disability and inclusion.

Ginny Thornburgh, of the American Association of People with Disabilities, likes to say that in congregational disability work, a good rule of thumb is, don't start with the elevator. Money divides people. Some leaders want it saved for a new furnace or roof, and others want it given to missions. Start instead with low-cost, easy successes. Some ideas:

Enlarge the print size in the bulletin. Change the wording in the bulletin to "Stand or remain seated" rather than "All stand." Train ushers so that they feel comfortable and are respectful in a variety of disability situations. Invite a congregation member with Down syndrome to be a greeter. Organize an employment support group for unemployed and underemployed people with and without disabilities. Invite someone who uses Braille to read scripture.

These and other creative, inexpensive ideas will emerge if people with disabilities are encouraged to lead the transformation of the congregation. Children and adults with disabilities, like so many others, long to know they are loved by God and by the people of God. The most important accommodation a congregation can offer a person with a disability is the sacred gift of friendship—respectful, unpatronizing, unrushed friendship.

Congregations may want to form "circles of support" around a child's family or an adult with a disability. People involved in these support networks, bringing a variety of interests and skills, gather, listen, plan, encourage, and sometimes make the seemingly impossible become possible. Such support networks, as the following stories of Barb Eiler, Steve Schoon, Izzy Rosen, Raymond, and Deb illustrate, can be built, at least initially, around a single person. Imagine a member of your synagogue, mosque, church, or temple—perhaps a former leader who has had a stroke but would like to attend services, if only she or he had a ride. Imagine what can be done to reach out to a young couple whose new baby has Down syndrome. How is the congregation preparing to honor, teach, and enjoy these people?

Additional ideas? Plan an adult education class on issues of disability, led by people with disabilities paired with professionals. Show movies with a disability theme, followed by a discussion. Offer respite services for families affected by disability. Include children with disabilities in religion classes and children's choirs. Move the site of a congregational committee meeting to the apartment of someone with a disability who is unable to leave home.

Each of the stories to come is replete with ideas like these—and with testimony to the enormous benefits, for both people with and without disabilities, of following the lead of some determined and inspiring exemplars.

1

A Spirit of Hospitality

Sue Montgomery

False starts—even bad beginnings—can sometimes lead to good endings. When care providers for people with intellectual disabilities in rural western Pennsylvania brought their members to some area churches, the group home residents were asked not to return—a painful rejection. A few church members had found the newcomers' sometimes noisy behavior disruptive, or they felt uncomfortable because of the visitors' physical characteristics or difficulty in speaking.

The caregivers then contacted the Reverend Sue Montgomery about holding a service for the residents at the Nickleville Presbyterian Church, a small congregation with a rich and profound sense of being a family. At first Montgomery was reluctant to hold a special service for the group home residents, which she saw as a way of separating and isolating people with disabilities. After hearing about their earlier experience, she changed her mind.

"I agreed to begin a ministry that would take place on Tuesdays for the group home men and women as well as their staff," Montgomery recalled. "The ground rules were simple—the staff must worship with the residents, and the staff and administrative personnel of the facility must work to integrate the residents into local congregations as much as possible. A new ministry at Nickleville was born."

The Nickleville congregation was receptive. It had, after all, called Montgomery, who uses a wheelchair, to serve as its pastor. And more than fifty years earlier, a family in the congregation had decided not to institutionalize their son when he was born with a disability. Their decision, Montgomery said, flowed from an understanding of what it meant to be embraced in the family

5

of God, including full integration into the church. The congregation's spirit of hospitality and inclusion had since been extended to all—to people who had disabilities, who were confronting questions of sexual identity, who had served prison time, or who were struggling with addiction.

Still, Montgomery acknowledged, some members of her congregation felt nervous about the new ministry, and some confessed that they were afraid of the newcomers. But four people stepped forward and committed themselves to the ministry, which the church called the Training Towards Self Reliance ministry.

Two years into the program, the gifts the men and women with disabilities bring to worship at Nickleville Presbyterian have been rewarding. The group home residents are considered active participants in the congregation. When they are included in morning worship services on Sunday, they are no longer thought of as visitors. The men and women of Training Towards Self Reliance (TTSR) are a part of the extended church family.

During their "Our Tuesday" morning worship services, they read the scriptures, some of them with a great deal of assistance and others almost unaided. Some have played the piano or sung solos for worship. Others have assisted with morning prayers. They are always in charge of receiving the offerings. One week one of the young men walked down the aisle shouting, "My preacher never lets me do this!"

"It was the defining moment of why we do what we do," said Montgomery.

Participants in TTSR and the group home staff have joined with Nickleville's regular members in preparing for the church's annual Christmas Eve service and program. Church members are often invited to parties at the group home, and the ministry has expanded to include life-cycle events. TTSR organizes hospital visits when a person living in the group home is hospitalized, as well as visits to funeral homes when a parent of any of them dies.

The Nickleville church has especially embraced the gifts of two men and one woman from the group home, who now come regularly to Sunday morning worship, church dinners, and other special events. One has asked to become a full member of the congregation, a significant development for someone living in a therapeutic community rather than a traditional family. The three sing in the choir on Sunday mornings and work in the kitchen during fund-raising and fellowship dinners.

Montgomery and other Nickleville Presbyterian members are discouraged that they have been unable to integrate the group home residents into more churches in the community, but the necessary sense of welcome and family doesn't seem to be there. It may be that smaller congregations—Nickleville has seventy-two members—feel a stronger sense of family. They seem to have a profound, intimate understanding that when a family member is born with a disability, the family adapts and includes that person, no matter what.

The congregation's group home ministry has now expanded to other group homes in the community, with both on-site worship services and services at the church. "Our Tuesday" worship attendance now includes fifteen to twenty persons with developmental disabilities and fifteen to twenty-five caregiving and administrative staff. Many staff members had never previously attended church in the community, so the ministry helped them learn worship behaviors and etiquette. They now demonstrate to the group home residents appropriate worship behaviors, such as remaining quiet during prayer, finding hymns in the hymnal, and assisting with the offerings.

"We have watched a young man be transformed from a passive, unresponsive participant to one who now actively participates in a variety of ways," Montgomery said by way of example. "This wouldn't have happened without hands-on support being given to him during worship. Worship in this ministry, as it should be in every congregation, is a time of communal nurture."

The TTSR ministry also involves people with disabilities in raising money for the town's local food pantry. Every week, said Montgomery, "one of our women, as she goes out the door, says, 'I hope the children get their peanut butter and jelly.' And each time, she is reassured."

"Is it easy?" Montgomery asks. "No, but the spirit of inclusion is there, and that can never be destroyed. Are there difficulties? Yes, but tolerance, understanding, and acceptance of differences overcome all the uncertainty and discomfort among regular congregation members. Have we had people afraid? Yes, and they chose to keep their distance. The fear is that at their ages and frail conditions they might be hurt by aggressive behaviors. Their fears are respected and acknowledged. The [group home] staff work with the men and women, and with that staff cooperation, we are assured that everything will be done to support both the men and women with the aggressive behaviors and the members of our congregation."

Sometimes the smallest things can make a difference. For example, the congregation modified the way it articulated worship. "Our speech is slowed to match the speech patterns of the men and women with difficulties speaking," Montgomery said. "We have learned to slow down. The Lord's Prayer is recited much more slowly and is no longer a running of the Indianapolis 500 in speed and pace."

In turn, as so often happens, the congregation has learned from the gifts of the men and women with developmental disabilities. Their questions and comments challenge others in the congregation to rethink who they are and why they do what they do in worship.

"Integrating and affirming the leadership gifts of these men and women has been a source of great joy," said Montgomery. "Now some actually argue over who is going to collect the offering, lead the prayers, or direct the choir. Yes, their choir is directed by one of 'them'! It's been exciting to see the growth of their gifts and leadership skills as they take on these important responsibilities in worship."

Some of the caregivers from the group home, Montgomery said, have found a spiritual home of their own at the small church. "As pastors, we have been called to minister to staff families in times of crisis and to support them in marriage as well. It is a ministry of evangelism in that staff who have experienced rejection of the men and women in their care [by other churches] also struggle. They ask, 'Why do churches do this?' and 'What does it mean to be a Christian when a disability affects participation and hospitality?'"

"When a church excludes one member of a family, the church excludes a whole family—sometimes two and three generations," said Montgomery. "In addition, as is so painfully witnessed here, the word spreads within a community about the rejection of the men and women of the group homes. That rejection affects the staff and their families as well. An astounding number of people are affected. The witness of the church—good and bad—is a message that is heard loud and clear."

2

Building Bridges

Bill Gaventa

People often ask Bill Gaventa how he got involved in ministry with people with intellectual and developmental disabilities. No one in his immediate family has a disability, although when he was growing up in Nigeria as the son of a Southern Baptist medical missionary, his family did adopt and raise a village boy who had been left to die in the "bush" because he was thought to be cursed or possessed by an evil spirit. And for a year his father served as the physician at a leprosy settlement in the jungle, where young Bill met people with all kinds of disabilities.

Still, following Gaventa's graduation from Union Theological Seminary, while he was a clinical pastoral education resident at North Carolina Memorial Hospital in Chapel Hill, it was against his preference that he was assigned to work part-time at its Division of Disorders of Development and Learning. The program trained graduate-level students who worked with faculty in a two- or three-day, multidisciplinary evaluation of children with suspected disabilities. Gaventa's first reaction was, "I can't do that. Send someone else." But participating in the program was part of a bargain he had made for another prime placement, so off he went.

"I had no idea what to do," he recalled. There was no formal job description, "so I simply started talking to families as they sat in waiting rooms, or in rooms behind a one-way mirror where they could watch the particular assessment going on. There were two questions that glared out at me. 'What does it mean to be a pastor to families with children with mental retardation, as the term was in those days?' And 'What does it mean to be a chaplain on a tightly defined, medical-model interdisciplinary team where there was no automatic place at the table for pastoral care?' And I began

10

to hear stories, occasional ones about how their pastor or church had been helpful, but most were about the lack of response or responses that hurt."

One family told him about their daughter, who had a developmental disability and who had gone to the family's church as a child. Their first disappointment came when she was asked to stay in the younger classes and not advance with her peers. The second injury came when the couple followed the best professional advice of the time and sent their daughter away to a residential school. They soon found that fellow churchgoers asked them about their other children, who were away at college, but never about their daughter with the disability. The third wound was the most hurtful. The church had a new pastor, and one Sunday when the daughter was home, the entire family went to church. As they were leaving, the new minister failed to shake the young woman's hand.

Gaventa, determined to make things right, visited the minister and found that he was in fact highly trained in pastoral care. The man said he had visited the family at their home, and they had never talked to him about their daughter or mentioned her needs. He thought they were a "proud, independent family" who preferred to handle things on their own. The minister's perception, Gaventa said, might have influenced his not reaching out to the young woman after the church service.

The gap in perception between pastor and family, Gaventa realized, was leading each side to expect the other to make the first move. The real pastoral care skill was simply being willing to bumble in, perhaps without the right words, and say, "Can you tell me about your daughter?"

"That was one of my first mental images of where the grace of God could be at work," Gaventa said. "The grace of God, it seemed to me, was like Jesus's response to the disciple's question about the blind man (John 9:1–4): 'Whose sin caused this—his or his parents'?' 'Neither,' replies Jesus; the man is blind so that 'the grace of God might be made manifest in him.'" In Gaventa's interpretation, Jesus was saying, "What you have here, disciples, is a opportunity to demonstrate the grace of God by moving toward this man and his family in love, without worrying about whose fault it was, without their having to ask, and perhaps without knowing what in God's name you are going to do. Your faith should be that God will provide."

Stories like this called to Gaventa, the one-time missionary kid, and ignited in him a passion for ministering to people with disabilities. The year after his residency at Chapel Hill, he took a part-time job creating a ministry network in North Carolina for people with disabilities, which evolved into his life's work. He organized the first "Mental Retardation Sabbath Sunday" in the state, working in conjunction with the Association of Retarded Citizens. On donated billboards and church bulletin inserts, the organizers pictured a pastor shaking the hand of a young man with Down syndrome, above the caption, "Remembering all people are God's people."

Not all the stories Gaventa heard—or experienced—had happy endings. Years later, after a presentation to a Down Syndrome Association conference, Gaventa asked those in the audience to share their faith experiences with him. One mother told of moving to a new community with her daughter, who had been labeled "microcephalic and moderately retarded," even though she had previously worked at a fast-food franchise. The two had gone church-shopping, and the daughter attended a youth organization meeting at one congregation. Afterward, the daughter came home and said, in her limited English, "No church, Mom. No more church." The mother recounted that she had gone into parenting mode, repeating to her daughter that they needed to find a church home as a family, that it was God's house. Whereupon the young woman said simply, "Well, it may be God's house, but he's not home."

From North Carolina, Gaventa went north to become chaplain of an old state institution, Newark State School in Newark, New York. In the early 1900s it had been called the "Newark State School for Feebleminded Women of Child Bearing Age." When Gaventa arrived, fifteen hundred people were living in a place where forty-five hundred had once been housed, a huge and haunting reminder of a bygone era. One of his first sermons to community congregations was, he realized later, a missionary message: "So Near, Yet So Far—A Report from a Foreign Land." While serving as chaplain of the state facility, Gaventa tried in small ways to get churches, seminary students, and others to visit.

Following the example of a Catholic chaplain in Buffalo, New York, Gaventa coordinated a first-time, one-day Friendship Fair as part of the Newark State School's hundredth anniversary celebration. He and other volunteers recruited more than a thousand people to participate, so that every resident could have a buddy for a day of music, games, and food. It began to rain halfway through the day, but no one cared. "Everyone got wet together," Gaventa recalled, "and you could just feel the invisible walls tumbling down. It also made me a believer in the power of celebration to bring down walls, with the great historical precedent of Jericho."

Gaventa's journey then led him to an interfaith chaplaincy at Monroe Developmental Center in Rochester, New York, where he bridged facility and community congregations and helped create a faith-based respite care program. His next move was to Georgia, where he worked for the Developmental Disability Council on family support and creative forms of respite care. Gaventa says he was looking for "places where God was already at work."

Part of his job, and part of his simultaneous volunteer work as executive secretary of the Religion and Spirituality Division of the American Association on Intellectual and Developmental Disability, was to find written and audiovisual resources related to ministries to people with developmental disabilities and their families—resources that were still scarce at the time. Through newsletters, exhibits at conferences, and other means, Gaventa shared these materials with clergy, congregations, families, and service providers interested in working with faith communities. Eventually he helped found what became the *Journal of Religion, Disability, and Health,* a professionally recognized publication for the growing number of people writing about theology, ministry, and disability.

In 1992, a job offer for Gaventa's wife, Beverly, drew the family to Princeton, New Jersey, and Gaventa found a professional home at the Elizabeth M. Boggs Center on Developmental Disabilities in New Brunswick, New Jersey, where today he is associate professor and director of Community and Congregational Supports. During his years at the center, Gaventa has developed a personal acquaintance with disability.

"Old habits of working too hard to establish myself in a new community, the sometimes unacknowledged struggles of transitions and moves, putting too much on my plate, and not practicing what I preach about taking care of myself took a toll," he said. "In the past twenty years I've experienced two, three- to four-month journeys into the pits of a major clinical depression. Or, as I sometimes say, experiential exercises in disability I had no intention of having, rather than doing. But they, too, have taught me in profound ways about the grace of God, through my family, friends, and therapists who walked through those valleys with me and helped me emerge to what has felt like a miracle each time."

Gaventa continues to write and lecture around the country, offering some clear, key messages about inclusion. "It is not so much about 'special ministries' to 'special people,'" he says, "but about hospitality to the stranger, for in a so-called normal world, people with disabilities are so often the quintessential stranger, and our task as hosts is to be open to the messages and gifts from God that the stranger often bears. It's about helping all people feel safe in congregational sanctuaries, seeing people with disabilities with gifts who are also called to serve, learning to communicate God's word through all kinds of strategies."

One of Gaventa's favorite recent stories is of two young adults with Down syndrome who trained to be ushers in a Catholic parish on the Jersey shore. After one Saturday afternoon Mass, the mother of the younger boy couldn't find him. (For Christians, the story of a mother looking for her young son in the temple after the service might sound familiar.) She finally found him talking earnestly to an elderly couple. It turned out that they had come to Mass that afternoon for the first time, searching for solace and answers, because their first grandchild had just been born—with Down syndrome. "Think of the incredible ministry done by that young man on that afternoon," Gaventa said.

"As interest in this intersection of faith, theology, and disability emerges and becomes more visible in many ways," said Gaventa, "my excitement about the intersections of theology, disability, and ministry is as strong as ever. One thing I have known for a long time is that my personal journey as a missionary kid was bridging two or more worlds and trying to find my own sense of place and home. The parallel, of course, is that seeking and building community has been my personal and my professional journey. The paradoxical question is, who has helped whom?"

3

When Faith and Disability Collide

Jacob Pratt

Sometimes, when faith and disability intersect, they also collide, and the best efforts and intentions can end up in frustration for everyone. Jacob Pratt, who was born with severe autism, is devoted to the Church of Jesus Christ of Latter-day Saints (LDS) and has done as much as possible to live fully as a Mormon. For its part, the church has done everything it can to help Pratt, a resident of Connecticut who serves as executive director of the Autism Spectrum Differences Institute of New England, Inc. Yet Pratt today faces a dilemma, because circumstances surrounding his disability conflict with his faith-driven desire to be married in the church.

Although Pratt has some behaviors that can be challenging, such as loud vocalizations during services and some movement difficulties that make it hard for him to eat without spilling his food, he has been accepted by most other members of his congregation. "I'm grateful that most did," he said.

Pratt's parents did not pursue priestly training with him in his teens, when it was age appropriate. So years later he worked with his bishop to become a priest, and he is now considered a full adult male member of his church. "This wasn't my parents' fault," Pratt said. "It just wasn't done at the time. I'm glad attitudes have changed."

Because he cannot communicate verbally, Pratt uses a keyboard voice synthesizer called Lightwriter, in addition to e-mail. Although some members of his church questioned whether his communication was really his or was typed by an aide, his supportive bishop was convinced that Pratt was intelligent and able to fulfill the church's requirement for demonstrating his faith. The hope and expectation was that with some modification and accommodation on the church's part, Pratt would be able to perform baptisms and participate, at least partially, in LDS outreach.

In the course of traveling around the region, making presentations for the Autism Spectrum Differences Institute, Pratt met a Rhode Island woman named Hope Block, who also has severe autism and communicates with a voice output device. Although Hope had been raised Jewish, the two fell in love and decided to marry. The problem is that Pratt and his fiancée both receive substantial support from their respective states, and if either moves to join the other, the one who moves will temporarily lose benefits and have to reapply at the end of a very long line in the new state. Neither can live in the community without ongoing support, so for either to be "wait-listed' is out of the question.

Compounding the problem, both Jacob and Hope have been told by their social services case managers that they cannot marry while maintaining residency in separate states. Such an arrangement would raise suspicion about what their living arrangements actually were, and if any suspicion of misuse of benefits exists, funds can be withdrawn. Problems like this are common, according to Bill Gaventa, associate professor of pediatrics at the Robert Wood Johnson Medical School, and also arise when parents or a sibling wants to move with a relative who has a significant disability.

Pratt's bishop is willing to marry the couple and even offered use of the church hall and other members' talents for the reception. But Mormon doctrine requires the bishop to submit the necessary paperwork to the state in which the marriage is performed, which would jeopardize the couple's support systems. Any marriage, the bishop said, would have to take place under both God's and man's law, or it would not be a valid Mormon wedding. Thus the bishop felt he could not perform a "church only" wedding, even if it was the only way the couple's support could be guaranteed. Pratt was told to come back to arrange the LDS marriage ceremony after he worked things out with the state.

Hope's and Jacob's families support a civil commitment ceremony, which would enable them to spend a few days together at a time, but Jacob is driven by his faith to have a church wedding, recognized by God. "I feel that to do otherwise would dishonor my beautiful Hope," he said, and would prevent him from being with her for eternity, according to Mormon doctrine. "I love my church, but I am not very happy with government right now."

"Everything Jacob says is true," added Hope. "I don't think government should interfere with my wedding plans."

Linda Rammler, Pratt's friend and colleague, is as frustrated as the couple is. "Jacob is embraced as a member of his church in all ways except when the state interferes with his ability to be married," she said.

On September 4, 2011, Jacob and Hope celebrated their love and commitment at a party at Rammler's home, joined by nearly fifty family members and friends. Jacob presented Hope with his grandmother's ring, which she displays as if it were a wedding ring. Having her wear the ring, while the two remain officially unmarried and continue to live apart, is the best they can do for now.

4

Access to Faith

Robin Gray

Some years ago, when Robin Gray was minister of the First Unitarian Universalist Church of Milford, Massachusetts, her congregation began a project to remodel their church for ease of use by people with disabilities. Among other things, they planned to create a new, wheelchair-accessible entrance from outside the building into the fellowship hall, where an accessible rest room has been fashioned a half dozen years earlier. A tougher decision involved what to do with the church's beautiful granite building, dating from 1900, which could be entered only by climbing eight or nine difficult stone steps. The only way to connect a ramp to the church from the parking lot on one side of the building required removing a stained-glass window in order to create an exterior door.

"We held our breath that the congregation would approve," Gray recalled. "And not only were those significant changes approved, but once the new ramp and doorway were built, that became the entrance everyone used, because it also led through the fellowship hall to the sanctuary on the same level." As usual, the best practice was to aim for an accessible entrance that benefited everyone.

As happens on the road to access and inclusion, building an accessible entrance at street level proved to be just the first hurdle for this small congregation. The lower level, where the kitchen, dining hall, and classrooms were located, was still reached only by a long flight of stairs. When the church committed itself to providing a free, weekly, soup-kitchen-style "Community Supper" for anyone in Milford who needed a hot meal, the question of accessibility arose again. Yet the congregation felt that it could not approve adding the cost of an elevator to the Community Supper's expenses. Volunteers who staffed the supper offered to serve meals in the street-level fellowship hall to anyone who couldn't get to the dining area—the best alternative available.

After several years, the congregation welcomed several members who found it extremely difficult to reach the lower level. At those members' request, and with Gray's support, the church's governing body approved a capital campaign to raise funds for a lift—a modified, simplified elevator. The lift could be installed adjacent to the street-level accessible entrance and take passengers to the lower-level dining area. But despite the efforts of the fundraising committee, only a tenth of the cost of the lift was pledged. The campaign ended, and the money was put aside for the day when the congregation would take seriously its role in creating a fully accessible building.

The failed capital campaign was a disappointment to all who worked on it. It created some hurt feelings, too, especially for people who had begun to anticipate full participation in activities on the lower level. Meanwhile, after thirteen years of service in Milford, Robin Gray moved to a new congregation in another city. But in Milford, "the story didn't end there," she said. "A dozen years after creating the accessible walkway and entrance, the church installed an elevator adjacent to the 'new,' popular entrance, finally giving everyone easy access to the fellowship hall and classrooms on the lower floor."

Despite the frequent jokes about Unitarians on the television shows *The Simpsons* and *Saturday Night Live* and the radio program *The Prairie Home Companion,* people sometimes say the denomination is "too intellectual," Gray said. "They mean, I think, that people with cognitive disabilities won't be comfortable at our worship and programs." Yet Gray has been minister in two Unitarian Universalist congregations where that assumption was tested and found false. Each church was in a small city, and each was located fairly close to a group home for people with cognitive, developmental, and emotional disabilities. Both congregations were small, and both became the church of choice for people from the group homes and their staff. In the first instance, the congregation had turned its parsonage into a group home, and the residents and staff could readily sense that they would be welcome at worship. The second congregation had no prior relationship with the group home, but the church was known in the community as one where differences were welcome.

The first time seven people of differing ages and cognitive abilities arrived at the worship service, they were quickly made to feel welcome. "There's no doubt that some of the issues raised in the sermons were of little interest to our new friends, yet the embrace of fellowship meant more to them than all the intricate arguments I could put forth from the pulpit," Gray said. "But then, I think that's true for everybody who finds their way into a church." Members of the congregation included the newcomers in activities outside of worship. They joined in Christmas tree trimming and caroling with the same enthusiasm they brought to Sunday morning services.

Some years later, in a new city, Gray's congregation was "adopted" by the residents of a group home. After a few initial visits, residents made their own choices about what to do on Sunday mornings, and some decided to continue their association with the church. Two became members. A weekly free meal offered by the congregation encouraged other people with mental health issues and cognitive disabilities, from both group homes and the community at large, to return for Sunday morning services. Some only visited, but for others, the church became their spiritual home. The key seemed to be that each person's concerns and contributions were accepted with an eye toward helping him or her find a unique place in the community.

5

Interpreting God's Word

David Kay

People become engaged with faith and disability through a spectrum of experiences and interests. Most often they have disabilities themselves or have family members or close friends who do, or they have an academic or theological involvement. Others may be in the medical, scientific, or caregiving professions, with an interest in the therapeutic value of spirituality. David Kay was drawn to the intertwined world of faith and disability by rock and roll—and romance.

In the late 1980s, shortly after Kay's rock band had broken up, he was playing a solo acoustic gig at a unique venue—a coffee house program at Bene Shalom, one of the nation's best-known deaf synagogues, in suburban Chicago. The backup American Sign Language (ASL) interpreter that night was an attractive young woman named Joanne Goldman. Although a hearing person herself, she was a member of the congregation's signing choir and part of a sign-language performance group.

One thing led to another, as these things tend to do—the couple eventually married—and Kay learned American Sign Language by immersion after becoming part of the synagogue community. "It was the connection with the deaf community that really gave me a sense of mission, a calling," Kay said, and he gave up playing rock music professionally to become a Conservative rabbi. The Bible verse that most resonates with him is Leviticus 19:14, which he interprets as "Show your fear of God by treating the deaf with respect" or, more expansively, "Do not take a deaf person lightly, or do not insult deaf people by underestimating them because of their hearing impairment."

In 1992 Kay became one of the three inaugural students in a pilot program launched by the rabbi of Bene Shalom to train Jewish leaders—rabbis and teachers—to serve in the Jewish deaf community. Ultimately, Kay, who was in the choir and served as cantorial soloist at Bene Shalom, enrolled in the Rabbinical School at the Jewish Theological Seminary of America, in New York City, where he sang in the school's a cappella group and was ordained in 2002, after delivering his senior sermon in both voice and sign.

Throughout the decade between his first involvement with Bene Shalom and his ordination, Kay conducted High Holiday services at the Rochester Institute of Technology/National Technical Institute of the Deaf—in voice and in Sign—and provided rabbinical and pastoral services to the Hebrew Association of the Deaf of New York. He attended the biennial conference of the Jewish Deaf Congress (previously known as the National Congress of Jewish Deaf), co-chaired a conference on facilitating Judaic content in Sign, and performed in a Sign performance group called People in Motion.

As the assistant rabbi of Congregation Ohev Shalom in Orlando, Florida, Kay decided in 2007 to both speak and sign his sermons from the pulpit on the High Holidays—Rosh Hashanah, the Jewish New Year, and Yom Kippur, the Day of Atonement, the following week. His hope was that along with hearing members, a small number of deaf and profoundly hearing-impaired worshipers would be in the pews. "This is something that is close to my heart," said Kay. "I hate to see anyone denied access to their Judaism."

Among Christians of many denominations, signing for deaf worshipers is increasingly common in churches and evangelical crusades. Some megachurches, with resources that better enable them to sustain deaf ministries, often send experienced signers to smaller congregations with just a few hearing-impaired members. Jewish communities around the country take a similarly collective approach on behalf of the estimated fifty thousand deaf Jews in the United States. In 2009, for example, the Jewish Federation of New York granted $5,000 to the Jewish Deaf Resource Center. The Jewish Federation in Columbus, Ohio, allocates $3,000 a year for deaf services, including High Holiday services rotating among different synagogues each year.

Another resource is Temple Beth Solomon of the Deaf, in Northridge, California, a fifty-year-old Reform congregation that claims the distinction of being among the first synagogues in the world established and run by deaf Jews. Both words and music are communicated in sign language to the sixty families who belong. In 1983 the congregation sponsored a conference and art exhibit memorializing the thousands of deaf people of all faiths who were sterilized or killed in the Nazi Holocaust during World War II. It also helps other congregations learn how to be culturally sensitive and accessible to deaf people.

But outside of congregations for and made up of the hearing-impaired, such as Temple Beth Solomon and Bene Shalom, it is still unusual for a spiritual leader like Kay to sign sermons while delivering them in full voice from the pulpit.

In 2007 Kay held an "alternative" High Holiday morning service at a rented Christian worship center up the street from his synagogue. He hoped the venue might help attract deaf people who were not members of his synagogue. "If you make services accessible to the disabled—before you are asked—people will come," Kay said. "If I want access to a building, the building needs to be unlocked. My goal is to unlock the building—that's the goal of the alternative service."

Kay signed his own lesson, emphasizing Judaism and the environment, after removing his white prayer shawl so it wouldn't distract people from watching his hands. The remainder of the service was signed by American Sign Language interpreters.

Jon Ziev, then forty-two, who had been deaf from birth, was sitting in the front row of the alternative service. He was pleased that for once he had not been forced to drive five hours from his home in Orlando to south Florida, which has a much larger Jewish community, to find a service with an ASL interpreter. "If there's a place that's accessible, that's where deaf people will go," said Ziev, a consultant and a nonprofit volunteer, as Kay interpreted for him.

Kay's task is daunting, according to Margalit Fox, author of *Talking Hands: What Sign Language Reveals about the Mind.* "It's pretty much impossible to speak out loud in English, which has one way of putting sentences together, and to sign simultaneously in ASL, which has a completely different way of putting sentences together." The way Rabbi Kay is meeting this challenge is valuable, Fox said, "because it will indeed allow many deaf people access to his talk."

Before the 2007 High Holiday services, deaf Jews had encouraged Kay to sign his teaching during the services. "Almost to a person," he said, "deaf people say, 'Sign for yourself—I'd rather get it from the horse's mouth—no offense.'"

What is the benefit of signing at services, when only a handful of people in the pews might benefit? It keeps those people from feeling marginalized, Kay explained, and it expresses the value a hearing speaker places on the visual communication that is deaf people's vernacular.

"I enjoyed the simultaneous comment when Rabbi Kay was speaking," Ziev said. "I am getting the point directly from the speaker, rather than through another. Otherwise, you lose meaning, and the sign-language interpreter can fall behind the speaker. You get the point exactly from the rabbi, and it's happening in real time."

Kay is not unique. In New York, one Hassidic Chabad rabbi can sign while chanting in Hebrew from the Torah scroll—which has no vowels or notes—effectively signing in two languages. Although not all congregations are so innovative, efforts to include deaf people are growing. The same year that Kay signed for his services in Riverside, California, there was a sign-language interpreter at Rosh Hashanah Eve services sponsored by the Chabad Jewish Community Center.

Historically, deaf Jews were treated as less than full members of the religious community, according to George Robinson, author of *Essential Judaism: A Complete Guide to Beliefs, Customs, and Rituals.* Today, deaf people are treated no differently from any other linguistic minority, Robinson said. "In Judaism, it is of paramount importance to respect the individuality, the personhood, of any human being."

In March 2009, David and Joanne Kay's son Jonah became a bar mitzvah at Ohev Shalom. Naturally, the family engaged ASL interpreters for both Friday night and Shabbat morning services. "It was particularly meaningful," said the rabbi, because "the fellow who had extended the invitation for me to perform at Bene Shalom nineteen years earlier—the deaf son of a lifelong friend of my mother's—was present for my son's bar mitzvah."

6

A Celebration of Faith

Jim Schwier

Jim Schwier's membership at St. Paul's Lutheran Church in Saskatoon, Saskatchewan, is hardly spectacular, but maybe that's the point. Some say the young man with Down syndrome has become one of the most devoted congregational greeters in all of Canada. Jim's father, Rick, a university professor, agrees, and believes his son has a divine mission.

"People have been telling me my whole life that God can see into my heart," Rick said. "If God is that smart, he can certainly see into Jim's soul. Jim doesn't understand the details, but he gets it. He understands there's more to this life, even if he doesn't always understand what that is. That's for us to worry about. But he knows when he belongs, and he belongs at St. Paul's."

All week while Jim works at the YMCA, he looks forward to church. On Saturday nights he and his father shine their shoes together, using the same shoe-shine kit Rick and his own father used before attending church in Indiana. The simple wooden kit is one of the most precious things Rick inherited when his dad passed away at ninety-two. Next, Jim picks out his church clothes to have them ready for Sunday morning. Should he go with the plain blue tie or with something a bit wackier? How about the Star Trek one? Then comes the offering envelope—he sometimes writes cryptic notes on it, messages perhaps legible only to God.

As a greeter at St. Paul's, Jim is solemn, often patting people on the back and shaking hands rather than speaking as he hands out bulletins. Yet he feels a vital part of the community and takes seriously his job of welcoming everyone each week. People don't seem to mind that he isn't vocal, and the greetings exchanged as they accept their bulletins are hearty and warm.

Rick and Jim had shopped around for a church, looking for a faith community where Jim would be accepted and welcomed. They tried a few before finding St. Paul's, where Pastor Mark Dressler, a young minister without pretense, was as happy to see Jim every Sunday as he was any other member of the congregation. During the service at St. Paul's, when Jim is not taking the offering, he sits next to Rick, sharing a hymnal and pointing out the proper verse to his dad.

The first time father and son took Communion together at St. Paul's was a revelation. As a new visitor to the church, Jim quietly studied what everyone else was doing in line in the church's center aisle. Rick whispered instructions to his son, recalling his own childhood, when his father worried about what Rick himself might get up to. But he got the distinct feeling that Jim was humoring him, as if to say, "Yeah, sure, Dad, I get it." Still, Rick was hoping Jim would do everything right when they reached the front of the line.

As the ushers invited their row to join the line, father and son both did their best to look contemplative. Jim seemed to be doing a better job, because Rick was more focused on Jim's getting it right. The pair eased themselves into position, kneeling at the railing. Jim was perfect—hands folded and head bowed, watching his dad out of the corner of his eye.

Jim held out his hand, accepted the host from the minister, and popped it in his mouth. "Mmmmmmm," he exclaimed, "good!" Suddenly, visions of wine and cheese with dinner guests at home filled Rick's head. Rick shot him "the look," the one that says "Stop what you're doing, or you will meet God—now!" Jim got the message but seemed confused about why it was sent. Then came the wine, which Jim knocked back with great gusto and appreciation, announcing with cup raised high, "Cheers!"

As they walked back to their seats—Rick sheepishly and Jim happily—Rick noticed that almost everyone they passed was smiling and nodding to Jim. They weren't the least bit bothered. In fact, they seemed to see something that eluded Rick in his cloud of embarrassment. Jim was truly happy with his experience of this celebration of faith. Jim got it right, and he showed his father a lot that day about what it meant to be devout. Rick knew they had found their church.

Jim's stepmother, Karin, a writer, is not a regular Sunday morning worshiper. But one summer weekend when Rick was out of town, she accompanied Jim to church, knowing that he was looking forward to attending and taking Communion. Karin, who was not raised in a church, explained to Jim that he should go to the rail by himself when the time came. As their pew was invited forward, Jim reverently folded his hands but then bolted for the front. As Karin watched between her fingers, he dodged people this way and that, up the aisle like a broken field runner, all the way to the front, until he was stopped and told he had to wait his turn. Later, as the congregation filed out into the Sunday morning sunlight, Pastor Mark shook Jim's hand warmly, thanked him for coming, and remarked that it was always good to see people so enthusiastic about their faith.

"We wanted to find a church where I felt we belonged," said Rick. "It's about the deep connections you see among the members. It's about finding a pastor who's the real deal, and people who know it in the congregation. You feel it. It's not something you analyze. It's intuitive. It's shaking hands with Art and Ed and Margaret every week. It's sitting next to Barry, and by coincidence it turns out you have season tickets next to each other at the University of Saskatchewan Huskies football games. It's those things that make community."

Rick elaborated: "To be completely honest, it's not entirely about being faith-based for Jim. It's as much about community as it is about faith, but perhaps there's not a great deal of distinction. I do worry about the faith side, and I hope Jim gets parts of that. But even if he doesn't get much of the truly spiritual part of it, the community part of it makes it worth being there every Sunday. And I've got to believe that God understands.

"We're there in a celebration of faith. Divine worship is about strengthening your faith. We don't know what it takes to strengthen Jim's faith, but don't you have to take a shot at it? Do we know what Jim gets out of it? Maybe not much, on some days. But we know he likes being there and he's in the proximity of faith. He sees and feels it practiced not just by his dad but by a lot of other people in the community. And isn't that enough? I think God's smart enough to figure it out."

Rick is confident that the Saturday night shoe-shine tradition will carry on and that his father—and God—are pleased.

7

A Place for Everybody

Hartmut and Susan Kramer-Mills

The historic First Reformed Church of New Brunswick, New Jersey, organized in 1717, sits literally at the intersection of faith and disability. Next door is the Elizabeth M. Boggs Center, a University Center for Excellence in Developmental Disabilities Education, Research, and Service and part of the Robert Wood Johnson Medical School. New Brunswick is also home to the Douglass Developmental Disabilities Center at Rutgers University. For Pastor Hartmut Kramer-Mills, a native of Jena, Germany, who began his theological education at Heidelberg University and is married to the congregation's American-born co-pastor, Susan Kramer-Mills, the church's proximity to these institutions is more than symbolic.

"A church is only on the map of the community," he said, "when its ministry is relevant to that community. In our diverse society, there's never one single map. With resources like [those nearby], it was clear that, among other maps, the 'map of special needs' was important for New Brunswick."

But it took one family, new to the church, to transform the congregation, whose seventy regular members often felt lost in a sanctuary that seats six hundred. Shortly after the Kramer-Millses returned from pastorates in Germany and took the pulpit in 2000, a wave of new members joined the church. Among them were a young mother and her four-year-old daughter. The woman introduced herself as Sandy and her daughter as Kathleen. Hartmut noticed, however, that when Sandy filled out her membership form, she also listed her eleven-year-old son, Walter, whom neither of the two ministers had ever seen.

Sandy explained that Walter had autism, a diagnosis of intellectual disabilities, and was nonverbal. His IQ was reported to be around fifty, which Sandy thought seemed high. What concerned her was that Walter might be disruptive of the church's worship life, partly because of his eating habits and personal hygiene. Sandy worried that bringing Walter along to church might add another burden to her life—the possibility of rejection by a church family.

Coming from Europe, with its heritage of official state churches, Hartmut was unfamiliar with the concept of a "church family" that might exclude newcomers. He believed the church was a public institution in which there should be a place for everybody. His idealism encouraged Sandy, and soon she brought Walter to church. He turned out to be a relatively calm child, although he did have significant support needs, such as help with standing and sitting, following the service, and calming down when he became excited. In addition, Walter needed structure. He enjoyed the repetition of the liturgy and the recognizable distinction between the worship leaders, who wore robes, and those in the pews, who did not.

Susan Kramer-Mills baptized Sandy during worship on May 5, 2002. In the following weeks the two pastors prepared for the baptisms of Walter and his sister, Kathleen. Because of Walter's fear of confined spaces—even the church's large sanctuary—the pastors and Sandy decided to baptize him outdoors. By custom, at midsummer First Reformed Church held a joint open-air service with other area Reformed churches, marking the conclusion of collegiate vacation Bible school, and this seemed a good opportunity to baptize Walter.

Still, the boy was anxious about events that took him outside his routine, so the pastors met regularly with the family at the outdoor worship area to rehearse the baptism. For several weeks they all went through the sacrament using an empty bowl on a camping table on the front lawn of a nearby farm, the only witnesses being a pair of cows watching over a fence. Finally, during worship on August 4, 2002, Hartmut baptized both Walter and Kathleen, surrounded by members of five other churches, all without incident.

At this point, bringing Sandy and her children into the church family was guided by little more than common sense and the church's innate sense of inclusion. To go farther and deeper, Hartmut and Susan needed to seek help in understanding Walter and autism and in providing the support the family required. It seemed only logical that the pastors visit Walter's school at the Eden Family of Services in Princeton. The school's director, David Holmes, gave them an introduction to autism and insights into the status of research on its origins, symptoms, and effects and into several schools of therapy. He also made suggestions about how the ministers could help First Reformed Church become more inclusive. Holmes's book, *Autism through the Lifespan: The Eden Model,* became the Kramer-Millses' guide in the months that followed.

The pastors also got help a little closer to home. They reached next door to Reverend Bill Gaventa at the Boggs Center (see chapter 2) and at his invitation joined the Autism and Faith Task Force, a group of lay people and clergy from a variety of faith traditions that Gaventa had helped organize as part of the Boggs Center's work. Through the task force the two pastors learned how other faith communities had integrated people with autism and how to apply those experiences at First Reformed. Ultimately, the couple also met with faculty members at Rutgers University's Douglass Developmental Disability Center and Rutgers Graduate School of Education.

The next step for the pastors was to apply what they were learning. Normally, children in the congregation began Sunday services with their parents in the main sanctuary and then, after a junior sermon, left for Sunday school classes. "While it seemed impractical to set up a separate Sunday school class for Walter alone," Hartmut wrote in the *Journal of Religion, Disability, and Health,* "we did not know how to integrate him in one of our classes, as all three of them consisted of much younger students. Instead, we decided to provide him with individual respite care" offered by student volunteers from Rutgers. "This would also allow his mother, Sandy, to remain in worship." Sandy readily agreed to the plan and joined a group of church volunteers who worked to make it happen.

Soon, the congregation's main committees were drawn into the effort, which had the collateral benefit of allowing the majority of the church's volunteers to become quickly acquainted with Walter and his family. The Worship and Music Committee was asked to consider an "emotional reversal" of the order of worship. Until then worship started in a reflective and meditative mode that eventually led to joy and praise. Now the pastors suggested allowing for worship to begin a bit more noisily, accommodating Walter when he needed to disrupt things, and to provide for reflection and meditation after the children's sermon.

The change was explained in the Sunday worship bulletin. Members accepted it well, perceiving it as giving everyone an opportunity to participate in ministry with Walter. In addition, the discussions that surrounded the change gave committee members a renewed sense of their role in determining the order of worship.

Almost immediately, church members embraced Walter, and four people appointed themselves his unofficial support team. He accepted this development readily and quickly grew familiar with the members of the team. It helped that the team stayed small, never with more than four members. The volunteers stayed with Walter during service and coffee hour and took him on short walks when he was restless. Other church members confided to the pastors their admiration for Sandy's care of Walter and Kathleen and for the fact that she made the family's regular church attendance an imperative.

At the pastors' suggestion, the church's finance committee agreed to raise funds to hire a respite worker to do what the student volunteers had been doing. The Christian Education Committee held garage sales and hosted breakfasts and dinners to solicit donations. The committee also appointed a small autism task force, with Bill Gaventa serving as informal adviser, to monitor all aspects of support for Walter. The task force received a small budget, so it became part of normal church administration. One of its first accomplishments was to establish a regular schedule of family events and excursions that would link Sandy and her family and a few other families from the Eden School with church families.

Ultimately, the autism task force was renamed the Special Needs Accessibility Project, and its mandate was broadened to reflect its members' awareness that other developmental disabilities existed besides autism. It also reflected its members' conviction that their work was really about providing access to God for people with special needs.

Still, the changes taking place at the church to include Walter sometimes met with resistance. As Bill Gaventa has written, the difference between welcome and rejection of people with developmental disabilities in houses of worship can be small. Church members occasionally called the pastors to complain about Walter's behavior during worship. One person voiced concern about whether the ministers were "turning the church autistic."

The pastors responded by publishing more of Walter's story and reports on the work of the special needs group in the church's monthly newsletter. Walter's family joined the church's Dutch Dancing Group, which further brought the boy into the life of the church. As a congregation, members read books such as *That All May Worship: An Interfaith Welcome to People with Disabilities* and *We Don't Have Any Here: Planning for Ministries with People with Disabilities in Our Communities.* Although one member did leave the church over the inclusion effort and other issues, what little anxiety and resentment existed in the church ultimately faded as Walter and his family became part of the fabric of the congregation.

In 2005 Walter reached confirmation age, but because of First Reformed's small membership, he was alone in his age group, and there was no confirmation class in which he could be included. The larger question for Sandy and the pastors was, in any case, what could confirmation mean to Walter? Hartmut believed that confirmation was foremost a remembrance of baptism, an invocation of the Holy Spirit, and an admittance into the confessing membership of the church. He and Sandy discussed what they wanted for Walter and "quickly found common ground," he later wrote. "We did not want to pursue Walter's confirmation only for the sake of the ritual. It would have to have meaning if we were to proceed."

The church's elders agreed, and they concurred that Walter's training should be flexible, consistent with their understanding of God's grace. They wanted to focus on Walter's potential for learning and growth in their faith. "At the time, this sounded well intended," wrote Hartmut, "but also very ambitious. How would we determine Walter's potential for growth of faith?" Again the church's neighbor, Bill Gaventa, offered some help, in the form of examples of curriculums from the Boggs Center library. Soon the group had a list of learning goals and objectives and a custom-made curriculum with illustrations, simple songs, and very simple texts.

When two church members who were also special education teachers reviewed the curriculum, they felt the lessons were in some respects too difficult for Walter and in others too simple, underestimating his ability. Drawing on their expertise, they revised it down to six lessons. On May 11, 2008, Walter, now eighteen, was presented to the Board of Elders. Accompanied by his mother's voice and Pastor Hartmut on the piano, Walter sang the Doxology and the Gloria Patri. The elders continued with a normal, if modified, confirmation class setting, asking Walter to distinguish a Bible from a hymnbook and an angel figure from a cross.

Having satisfied the elders, Walter was confirmed a week later, on Trinity Sunday, May 18, 2008. While using the traditional order of worship, the pastors were determined not to have Walter experience worship as a passive recipient. They included a Sunday school skit before the sermon, written by Susan and called "Weedy Creation." The plot followed the creation story of Genesis 1 and required Walter to hold up a sign for the congregation after each completed part of a very diverse creation. Seven times he performed this, exclaiming each time, "It is good!"

The confirmation ceremony, too, was tailored toward Walter's strengths. Instead of the usually required verbal vows, team members prompted the young man to act out his vows. A member read the four professional questions, but instead of answering "I do," Walter handed her, after each question, one of the objects he had used during his confirmation class sessions: a wooden cross, a Bible, a figurine of an angel, and a figurine of Jesus. In the end he received the blessing while kneeling in front of the holy table, something that had also been rehearsed. It was a joyous day, and representatives of many agencies and nonprofit groups joined the worshiping community for the event. The service was followed by a party in the church's fellowship hall.

"Today, Walter is an integral part of the congregation at First Reformed Church," Hartmut said, and working with him has connected many groups and individuals within the congregation. "It has also opened our eyes to people with other needs," the pastor said. These include Latino schoolchildren in New Brunswick, some of whom First Reformed has integrated into its congregation, and homeless men, for whom it provides shelter in rotation with other area congregations. For many years now, as many as fifteen homeless men have slept in the church's fellowship hall for two weeks each winter.

"Anybody working toward including a particular group," said Hartmut, "soon discovers that inclusive ministry does not stop there. It leads to many other groups, whose access to the holy table deserves equal attention."

8

Gathering Karma

Vidya Bhushan Gupta

As a Hindu priest in New Jersey and a physician specializing in neuro-developmental disabilities, Vidya Bhushan Gupta was able to provide unique counseling to the Hindu father of a child with a disabling condition. The man's adult daughter had attention deficit/hyperactivity disorder (ADHD) with severe nonverbal learning disability, her perceptual IQ ranging between 70 and 100. In recent years she had also developed bipolar disorder and, at thirty-three, lived at home and was unable to cook or live independently.

For many years, the father told Gupta, he grappled with the question of why this had happened to his family, at first trying to find an answer in something he or other family members had done wrong. For the man as a Hindu, this faultfinding extended to deeds done during past lives, in what his faith tradition calls "karma." But this only brought him guilt and then clinical depression. In addition, finding fault with others, including his wife and her family, brought rancor to his marriage and his relationships with his relatives.

Although he did not discuss his daughter's condition, the man's Indian immigrant friends were aware of it. Still, they asked him no questions, to avoid hurting his feelings. A parents' support group also existed at the family's temple, but members were reluctant to announce their problems directly. In the Hindu community, visible physical disabilities are accepted more easily than mental and behavioral disabilities. Nevertheless, a few parents of children with autism and Down syndrome had come forward to ask for help in connecting with useful resources.

With Gupta's help, the man came to recognize that he might never be able to find a rational cause that he could attribute to someone else, so that he could unburden his conscience and relieve his personal guilt. Similarly, Gupta pointed out that the man's persistent anger and frustration were futile and unhelpful in dealing with the task before him. Ultimately, dealing with his daughter's disability brought the man closer to his wife and to his other child. He ultimately found refuge in God—not to find an answer, but to deal with the stress of living with a child with disabilities.

"I urged him not to blame God or beg him for redress," Gupta said, "because the Hindu concept of karma posits that God does not perform karma for people. Only *they* do. After all, God is just and merciful. 'Just,' because God maintains order, which we call *rita,* in this world without any favors. 'Merciful,' because God is always ready to give guidance, love, and support to anyone, irrespective of their past deeds.

"By performing better karma in this life in the process of managing the daughter's disability with equanimity, the man will gather good karma for his future *samsaaric* journey [cycle of birth, life, and death]. The expectation is that the daughter, too, will benefit from her father's efforts. She, too, is suffering, and her father's faith urges him to have compassion, or *daya,* for her, even when she reflects hate and anger on her parents. Although the man still experiences grief when someone else's daughter gets married, he can overcome the crisis with God's grace."

Hindu scriptures do not specifically deal with the issue of disability, Gupta explained. However, many tenets of Hinduism are pertinent in dealing with it. Hindus believe that the real self is the spirit, which resides for a lifetime in the temporary container of the body. This spirit, or divine spark of consciousness, called *atma,* is similar in essence to the universal consciousness, or God, called Brahman or Parmatma. Thus the body can be disabled, but not the spirit, so there is no question of discrimination. People with disabilities are like the divine. An anecdote in Hindu scriptures talks of a young man with eight physically disabling conditions who is barred from entering the court of a king because of his youth and disabilities. The king, on hearing this, apologizes to him and allows him to compete in a theological debate. He seats him with other Brahmans in his court and showers him with gifts and honor when he defeats the others.

One of the cardinal virtues of Hinduism is *daya,* or compassion toward other beings, both human and nonhuman. All Hindus are required to be nonviolent in body, mind, and voice to other people, including persons with disabilities. During India's medieval times, Gupta said, people with disabling conditions were not treated well, particularly in matrimonial matters. But the popular culture is changing, he believes, and becoming more accepting of people with disabilities.

Gupta is not alone in his effort to reach out to Hindus with intellectual disabilities who may be reluctant to seek help. He is trying to make Hindu religious congregations more welcoming to people with intellectual disabilities and has established a support group for parents of children with such conditions.

"Hindus in New Jersey who are affected by mental illness, whether as family members and caregivers or by having a serious mental illness themselves, often turn to religious leaders for support," according to Aruna Rao, director of educational programs for the National Alliance on Mental Illness. "Most religious leaders provide some degree of spiritual counseling, but they rarely have any understanding of the medical and social issues and the resources these families need to sustain themselves and their loved ones. Swami Tadatmananda Saraswati is one of the few members of the Hindu clergy who provides personal support, understanding, and religious guidance to families in need."

Rao recently nominated Swami Tadatmananda for an award from the New Jersey Coalition of Statewide Ministries, which he won. Tadatmananda is the resident spiritual leader, or swami—someone who has mastered Hindu scriptures and philosophy and is a descendant of teachers—of the Arsha Bodha ashram (spiritual retreat) in Somerset, New Jersey. The ashram serves Hindus in central New Jersey and brings together a congregation of about five hundred from several counties for weekly worship and religious education. Tadatmananda sees an average of two to three individuals or families with disabilities each week for counseling and spiritual guidance, according to Rao.

"Many families are unable or unwilling to seek out mainstream social services or support," Rao said, "and he is instrumental in directing them to resources that will enable them to cope with disability-related issues. He provides access to a mental illness support group to hold their monthly meetings at the ashram, and he frequently attends the groups to provide support to participants."

Tadatmananda's work goes beyond counseling. In his weekly addresses at the temple, he often discusses the issue of mental health, including depression, which is a common and unaddressed illness in the Hindu American community. He stresses that mental illness is a biologically based illness of the brain and that treatment is available for those who need it. This direct acknowledgment does a tremendous amount to address the stigma attached to admitting mental health problems in the community.

"Swami Tadatmananda also addresses mainstream audiences to provide an important perspective for social workers and other providers about the Hindu outlook on disabilities, suicide, mental health, and other issues that are difficult for providers to address directly with their clients," said Rao.

9

Telling the Story

Cindy Merten

Adaptive technology has almost become a ministry in itself for people like Cindy Merten, director of Christian education at First Presbyterian Church of Birmingham, Michigan. "Inclusion really is one relationship at a time in our church," said Merten, who also serves on her denomination's Presbyterians for Disability Concerns Leadership Team.

Merten became concerned that some children with disabilities in the confirmation classes she taught were feeling left out. Most students in the class made public presentations of their "faith statements" to the congregation, in the form of either a verbal statement or an artistic representation such as a poem, collage, song, or painting. Because this was difficult for students with disabilities, Merten began using a small, inexpensive electronic device called a Talking Photo Album. The twenty-four-page album has transparent sleeves to hold pictures or drawings, and the user can record a ten-second message on each page. For young people in the class who were unable to speak, Merten recruited friends and family members to make recordings about their faith.

One class member, Elizabeth, who was unable to speak, was presented to the congregation with her "talking book." "Elizabeth doesn't have speech," her mother said, "but she certainly has a lot to say." A member of a different class, Derek, was a thirteen-year-old boy who had developmental disabilities and was visually impaired. He was enrolled in the church's confirmation class along with his twin brother, who wanted to help Derek, an auditory learner, participate. So Merten created a book for Derek in which her recorded voice told the story of the birth of Jesus, with Christmas carols playing in the background on each page.

A woman in Merten's church who was visually impaired used what is called a Dymo Braille gun to create labels to add to the pages. Along with the book, Merten and her colleague supplied a child's Nativity set, to add tactile manipulation to the story. Derek could then push a button on each page of the book to listen to the story and the music. As the story unfolded page by page, a different piece of the Nativity set was placed in his hands for exploration.

Derek didn't know the other members of the confirmation class very well, so Merten had the others record greetings to him on each page of a Talking Photo Album, introducing themselves so that Derek could become familiar with their voices. Merten's goal was not only to help Derek know the other class members but also to give them a way to interact with him more comfortably. Derek loved the book and listened to it frequently at home. Other kids in the confirmation class who had siblings with disabilities saw the book and asked Merten if she would make one for their brother or sister. "Now," said Merten, "we are in the process of creating these books for every child and young person with disabilities in the church, to help them learn more about their classmates and feel more included."

In another example of the way individualized adaptations can expand opportunities for inclusion, Merten worked with Sean, an eight-year-old boy with autism, to create a social story about taking Communion. Earlier, Sean had participated in a class meant to instruct children in the sacrament, but when the day came to try it, he had a meltdown. "There was so much to the logistics of it," Merten said, "that we hadn't even thought to prepare Sean."

The class instruction had focused on the meaning of Communion, but now Sean's mother helped Merten see that it was the details of the process that he needed to learn. The two women collaborated to write a simple story describing every step of the event, and they recorded it on the pages of a Talking Photo Album. Sean enjoyed taking digital photographs, so Merten had him take photos of Communion and used them to illustrate the book. Sean studied the book with his mother at home and grew comfortable with the idea of participating in the sacrament with his peers. "I think it will also be useful for teaching all our second graders the simple steps we as adults take for granted," Merten said.

With these experiences under their belts, Merten and others at the church launched two other programs that included young people with disabilities. A drumming group for youths in grades six through twelve involved ten boys, including Derek and several others with autism or attention deficit/hyperactivity disorder (ADHD). They help lead worship at the ten o'clock service on Sunday mornings and at the monthly "Rejoicing Spirits" service, an inclusion service that welcomes and celebrates the gifts of people with developmental disabilities (see chapter 13). New relationships in the community and connections with residents of group homes emerged from this new ministry. The church is now adopting one of the homes and plans to provide ongoing spiritual care to its residents. What began as a children's program has become a whole church ministry at First Presbyterian Birmingham.

"Inclusion surely is about building relationships one person at a time, and offering a welcome where our embrace is as wide as God's love," Merten said.

10

The Joy of Giving

Dennis Schurter

For thirty years the Reverend Dennis D. Schurter served as chaplain at Denton State School (now Denton State Supported Living Center), a state-run residential facility for adults with developmental disabilities in Denton, Texas. During his ministry he worked closely with congregations in the area to assist them in including people from his facility in their churches. Many of these activities were successful, he says, thanks to the loving ministry of members in various congregations.

In the late 1980s Schurter organized what he called the REAL/LIFE Network—the name was an acronym for "Religious Educators and Learners Linked in Faith Experiences"—to create a support group for teachers of Bible classes for adults with developmental disabilities. The network included volunteer teachers from six Protestant congregations in the area. They met quarterly to share resources and discuss the mutual concerns and joys of their ministry.

At one REAL/LIFE Network meeting in 1999—which Schurter himself missed—members planned a joint Sunday morning retreat for all the people in the participating congregations' classes, to be held at the Singing Oaks Church of Christ. The program, called "Son Day Retreat," was centered on a theme and five "learning centers." As five groups of participants worked their way through the learning centers during the morning, teachers from each congregation taught a brief lesson to each group. Singing Oaks planned a lunch for nearly eighty participants and volunteers, and Schurter conducted the closing activity. The retreat finished by one o'clock that afternoon, when everyone returned to their group homes or residences. "It was a grand morning for everyone—the participants, their teachers, and congregational volunteers," said Schurter—and the event has taken place every year since then.

In 2006 the REAL/LIFE Network launched a local fund-raising effort so that class members could send food and Bibles to Iraqi Christians through the Global Aid Network of the Campus Crusade for Christ International. The teachers wanted their students to experience the joy of helping others and sharing God's word with people in another part of the world. Five network congregations cooperated in the effort.

They began by passing out to their members what they called "Bags of Blessings," small cloth bags holding Hershey's Kisses and a note explaining their project. Some donations came from church members, and the group held several fund-raising events, including fellowship meals served by Sunday school members, car washes, and a large garage sale at the social hall. The adults with disabilities participated in many of these activities, working at the garage sale and car washes. Working together, members of the network, church members, and residents from the Denton School raised $4,300—enough to send more than one hundred "Bags of Blessings," each containing food and a Bible, to one Iraqi village. Everyone involved, said Schurter, was "excited to reach out to others with God's love in such concrete ways."

As often happens with programs like REAL/LIFE Network, its benefits and expertise have filtered throughout congregations in the Denton area. For the past twenty-five years, for example, volunteers at First Christian Church, Denton, have organized a ministry called the Rainbow Class, an outgrowth of REAL/LIFE, which has participated since 1999 in the Son Day Retreats. Members of the class—all adults with developmental disabilities—play bells during worship services, help prepare Communion, set tables for fellowship dinners, host annual cookouts at a teacher's home, and sing at occasional services. One Rainbow Class study segment, lasting several months, was titled "Women of the Bible."

Rainbow Class members often take active roles in worship, leading the lessons, playing "Amazing Grace" on the piano along with the organist one Sunday a year, and pledging to the congregation's budget. At Advent, the class participates in the "hanging of the greens," a winter tradition that originated in England.

"The first year we were invited to participate, one person was asked to light the lights on the tree, and he was so excited he skipped up the aisle," said Linda Morrow, one of the ministry's leaders. "Since then we have either helped decorate the tree with chrismons [Christian symbols formed from two Greek letters, also called Chi-Rhos] or hung door wreaths. People realized how little it takes to excite some of our folks and make them feel a real part of the worship.

"Over the past twenty-five years the members of this class have become more and more a part of the life of the congregation and not just attenders on Sunday morning. The congregation is much more comfortable around 'us' and makes us feel welcome. Some of our ladies come from a group home. Those ladies attended church school for only several months, then told their house parent that they wanted to stay for worship as well and have attended worship for several years at this point."

The church made preparations to smooth the way. "We asked our congregational folks to invite our folks [with disabilities] to sit with them in the sanctuary during worship," said Marilyn Reeves, a teacher in the Special Populations ministry at Singing Oaks Church of Christ. "What we found is that our folks liked sitting together and they liked sitting with us. We all sit together and we do this to this very day." When the newcomers participated in area Special Olympics events, they were acknowledged from the pulpit the following Sunday. They also received practical instruction in church doctrine and practice.

For many people with disabilities, who may be unable to work and trying to survive on a tight budget, the issue of supporting their faith communities is a sore point, if not a cause for embarrassment. But in Denton, most members of the Rainbow Class had jobs of some sort, so they were taught the church's concept of tithing. At first they were asked to contribute a nickel a week to the church, and this was gradually raised to a quarter. Their contributions were designated for specific charitable projects such as buying caps and mittens, which class members picked out, for poor schoolchildren.

"Our folks learned the joy of giving, both of themselves and of their means," said Reeves. "They have very caring hearts and love helping others. We have now upped their giving to a dollar a week and they bring a canned good for our food pantry as well to feed the homeless."

For Bible study on Sunday mornings, the class uses Friendship Bible Study material from Friendship Ministries (see chapter 15), in conjunction with handicrafts. Once, when the class was studying the story of Lazarus, Morrow had her son wrap himself in cloth strips and hide in the classroom closet. When the time came in the story for Lazarus to come back to life, she opened the closet door, and there was Lazarus coming back to life. The class was amazed and talked about it for weeks.

Like congregations everywhere, members of the Rainbow Class have observed the passage of life-cycle events. They make cards and send them to other members who are ill. On one occasion, the class held a well-attended wedding shower for two members, residents of a group home who were living together and decided to be married by the bride's brother, who was a pastor.

When one of the group, a woman named Leslie, died suddenly, her parents asked the group to sing at the funeral, where they led the music, along with several residents of a group home. The service, which was held at First Christian even though the family did not attend there, was quite an experience, Morrow recalled. Some of the out-of-town visitors who came for the service were so moved by the church's gesture in holding the service that they made a donation to the Rainbow Class. Lasting bonds were formed. Regular members of the church began to pick up visitors from their residential communities and bring them to services, as well as take them shopping, to religious retreats, and to movies.

Members of the Rainbow Class "are constant in inviting their friends to come with them to Bible class, and we are never surprised to find new faces any Sunday," said Reeves. "They are truly a joy and we have learned so much from them."

11

Circles of Support

Barb Eiler and Ben Smith

Sometimes the smallest efforts to include people with disabilities can yield gratifying results, as they did for Barb Eiler at East Goshen Mennonite Church in Indiana. Eiler was born with the hereditary bone disease osteogenesis imperfecta (OI), which causes extreme brittleness of the bones. At birth she had sixteen fractures throughout her body, which were not found until she was two weeks old. Although she grew to be only four feet, three inches tall, suffered frequent broken bones, and sometimes used a wheelchair, she graduated from college and began a career as an elementary school teacher. She married and raised two children, one of whom also has OI.

"God gave me very special parents who believed that God had a special place for me in this world," she wrote in *Timbrel,* a publication for Mennonite women. "They never believed the doctors who said I would never sit or crawl—let alone walk—in my lifetime. And at the age of sixty-two, I am still walking and living a very full life. Yes, there are difficulties, and I often have pain, but I am so thankful for each day that God allows me to continue walking."

Despite support from her family, Eiler often felt isolated in school. Her condition kept her from sports, for fear that she would break more bones, and she was unable to climb the steps to the second-floor lunchroom. On snowy or icy winter stays, other students left her behind as she carefully negotiated the walkways between school buildings. "As I recall those high school days, I remember that I questioned my faith in God, but ultimately, my faith was strengthened," Eiler wrote.

Throughout her life Eiler has found support from East Goshen Mennonite Church, and several years ago she was asked to lead Sunday worship at the congregation. After several weeks members told her they enjoyed her leadership, but because of her short stature, she was hidden by the standard-size podium. Mennonites are known for their carpentry skills, which they often put to use during disaster recoveries, so someone made her a simple step stool, and the problem was solved.

Later, when East Goshen built a new sanctuary, a congregation member named Mike Grieser, who is a gifted woodworker, called Eiler to ask her to inspect a new podium he had built. When she did, she was surprised to find that Grieser had built in an easily pulled-out step for her at the base. As often happens when a congregation makes an effort to include worshipers with disabilities, there were some unanticipated beneficiaries. "Children can also use this step with ease," Eiler wrote. "This act of helping to include me and children in our worship service has been a great gift of including shorter people in the service."

Eiler says she has learned a number of lessons from being a person with a very visible disability: "I encourage others to look at individuals beyond their handicaps. You may be uncomfortable or unsure of what a person is capable of doing. Don't assume; rather, take the risk and ask the person if they wish to be involved. I encourage parents to allow their children to ask questions when they see someone who is different from them. I would prefer they ask me why I am short, or why I have a limp when I walk, rather than for them to feel I am not a real person. Adults have questions, also, and there is nothing wrong in asking the questions."

Another midsize Mennonite congregation, Pleasant View Mennonite Church, north of Goshen, has also been intentional about being accessible and inclusive to everyone, regardless of physical or intellectual abilities. The congregation places a high value on involving everyone in its worship services, as well as in other areas of the life and ministry of the church. To accomplish that, Pleasant View provides accessible facilities, including parking, doorways, and bathrooms, and has installed a permanent ramp to the sanctuary podium and a handrail along the steps to the podium. The congregation holds Christian education classes on the church's main floor, offers large-print verses for hymns via video projection, and provides an enhanced audio system for people who are hard of hearing.

And just as East Goshen reached out to Barb Eiler, so Pleasant View has taken a bigger step to reach out to one particular family. More than a decade ago, Phyllis and Jim Smith's son, Ben, was diagnosed with schizophrenia. After years of learning and heart-break, crisis and intense involvement, the couple came to the congregation and asked whether a small group could be organized to help the family. After listening to them and praying with their minister, members consulted a booklet called "Supportive Care in the Congregation," prepared by a task force of the national Mennonite Church's Central Committee. Using that resource as a guide, the group began by educating the congregation about schizophrenia. The Smiths gave talks to five different Sunday school classes, followed by a Sunday evening presentation.

One man who heard the presentation, Clay Shetler, said he was inspired by the parents and the open way in which they shared their family situation. "What motivates me has to do with what we promise each other when we bring new members into the church," he said, according to *Connections,* the newsletter of the Anabaptist Disabilities Network (ADNet). "We make this commitment to care for each other. We have a responsibility to help."

The first thing the congregational support group did was to help clean up Ben's apartment and make the space more livable. They also worked to move Ben to temporary housing while a lo-cal social service agency renovated his building to provide quality, low-income housing and make it accessible. That made it possible for Ben's father, who uses a wheelchair, to visit him at home for the first time.

The church support team then turned its attention to trying to help Ben with positive social interactions in settings he could handle. Because Jim and Phyllis travel frequently on church busi-ness, they were concerned about Ben's needs when they were out of town. When they are away, Shetler, the team coordinator, tries to make certain Ben is invited to participate with church members in activities such as softball games, fishing, church dinners, and

Frisbee golf, which he enjoys. A team member brings Ben frozen ready-to-eat meals.

Both work and worship for Ben continue to challenge the team. One member helped him get a job for a few months, but nothing long-term has materialized.

Although Ben doesn't feel comfortable at regular worship services, members of the support team want to bring him into the congregation's spiritual life in ways that he might find accessible and meaningful. One team member suggested that someone might stop by every week or two to share a Bible verse or pray with him, if Ben felt comfortable with that arrangement. "We could make that church for him," said team member Ruth Sellers, although this is an issue the group is still feeling its way through.

"We don't have it completely figured out as to when we are being helpful," said Shetler. "We are in new territory. We want to hear stories from other churches that are doing something like this." The support team has also discussed what additional role it might play if Jim and Phyllis were no longer able to help Ben.

The Smiths are grateful for everything their faith friends have done for their son. "Our family has been blessed by the gracious support of the caregiving network of Pleasant View Mennonite Church members," said Jim. "They surround us with love when needs arise and with their ongoing spontaneous expressions of care for our son. We encourage every congregation to consider developing a network of support for the vulnerable individuals and their families in their midst who need occasional assistance with a long-term commitment for caring ministry."

12

Finding Acceptance

Lucas McCarty

There is no real limit to what a worship community can do—to the barriers it can surmount—when it chooses to welcome people with disabilities, especially with the help of new, affordable, electronic technology. In the rural Mississippi Delta, a young white man named Lucas McCarty, born with severe cerebral palsy, has found a faith home at Trinity House of Prayer, a small, exuberant, cash-strapped, African American congregation that has embraced him. The son of a teacher, McCarty uses a wheelchair but also gets around by walking on his knees, with the help of pads worn over his blue jeans. He shouts and makes noises, but for the most part he communicates with a device called a Delta Pathfinder, using a keyboard and an icon-based language called Minspeak to synthesize speech.

Until 1996, when he was ten, Lucas worshiped with his family at a predominantly white, middle-class church near his home in Indianola, Mississippi. Although he lived in one of the most historically segregated regions of the United States, the boy was fascinated from an early age with African American culture and its particular strain of gospel music.

In their inspiring book *The Year of Our Lord: Faith, Hope, and Harmony in the Mississippi Delta,* novelist T. R. Pearson and photographer Langdon Clay described how McCarty came to Trinity. John Woods, an African American employee of McCarty's grandfather, a catfish farmer, brought Lucas to the tin-roofed structure across from a rice field, correctly sensing that the boy would be welcomed there. Trinity is a congregation, Woods told Pearson, whose members know about personal challenges and setbacks: people struggling with poverty, former drug addicts, recovering alcoholics, sometimes violent people familiar with the insides of

jails and prisons. In short, the kind of people Jesus preached to—
and loved.

Lucas, who loves music, was immediately embraced by the congregation and was in no way considered out of place or disruptive.
He joined the choir, sitting in the first row of the loft, leaning
on the railing as he participated in worship, singing with his eyes
closed and his arms raised. Trinity House of Prayer sees plenty
of shouting, speaking in tongues—*glossolalia* is the theological
term—and collapsing to the floor, "slain in the spirit," during its
ecstatic, three- to four-hour services. It is a place, one congregation member told Pearson, where there is sometimes "too much
joy."

"Without doubt," Pearson wrote, "Trinity's members treated
Lucas with unstudied compassion. Instead of thinking Lucas diminished by his condition, his friends at Trinity seemed to consider him blessed by it, almost anointed. . . . In too many churches
I've known, Christian living is treated as a dutiful sideline, but
there is a palpable happiness infusing worship in this Delta church
that I, for one, find consoling."

Once, an entire service at Trinity was dedicated to Lucas. "I
am white on the outside but black on the inside," McCarty told
Pearson. "When people look at me, I want them to know that I am
not just a boy in a wheelchair." Still, this is a Pentecostal church
that believes in faith healing by touch—the "laying on of hands."
"One Sunday," Pearson wrote, "when the olive oil comes out and
Bishop [Willie B.] Knighten wades into the congregation, who's
to say Lucas McCarty won't rise and walk?" But he doesn't, and his
faith is not questioned because of it.

The relationship between a young white Southerner with a disability and a black Pentecostal congregation is less unlikely than
one might expect. In the 2011 memoir *House of Prayer No. 2,* Mark
Richard, a white man, tells of his own experiences growing up
with physical and intellectual disabilities in southeastern Virginia
in the 1960s. Before going on to a successful career as a novelist, Richard felt a call to ministry but was thwarted in his efforts
to enter a seminary. On a visit home he found that his mother

had joined a local, predominately African American Pentecostal congregation that was planning to build a new church. In helping to build the new structure, Richard, like Lucas McCarty, found acceptance and spiritual fulfillment.

13

Getting Involved

Rejoicing Spirits

January of 2003 marked a turning point in Susan Crawford's life, she told *Breakthrough* magazine. "I was a member of St. Paul's Lutheran Church in Exton, Pennsylvania, for about two years and only peripherally involved, helping with a few activities here and there. I wanted to be more active, but didn't know how to best serve the Lord." Then she attended a class held at the church, titled "Identifying Your Spiritual Gifts." While praying for her spiritual calling, Crawford felt an inspiration from the Holy Spirit—a strong desire to explore the idea of developing a worship service adapted for people with intellectual and developmental disabilities.

Crawford confided in her pastor, who encouraged her and suggested she contact Cynthia McCurdy, whose daughter, Katie, had Down syndrome. Since birth Katie had been an active part of her family's faith life. She attended Sunday school and vacation Bible school at St. Paul's, made her first Communion and confirmation, and was active in the teen theater group. "I carry the banners, kind of like a spirit does, too," Katie explained in the documentary *Creating Room in God's House,* which aired on PBS. "And the Gospel—I have to read the Gospel. I have to study for it. Then I read the Gospel to everyone."

McCurdy was aware, however, that many of Katie's peers and their families were not having the same positive experiences at other churches. She said, "Over the years, I heard stories from families that they were asked to leave, were told not to come back, or that they just didn't receive the kind of support needed and necessary while navigating the challenges of raising a child with a disability. Many families felt, if we can't get the love and support we need at church, where can we get it? This left many of them feeling even more isolated and disillusioned with organized religion. In other families that I've talked to, there have been numerous instances of 'We don't know what to do with your kind' or 'Please don't come back.'"

Crawford agreed. "I realized that people with disabilities were missing from communities of faith. It isn't that people with disabilities don't have spiritual needs and desires—they certainly do! They just weren't being invited and welcomed into houses of worship."

Both women felt moved to action, and with their newly recruited team they founded the Rejoicing Spirits ministry, which has grown to twenty-eight churches in five denominations, spread across ten states. "Originally," said Crawford, "our efforts were focused on our local community. However, a few months into this outreach we were contacted by another church that wanted to follow our model, and then another. We began to realize that God had bigger plans for Rejoicing Spirits."

St. Paul's pastor, Mark Singh-Hueter, embraced the Rejoicing Spirits service concept. "Everything is presented in a way that is really much more interactive," he said, "whether worshipers are in the choir, or part of the skit, or doing Bible readings—everybody gets to use their gifts and get involved."

Others soon became involved and spread Rejoicing Spirits to other congregations. Susan March first brought her son Joshua, who has a developmental disability, to the St. Paul's service, where, like many others, he found a caring, concerned, and loving environment—including a "no shushing policy." What March also found was an opportunity to network with other families affected by disabilities. Rejoicing Spirits brought her back to her own church, too, which she had stopped attending after Joshua was born. That church now has a Rejoicing Spirits ministry of its own.

"We've been very fortunate to make some new friends and rekindle friendships with some old friends," March said. "We are so blessed that Joshua was born in a time and place when people with 'differences' are better accepted in the community and that there are programs in place that give each and every one of us the chance to be everything we can be."

"I would not feel comfortable just walking into any church for a service, because of the noisiness," continued March. "We usually make some kind of a scene, but here at Rejoicing Spirits we really don't have to worry about it. A lot of times when we're out in public, Joshua does experience a lot of stares. So we find that we really don't go to many public places or events. Rejoicing Spirits is wonderful, because not only does Joshua get time to come and be exposed to worship, but I get to come back to church, too."

Karen, the mother of a young teenage boy with Down syndrome and autism spectrum, sometimes wondered whether her son, Freddie, was developing spiritually at their home church on Sunday mornings. She and her husband had to take turns engaging their son to keep him from being distracted. Then they heard about the Rejoicing Spirits ministry at St. Paul's, and they were not disappointed.

Freddie enjoys singing with his peers in the front of the church, leading the congregation in prayer and Bible readings, and participating in Bible lesson skits. These activities engage his attention and interest to the point that he no longer needs his parents to keep him focused throughout the service. The relaxed structure of the service enables him to feel free to be himself during worship. As a result, Freddie is more responsive during the service and, his parents are convinced, more open to receiving the messages of God's love. Freddie is eager to attend each service and often surprises his mother and father with his initiatives to participate, even though occasionally he doesn't understand what he has just volunteered to do.

One unforeseen benefit to Karen's family is the way their son's experiences at Rejoicing Spirits services have helped him to become more involved at the family's home church services, where Freddie now participates more and is much more interested in attending. "It's a joy to watch him grow in this way and become a fuller participant in his community," Karen said. With his family by his side, he "has an opportunity to develop his own unique spirituality and relationship with God."

One volunteer, a teenager named Ally, said her experience with Rejoicing Spirits had inspired her to pursue a career in occupational therapy. Before she formed friendships with Rejoicing Spirits worshipers, Ally had been considering a different career path. Others at St. Paul's, who had no previous personal relationships with people who had intellectual and developmental disabilities, have experienced changes in attitude because of their involvement with Rejoicing Spirits.

Paul, now a faithful volunteer, was drawn to the ministry because several of his family members were participating—but he had his doubts. "I knew myself well enough to know that I couldn't possibly relate to our special guests," he recalled in a newsletter testimony. "Wouldn't they and I be very different from one another? What would I say? How would I react? But my daughter and my wife were involved, and I thought, maybe, just maybe I might—uh—join them? Maybe. Then I stopped thinking and just listened. From somewhere a still, small voice said, 'Paul, you've got to do this.' 'Why?' I asked. 'Because you're afraid,' said the voice. And so I reluctantly volunteered."

Tentatively, Paul agreed to supervise parking for the services. But it soon dawned on him that he was more than a traffic attendant—he would be the first point of contact for people attending the services, the first person to greet and welcome the worshipers. Over time, he grew more comfortable attending the services.

"I've learned that our guests and I are not really so different one from the other at all. If they are special, they are special in ways that all God's children are special. I see them for what they *can* do and not what they *can't*. Isn't this how we are to see everyone? And isn't this how we would like to be seen ourselves?"

Crawford and her team developed a guidebook, *How to Start a Rejoicing Spirits Ministry*, to encourage and equip Christian congregations of all denominations to start their own disability outreach ministries. The guidebook outlines key topics such as setting up an initial feasibility review committee, launching the first worship service, reaching out to the community, and carrying out follow-up activities. It includes examples of invitations, letters to provider agencies, newsletter articles, press releases, and a worship bulletin. Additionally, Crawford's group mentors new Rejoicing Spirits host churches, sharing the many lessons the team has learned.

"Ideally, all people of all abilities should be invited and welcomed into the fabric of a faith community of their choice," Crawford said. "However, the reality is that most houses of worship are simply not equipped to do this for a variety of reasons. First, many people don't believe that people with intellectual and developmental disabilities are spiritual people. These doubters just need to join us at one Rejoicing Spirits service and they will realize that a person's cognitive abilities have no relationship to their spiritual capabilities. Second is their fear, fear of the unknown, and their lack of knowledge and experience with people with disabilities.

"With all the other issues that face our congregations, the easiest one to put off and avoid is full inclusion. It's been our experience, though, that congregations are willing to take on an outreach-evangelism ministry such as Rejoicing Spirits, and when they do, everyone realizes 'that we are not so different from each other at all and that God loves each one of us equally.' Rejoicing Spirits, as an intentional, inclusive outreach ministry, has created visibility, raised awareness, and fostered education, which has led to acceptance and friendship."

The ministry believes that religious communities provide some of the few opportunities people with intellectual and developmental disabilities have to develop friendships and interact independently with others outside of their individual or group homes. Too often, people with disabilities spend their lives feeling as if they are being shadowed, told what to do and how to do it. Rejoicing Spirits encourages free expression and full participation. Worshipers who are nonverbal and may have the ability to communicate only in noises are given handheld instruments to convey their spirituality and joy. All are accepted and celebrated.

"We created a welcoming environment for all children of God, filled with lots of music and joyous singing along with brief, meaningful messages," Crawford said. "Participants feel accepted and part of a love-filled community. We want everyone to learn about God and his love for each of them. The service provides fellowship with other Christians and the opportunity for friendships to develop.

"Rejoicing Spirits can be a stepping-stone for worshipers who want to transition into a fully integrated church community, which we believe is the ideal situation. For others, the Rejoicing Spirits worship service may fully meet their current needs and desires. But no one is excluded from this worship experience; anyone who is already integrated into a church community is also invited to this unique worship service."

"When I see individuals of all abilities feeling free to be themselves and to worship as God has intended them to be," Cynthia McCurdy said, "I feel the Holy Spirit moving within everyone."

14

Reunited with the Past

Isadore Rosen

Helping just one person, even relatively briefly, can have a profound effect. When Isadore Rosen—known as Izzy—was twelve, he was sent to live in a Minnesota state residential treatment center for people with intellectual disabilities, then called mental retardation, and since then he had never again heard from any family members. Yet when he was in the middle of his ninth decade and planning for the end of his life, he told Shelly Christensen, then a young program manager for the Minneapolis Jewish Community Inclusion Program for People with Disabilities, that he wanted to be buried with his immigrant parents. The problem was, he couldn't remember their first names, and there were lots of Rosens in the Minneapolis–St. Paul area.

Izzy was unknown to the Jewish community when Christensen first met him through a residential supervisor at a group home. She got to work tracking down the family and, by combing through funeral home records, located their graves in a small Jewish cemetery in St. Paul. In the process, she learned that Izzy had lived in one facility for sixty years, that he had once held a job outside the facility, and that he had just once been visited by a rabbi.

Christensen, who would later write *The Jewish Community Guide to Inclusion of People with Disabilities,* said she used her search for Rosen's parents' grave "to open a portal for Izzy to finally become a member of the Jewish community. I needed to meet Izzy to get to know him personally. Until then I wasn't sure how to engage him to participate in Jewish life in our community."

When she walked in the front door of the facility, Izzy was sitting, gently rocking, in his reclining chair in the living room. He wore a Yankees baseball cap, and as Christensen greeted him, she was reminded of many other Jews of her grandfather's generation.

Izzy was friendly, smiling and speaking occasionally, completely engaged. Christensen explained that she had come to visit him from the Jewish community. His whole face lit up as he broke into a broad smile and replied, "I'm Jewish!" From that moment the two forged a partnership to bring Judaism back to Izzy's life.

Christensen invited Izzy, his housemates, and his facility's staff to her agency's annual Passover seder for people who have developmental disabilities. This lively gathering, celebrating the Israelites' freedom from Egyptian slavery, was an adaptation of a traditional seder. For example, the group did not read from the Haggadah, the book used to conduct seders. Instead, Earl Schwartz, a community teacher, brought his guitar and played traditional songs and told the story of Passover in his own unique way. After songs and a creative telling of the story of Moses and the Israelites, the group ate a traditional Passover meal with all the trimmings: chicken soup, matzo balls, chicken, and *haroset*, a mixture of apples, nuts, spices, and wine that symbolizes the clay used by the Israelites to make bricks in Egypt. The celebration concluded with more joyful songs, which many people had learned in childhood.

The first seder Izzy attended was on a Monday night, and the effect of the experience was so great that the following Monday—and every Monday after that—Izzy brought his shoes into the living room and put them on. When staff asked him where he was going, he replied, "To the seder!"

Jewish Family and Children's Service gave Izzy Shabbat candlesticks and an electric menorah for Hanukkah, to use at his group home, and Christensen led a "Basics of Judaism" workshop for his staff. As the diverse group of staff members learned about Jewish food, Christensen used both English and Yiddish names for things like matzo balls (*knaidlach*). When Christensen looked at Izzy during these sessions, he had tears in his eyes and said, "Mama, Mama . . ."

"Izzy's connection to his childhood and his family was made through Jewish memories that had endured through decades of absence," Christensen said. "No wonder he wanted to go back to the seder and to his memories of early life. There lived the comfort of being with his family, where Judaism was built into the food they ate and the language they spoke. The truth is that as Jews we forgot the Izzys of this world. Shut away, invisible, it was time to bring Izzy back to the community."

As he neared death, Izzy made his final connection. Christensen contacted Izzy's case manager so that arrangements could be made to purchase a gravesite near that of his parents. On the day they found the location, Izzy and the case manager made a trip to visit his parents' resting place. Ironically, the cemetery was located just two miles from the group home where Izzy had been living for twelve years.

Soon afterward, Izzy's health began to fail rapidly and he was placed in a nursing home following a lengthy hospitalization. The Twin Cities Jewish Healing Program sent a rabbi to visit him. About a week later, a second rabbi went to see him with the purpose of reciting the Viddui—a confessional prayer recited when one is close to death. A day later Izzy died.

As the case worker was arranging for Izzy's burial, which was to take place at county expense, she called Christensen in a panic. A Jewish burial would cost more than a "standard" burial, and the county refused to pay the difference. A call to the director of Jewish Family and Children's Services assured Christensen that the community would find a way to cover the difference. Once Izzy had been "reunited with his Jewish past, we would not let him go again," she said. "And so Izzy was buried in the age-old Jewish tradition."

Ten people gathered at the graveside service on a snowy morning: Izzy's housemates, facility staff members, Christensen, and the officiating rabbi, who, during the eulogy, recalled having visited Izzy many years before in the institution. The staff members shed tears. Izzy would be missed.

"According to Jewish custom, the rabbi took the shovel, pointed it downward, and, with the back of the shovel, scooped up dirt to throw on the casket," Christensen said. "The practice of literally burying the dead is a way of saying good-bye and showing respect.

But using the back of the shovel instead of the front signifies that the death of this person means that life will never be the same. It honors the person who died. Afterward, each person shoveled dirt onto Izzy's casket."

After the service, people returned to the group home for a traditional meal, the *seudat havra'ah,* or meal of consolation. As they ate together, the mourners shared their memories of Izzy. Sitting in the living room, Christensen recalled the first time she and Izzy had met. Someone handed her a picture of Izzy sitting casually with a big smile on his face, a photo she cherishes because it reminds her of an exceptional man who knew himself as a Jew and who, in his way, demanded that he be regarded as such in his final years.

There was one more thing for Christensen to do. When she returned to her office, she sent an e-mail to all the rabbis in the Twin Cities. She told them Izzy's story and asked each one to read his name aloud from the pulpit during the period of *sheloshim,* the thirty days of mourning following a funeral. In this way, Izzy would be remembered by his Jewish community.

"Even if no one had ever met him, the respect and honor given to him was a sure sign that he was invisible no more," Christensen said. "The brief time that Isadore Rosen spent as a member of the Jewish community is a testament to the importance we must place on ensuring that older adults with disabilities have the opportunity to belong to their own sacred community."

15

The Gift of Friendship

Deb

Poverty frequently compounds the effects of disability. As a young teenager, Deb, who has a moderate intellectual disability, was taken into state custody in Grand Rapids, Michigan, after her parents divorced. She was placed in foster care, but her first foster family was evicted from their home. Deb was placed in another home, which she didn't like, so she ran away. "They weren't very nice," she said. "They didn't want to take care of somebody sixteen years old."

According to her guardian, Deb then gravitated to the Heartside area of Grand Rapids, where most of the community's homeless congregate. After a few weeks there, she went to her mother's house and said, "I need a bed." But after a month her mother "kicked her out," so she returned to Heartside, where she began eating at God's Kitchen, a rescue mission sponsored by area churches. It was probably there that Deb learned some of what she knows about God.

Deb was befriended by Nella Uitvlugt, executive director of Friendship Ministries, an interdenominational, international ministry for people with intellectual disabilities that focuses on one-to-one mentoring and Bible studies. The program is active in twenty-eight countries, serving approximately seventeen thousand people with intellectual disabilities in more than sixty-five denominations.

Uitvlugt asked Deb if she had ever been attacked while she was homeless. "Deb looked right at me," recalled Uitvlugt, and immediately said, 'Jesus kept me safe!'"

Deb was later placed in a group home affiliated with Friendship Ministries, and for several years she attended Friendship on Tuesday evenings. She was then moved to a new group home that had no access to a church. A year later, she moved back to the original group home. She was excited to be a part of Friendship again and to worship on Sundays at Plymouth Heights Christian Reformed Church, where Uitvlugt was a member.

On Tuesdays, Deb spent time with a Friendship mentor, and at Sunday worship she was befriended by a woman named Anna, who ensured that Deb found the songs in the hymnbook and knew when to participate in prayers. They prayed for each other, and when Anna learned that Deb liked to crotchet simple items, she provided Deb with yarn.

Through contact with Deb's guardian, church members learned that she had probably never been part of a faith community. In the spring of 2010, they asked Deb whether she would like to become a full member of Plymouth Heights Church. A thoughtful and careful person, she asked if she could think about it for a couple of days. When asked again, she nodded vigorously and said she wanted to join the congregation. Normally a quiet person who displays no emotion, Deb seemed to glow when she shared her decision.

The pastor led a three-session membership class for Deb and five other people with intellectual disabilities. In one session they studied God's creation of the world by taking a "Creation walk" through the church gardens. In another session, they learned about Jesus as Savior by building a large wooden cross, and in the third they lit candles to represent the Holy Spirit. During the sessions they painted a colorful banner, which they presented to the congregation during the worship service at which they were baptized. Later the painters signed the banner and sent it to a mission program in Cuba sponsored by Friendship Ministries.

Because Deb had no family contact, her guardians joined other members at the service. "Deb's testimony during this service was simple and yet profound," Uitvlugt said. "She told the congregation that she loved Jesus, that Jesus loves her, and that she was thankful to have a good home with food to eat." After the service, the congregation celebrated with a special cake.

The next goal for new members like Deb was to explore how best to use their individual gifts. Deb participated in worship on several occasions and then was asked to share her thoughts about Thanksgiving during the church's Thanksgiving service. She said she felt honored and would be happy to do so. Thanksgiving that year "took on a new depth for me," Uitvlugt said, "as I thought about who I was really asking to share thoughts about being thankful. What would Deb share? Would she be too shy when she got on the platform?"

Uitvlugt arranged for Deb's group home manager to help her get a haircut, suggest what she might wear, and make certain she wrote a list of the things for which she was grateful. On Thanksgiving Day, Uitvlugt and her husband, Eric, picked Deb up early, and she told them she was excited to spend the entire day with her friends from the church. In the car she gave Uitvlugt her list of things she was thankful for. First on the list was, "I am not hungry." Deb told her friends she was thinking of people overseas who were hungry, remembering that when she was about sixteen, she herself had been homeless and hungry. The second thing on her list was new shoes. She was thrilled that they had laces rather than Velcro and that she had chosen them herself.

With great dignity, and with Uitvlugt's help, Deb shared her list with the congregation and then joined Uitvlugt's family for Thanksgiving dinner. The following Sunday, the experience was still so vivid that she told another member about the elegant meal. She had enjoyed filling her plate with her own choices, having some wine, and celebrating Thanksgiving with a family.

Recently, Plymouth Heights Church held the annual Friendship Ministries worship service in Grand Rapids. Deb was asked to serve as one of the people who stood in the front of the sanctuary, holding a flower vase to receive flowers brought in by other members as part of the May theme the pastor was using in sermons.

"As Deb's faith journey continues, it is delightful to see her develop this spiritual aspect of her life," said Uitvlugt. "Recently her prayer request in Friendship was that she was thankful for the beautiful yellow flowers that are blooming outside the window at the group home. The smile on her face shows so clearly that she is happy and secure in her life."

16

Intending to Include

Kelsey Johnson

Even the most modest efforts can send a powerful message.

St. Luke's United Methodist Church in Bryan, Texas, proclaims its intention regarding inclusion in no uncertain terms in its new members' packet and on its website: "St. Luke's strives to model God's design for a community where individuals—no matter their differences—know they belong and can worship together."

Worship bulletins at the 150-member congregation incorporate graphic symbols as a way for people to follow along and comprehend the order of service. For example, praying hands are listed beside prayer times and musical notes next to songs and hymns. In addition to people with disabilities, in particular intellectual disabilities, these symbols aid children who cannot yet read and worshippers whose first language is not English, according to Kelsey Johnson, Communications Specialist at the Center on Disability and Development at Texas A&M University, who is also married to the congregation's associate pastor of music and worship.

In the Sunday school classrooms, a "visual schedule" is posted for children with disabilities, so they can follow the order of the morning's activities. There is a magnetic strip with laminated cards with a graphic symbol and word (e.g., "Game" with a symbol of a pair of dice) that can be shuffled according to the schedule. "We consulted with the parent of a young child who has several disabilities to integrate him into Sunday school with the assistance of our volunteer teachers," says Johnson. "He receives accommodations like larger copies of handouts, and we are mindful to stock only allergy-free art supplies and snacks."

While Johnson is quick to say that none of these measures are incredibly innovative, "they are ways we tried to think through inclusion issues and make our church as accessible as possible."

17

Elevators to Inclusion

Bill Zalot

Bill Zalot, a lifelong member of St. Michael the Archangel Catholic Church in Levittown, Pennsylvania, a fifty-year-old congregation outside Philadelphia, uses a wheelchair as a result of cerebral palsy. When he was invited to join the parish's outreach committee, he was gratified until he found that it met in the basement social hall, which was accessible only by a flight of stairs. For the first few meetings, church members carried him down the steps and back up again.

"I was afraid they might drop me or hurt themselves," he said. So he reluctantly left the committee; the priest at the time was unreceptive to making any changes beyond a makeshift ramp to the first-floor sanctuary. Zalot took his concerns to the archdiocese office that advocates for people with disabilities, which was supportive and sympathetic. Things did not really begin to change at St. Michael, however, until a new priest, Richard Powers, was appointed. "His whole attitude was that he really wanted me involved in the parish," Zalot said. "He really wanted this to be an inclusive community."

But reaching a goal like that can require investment and sacrifice.

If there is one word that strikes terror in the hearts of congregations that consider becoming welcoming and accessible to people with disabilities, it is *elevators*. They are the ultimate big-ticket item—costing $250,000 or more to purchase and install—and they are frequently the stick opponents use to beat down a faith community's efforts to become fully inclusive. Because existing small- or medium-sized congregations—the overwhelming majority of houses of worship in the United States—are effectively exempt from provisions of the Americans with Disabilities Act, the "elevator issue" is also a straw man.

Some larger, older congregations, as well as newer mega-churches, have found that installing or building with elevators (or less expensive chairlifts) has been a surprisingly effective and popular marketing tool. New Catholic churches and those undergoing major renovations are required to be fully accessible, under the document "Built of Living Stones: Guidelines of the National Conference of Catholic Bishops." Catholic parishes tend to be larger congregations, often with ten thousand members or more, and often are attached to parochial schools. Today, the Archdiocese of Philadelphia has 286 parishes, and 86 percent of their churches are considered accessible, including more than thirty that have elevators—despite some initial and familiar resistance.

Still, some existing parishes have found that efforts to purchase and install elevators can have a surprisingly broad base of support. "Parishes say, 'We could never do that,'" said Sister Kathleen Schipani, who has overseen the archdiocese's accessibility ministry for more than sixteen years. "But one step at a time they can raise the funds, one project at a time, and make their whole parish accessible."

That's the way it happened at St. Michael the Archangel, under the leadership of Father Powers, encouraged by Bill Zalot. A special campaign raised enough money to install an elevator to the basement; a new, sturdier ramp into the sanctuary; assistive listening devices in the pews for people with poor hearing; and fully accessible rest rooms. A member of the congregation built a portable ramp so that Zalot and others could reach the altar and serve as lectors, reading Scripture. As a result of these changes, the parish's services began to draw more people with disabilities, including some, such as Zalot's girlfriend, who weren't Catholic. The Mass held at five-thirty on Saturday afternoons has become especially popular. In addition, Zalot has been able to join the Knights of Columbus, which meets in the parish social hall. "I feel more a part of the parish and the parish community," Zalot said.

Among Zalot's and Powers's unexpected allies—and beneficiaries—were members of a seniors group that used the hall for regular bingo games, as well as young families with strollers who previously had difficulty navigating the stairs. Throughout the diocese, increasing numbers of people became unintended beneficiaries as other parishes learned of the improvements at St. Michael and began making similar changes. At one Philadelphia parish, a new priest told Sister Schipani that if it hadn't been for recent renovations, his mother would have been unable to attend his installation.

18

Welcoming Whosoever Walks In

Liz Lang and Raymond

For many faith communities, welcoming some inevitably means welcoming all. In the 1980s, Liz Lang's Seattle church, Findlay Street Christian (Disciples of Christ), heatedly debated whether to compose a declaration that they would welcome gays, lesbians, bisexuals, and transgendered people in all levels of membership in the Disciples of Christ congregation, in order to become what is known among the Disciples of Christ and other mainline Protestant denominations as "Open and Affirming." At one point, an elder spoke up to report a dream she'd had the previous night. "When I woke up it was as if God was saying to me, 'Whosoever believes shall not perish but have everlasting life.' I really knew inside me that the 'whosoevers' were anybody, all inclusive." The much beloved elder set the tone at Findlay Street for the next twenty-five years and beyond. "We clearly understood that whosoever walked in the doors of our little church must be welcomed, because they had been brought here by God," Lang said.

This decision was particularly significant for Lang. Years earlier, another church had welcomed her when she sought refuge from her dysfunctional home. Members later told her she was the church's first "orphan" and that the experience had turned out so well that taking in other alienated children became their ministry. Seeking a welcoming church, Lang and her partner, Louise Petrasek, arrived at Findlay Street Christian Church just in time to participate in the development of the Open and Affirming ministry.

Thus it was easy for Lang and Findlay Street to welcome Raymond, who has Asperger's syndrome, a mild form of autism. His brain wiring makes it impossible for him to connect with people in the way most others do, because he doesn't read social cues.

The training that is now available to children with Asperger's was unavailable to him during his childhood. "In spite of that he has grown in his abilities to interact socially and is definitely an important part of our church," Lang said.

When Raymond first arrived at Findlay Street Christian Church, he appeared slightly disheveled. He didn't quite look people in the eye, had a kind of ungainly, stiff posture, and seemed a little lost. "We soon had to deal with some unusual behaviors," Lang said. "We learned that stopping him from telling a long story about electricity was difficult. One day when some little thing went wrong he had a meltdown, where he flapped his hands and cried, 'I'm sorry! I'm sorry! I did it wrong! I deserve to go to jail!'"

But over the years such explosive outbursts have become less frequent. Certain people in the congregation have connected well with Raymond, and one or another will go to him when he does get upset, helping him move into a quiet room and get control of himself. Facilitated by a mental health specialist, the elders discussed some particularly difficult situations and developed plans that anticipated when Raymond might have problems. One of those situations is when the pastor is out of town. At those times a couple of elders make sure to connect with Raymond before the service and sit near him during it.

"We have been astonished by his ability to pray," Lang said. "In fact, it's been noted that he is quite a prophet. During the prayers of the people he is able to construct a prayer that ties together the sermon topic with needs of people around the world. He clearly tells God what is needed to build God's realm on earth."

One summer, a team of people from the church helped Raymond clean his house. He had been unable to make any decisions about what to throw away after his parents died twenty years earlier, so there was much to dispose of—draperies that hung by a thread, for example, and a threadbare carpet in the living room. A congregation member worked with Raymond to help him keep his anxiety at a manageable level, checking in with him about each item the team thought should be given or thrown away. This person gathered up all of Raymond's mother's jewelry and created a shadow box to display some of the prettiest pieces. Because of Raymond's dust allergies, the congregation bought him a new mattress and bedding, along with allergy covers and an air cleaner.

During the cleaning, one team member came across a Christmas stocking that Raymond had hung in his childhood. The next Christmas, church members surprised him with it, cleaned up and filled with Christmas goodies. He left several phone messages asking when he could deliver the empty stocking to be kept for the following year. It is now a tradition.

"We have learned that Raymond flourishes when he has specific tasks each Sunday," Lang said. "So he manages the sound system, distributes the hymnals, and helps an elderly member pour leftover coffee from the coffee hour into her thermos. Raymond offers thoughtful questions during meetings about our building project and is invited to share his special knowledge in other ways."

Just as Raymond, now forty-five, has specific tasks, so congregational members seem to have specific ways in which they reach out to him. One has him do electrical work at his house, another makes him an annual birthday cake, and yet another continues to organize cleanup projects at his house. Others remind him when it's time to get a haircut or wear a different shirt.

"Perhaps the greatest gift of his participation with us," Lang said, "is that each of us has grown in compassion. This gift of the Spirit has come from that decision to become an Open and Affirming congregation."

19

A Safe Venue

Military Veterans

Wounded warriors returning from Iraq and Afghanistan pose great and growing challenges to America's faith communities, as outlined in reports with titles such as "Beyond the Yellow Ribbon: Ministering to Returning Combat Veterans" and "Welcome Them Home, Help Them Heal." Religious groups hope to do a better job with these veterans than they did a generation earlier, when troops came home from Southeast Asia and were in many cases ignored or left to fend for themselves. The need is especially great for veterans with amputations, post-traumatic stress disorder (PTSD), traumatic brain injury (TBI), substance abuse, and depression.

While serving in the U.S. Army in Iraq, Tim Pollock was hit in the left eye with a bullet that blew away half his skull. Beyond the pain and the physical devastation, the wound left him feeling miserable, with no reason to live, because it forced him to retire from a career in the military that had given him pride and a sense of worth. Already a high-functioning alcoholic, he stopped drinking but began smoking marijuana. Six months after he was shot, he began having seizures and considered suicide.

"But then I started to go to church, the place to worship my God," Pollock wrote on his website, "our God, the one that brought me back to life twice in Iraq. I liked church but that wasn't enough for me. I needed a group to talk to about the military, but I wanted to talk to people who are God loving and can help me with my depression."

One Memorial Day, Pollock's pastor asked all the veterans in his Columbiana, Ohio, church to stand and be recognized. After the service, a good friend of Pollock's invited him to a meeting of a group called Point Man Ministries. "So I went, and the more I went to the meetings the happier I got. I walked away from mari-juana, and I'm clean, happy, and full of the Holy Spirit," he wrote. Since then Pollock has become active in Point Man Ministries, working with other veterans with PTSD, TBI, depression, and mo-bility issues. He also visits fellow vets in the hospital.

A descendant of three generations of Protestant theologians, Benjamin Story grew up in Virginia attending both mainline and evangelical churches. He loved reading and studying Scripture, but after graduating from Old Dominion University, he diverged from family tradition and chose a different path, serving for a year in 2005–2006 as a U.S. Army infantry officer in Iraq. There, he saw combat while his company provided security for convoys, in the process taking casualties. When he returned, he enrolled in an MBA program at the College of William and Mary, but he was hampered in his studies by an inability to focus, a result of PTSD. Still, he graduated cum laude and went on to a career as a consultant.

The family's hereditary pull of mission and ministry manifest-ed itself when Story met a twenty-seven-year-old fellow combat vet-eran in his congregation at City Church in Washington, D.C. The young man seemed to be struggling to find a reason for living. "I met Alex at a Wednesday night Young Professional's group," a church program, Story recalled. "I approached him after the group to introduce myself. When he looked up, I immediately sensed his past—his stare shared a common pain with me. I asked him about his life, and he mechanically responded that he had been a marine, an infantryman, and now he was out." Story then shared his own experience, and Alex's countenance changed. The two vets began a long conversation, which developed into a deep friendship.

On the front porch of Story's house several months later, the two men smoked cigars and shared stories of their lives while Story's wife made dinner. Alex was rough-edged and unfamiliar with proper church etiquette. Although he was comfortable chat-ting on Story's porch, he occasionally got dirty looks from church members when he dropped the "F-bomb" in casual conversation, as he had grown accustomed to doing in the military.

Over time, Alex shared with Story his experiences overseas, his traumatic childhood, and his attempts at suicide. In Iraq in 2005, Alex experienced the "Wild West," marine slang for the city of Ramadi in Anbar province. He lost several of his closest comrades in combat, and then several more to suicide. Unlike Story, Alex had no one waiting for him at home, so when his unit returned to the United States, he stood alone on the runway as the rest of his unit rushed into the arms of loving families. After being discharged from the marines for attempting suicide, Alex was left with nothing. He wound up in a Veterans Administration hospital, where a caring chaplain took him under her wing, leading him to Story's church.

"Alex trusted me because of our shared experiences," Story said. "He was tired of being labeled by psychiatrists and was tired of taking medications. Alex and I spoke daily as I began to fill the role of a father in his life."

For a year Alex had serious bouts with depression, due to his PTSD, which eventually led to involuntary hospitalization and six months in a psychiatric ward. Eventually, prayer, encouragement, and advice seemed to help him get partially on his feet. After his medications were properly balanced, he was accepted to college and is now on the dean's list. His goal is to earn a Ph.D. in psychology. Although his mental condition has improved, he is far from "healed."

"I thank God for every step toward improvement and celebrate each small accomplishment," Story said. "I hope and believe in a complete person for Alex, but I recognize that his wounds are deeper than mine and will take much longer to heal." Alex attends a church near his campus and seems to have made new friends in that community.

"Combat creates a sort of poison in the conscience," Story said, "which if left to fester will ruin a man. Finding a safe venue to vent these thoughts is the first step toward recovery," and a caring faith community can fill that role.

The Reverend Carol Ramsey-Lucas, an American Baptist chaplain at the Veterans Administration Medical Center in Washington, D.C., has observed Story's relationship with Alex as a staunch ally, friend, and supporter during the younger vet's recovery. "Ben Story is very humble, but his dedication to Christ and to his fellow soldier has helped to bring about profound healing" in Alex, she said.

"As soldiers return home from Iraq and Afghanistan," Jeffrey MacDonald, a religion journalist and author, wrote in *USA Today,* "congregations are discovering how spirituality can help veterans afflicted with postwar stress. But many pastors remain unsure how to help when veterans contend with chronic nightmares, outbursts, and panic attacks."

Martin Davis, director of the Alban Institute's Congregational Resource Guide, and Kimberly Loontjer, assistant director for ministry programs at Wheat Ridge Ministries, which funded the "Welcome Them Home" report, have also studied the issue. "America has a rich tradition of supporting neighbors through religious congregations," they wrote in the *Washington Post.* "Hearing a call to serve, congregations are now finding they're uniquely equipped to provide much of what this generation of young veterans needs.

"If a returning soldier or veteran is hospitalized, for instance, members of Rosemount United Methodist Church in Rosemount, Minnesota, will give the at-home parent a break by watching the kids for a few hours. Other congregations rally volunteers to help with transportation or odd jobs. Such simple yet valuable services are typical of hundreds of burgeoning ministries available to military families in America's congregations.

"By attending to basic needs, congregations give veterans more than a little help here and there. They offer opportunities for veterans to be contributors, not charity cases."

As MacDonald, Davis and Loontjer, and others report, congregational assistance to veterans with physical, emotional, or intellectual wounds takes many forms. The following are some examples:

- In New York City, Times Square Church members were trained to minister to returning veterans, including those with PTSD, by Bridges to Healing, an affiliate of Campus Crusade for Christ's Military Ministry.
- Outside Washington, D.C., the Sanctuary provides a faith-based refuge and spiritual guidance for veterans dealing with PTSD.
- In Colorado Springs, Colorado, a community with many military connections, Calvary United Methodist Church's congregational leaders have been trained to recognize those with PTSD who could benefit from help.
- In Goodyear, Arizona, Skyway Church has organized a veterans support group led by John Blehm, a Vietnam veteran who has PTSD.
- In Maple Grove, Minnesota, at Lord of Life Lutheran Church, an Iraq and Afghanistan vet named John Rodvik has taken the lead in raising money to enable local veterans to buy rehabilitation equipment, as well as in organizing dinners to honor veterans who are members of the congregation.
- In Lincoln, Nebraska, Messiah Lutheran Church's associate pastor, John Kunze, counsels military couples, and the congregation maintains a referral list, including a mental health counselor, for veterans in need.

"Even with God's help, congregations face limits," Davis and Loontjer wrote. "They cannot make transitions to civilian life easy for any returning veteran or family. But they are well positioned with caring, organized people in every hamlet, suburb, and metropolis where veterans back from the front lines are making new lives. When they're brave enough to try, congregations help ensure that life in America is manageable, joyful, and meaningful for a class of people that deserves nothing less."

20

Looking for "That of God"

Kevin Camp

Soon after Kevin Camp was born, his parents noticed that something was not quite right. He cried too much, slept too little, and clung too tightly. He was extremely shy as a child and had irrational fears, but he was also precocious in his verbal skills, musical talent, and insatiable intellectual curiosity. His mother, Deborah, and father, David, continued to worry, but doctors and teachers chalked it up to Kevin's "just being one of those quirky gifted kids."

Kevin grew up in a Protestant family, although his mother and father were skeptical of organized religion. Like many other parents, they attended church because they believed their children needed its moral teachings and ethical guidelines, and they themselves were seeking a social network with a spiritual aspect.

"We raised Kevin and his sisters in the Methodist Church," Deborah said. "That's what good Southern parents of my generation did—raise your children in the church! Kevin took his religious studies seriously and appeared to enjoy learning familiar Bible stories. Of course, Methodists aren't much for hellfire and brimstone, preferring to emphasize God's love and grace.

"We weren't a particularly religious family. We didn't hold family devotional time, openly profess our faith, say the blessing at every meal. We just went to church and Sunday school on a fairly regular basis. At times David and I would become active in the church—teaching Sunday school, serving on committees, organizing events." Then congregational infighting caused them to withdraw.

Kevin's first experience with chronic illness, disability, and faith came in his Hoover, Alabama, elementary school, outside Birmingham. A girl in his class got cancer and had to undergo regular chemotherapy treatments. Her hair vanished, and she wore a hat for the rest of the year. All this was explained to Kevin and the other students on days when the girl wasn't in school. "I knew that her ailment had to be serious because of the extra effort teachers made to prepare us," he recalled. "The more overtly religious among my classmates informed everyone that they were praying for her health and survival. Not being raised especially inclined to such public demonstrations of faith, I wasn't quite sure what to pray for or what not to pray for, in all honesty."

Somewhat detached, Kevin could conceptualize the girl's discomfort and inconvenience but was unable to apply this sensitivity to his own life. He nodded his head when the girl talked about the medication she had to take in staggered fashion throughout the day, but that was the extent of his understanding. His full, personal realization of disability arrived some years later, when he was in his early teens.

"The wheels fell off the wagon in adolescence," Deborah said. "During his sophomore year in high school, what began as irrational behavior at school and at home quickly spiraled down into a major depressive episode. The manic periods were the worst." As Kevin recalls that period, by the age of fifteen he found himself with an undiagnosed anxiety disorder coupled with demoralizing bouts of severe, lingering depression. These worsened with the passage of time, as did their frequency. For the family, the next ten years were a blur of psychiatrists, medications, and hospitalizations. They returned to religion and church.

"During the first years of Kevin's identified illness, his father and I joined a more evangelical, nondenominational church and dragged the kids along," Deborah said. The couple was under incredible pressure—caring for Kevin, fighting insurance companies, raising their other children, and caring for elderly parents.

"The interesting phenomenon about evangelical churches in the South is that they take good care of their flock," Deborah said. "More liberal churches such as the ones we had previously attended were more laissez-faire in this area. David, Kevin, his sisters, and I needed to be taken care of, and the good people of this church did just that. They brought meals to the house when Kevin was hospitalized, they held prayer vigils for him, they visited him in psych units—which are not pleasant places—and they let me know how much they loved me. I didn't care for the theology that much, but I needed that support system. Kevin eventually rejected their theology and joined the Unitarian Church. David and I and the girls gradually stopped attending this church or any other, for that matter."

Kevin soon found himself praying that his pain would lessen and that he might have his life back. "These prayers appeared to have no effect whatsoever, at least at first, and I eliminated prayer from my daily routine, except for in the worst times when seeking a distraction from a silent but troubled mind," he said. "Depression slows thought processes and with it the desire to engage with the world. Sadistically, a slowly building depressive episode slowly removes the joy of life and the motivation to keep fighting. Any conversation with God pulls the mind away from omnipresent pain."

"I felt distanced from God in those days, openly wondering whether he had abandoned me or whether I was being punished for some transgression. My father, a severe skeptic of organized religion, adopted this same attitude himself, I suppose as a means of coping. As I read the Gospels, I even allowed myself to question whether there was something to the idea of demonic possession in a literal sense. When medical science proved to be of insufficient help, I longed for someone to set the demons inside me free." He was seeking solid answers, he said, but diseases of the brain are still poorly understood. "The brain is a complex organ. Only a fraction of its mysteries are understood with any certainty, which is why mental illness of any kind is a massive challenge."

When—rarely—Kevin sought solace in Scripture, he turned to the book of Job, an obvious choice, where many who undergo periods of sustained suffering find comfort. "I was always afraid that what I read encouraged self-pity as I applied it to my own condition," he said. "I was, after all, a teenager, a time of usually harmless self-absorption, and with it great personal exploration. In a moderate but pronounced rebellion against the institutions and traditions of my childhood, I vacillated between periods of great faith and great agnosticism. This was all very normal, but the intensity and difficulty of my diagnosis were anything but."

Things were looking up by Kevin's senior year, and for the first time in a long while, he was beginning to enjoy himself. But a misdiagnosis and a new medication brought the worst depression he had ever faced. Just before Thanksgiving, following several half-hearted attempts to take his own life, Kevin made a serious attempt, collapsing on his basement floor.

"Yet something made me cry out for my parents, who were only one flight above me," he said. "Suicidal thoughts, to me, always reminded me of some eternal struggle between good and evil. It felt like the forces of darkness were encouraging my death, but at the last minute, those of lightness took control of my body. I've sought to ascribe this experience to many things over time. Perhaps God sent angels to rescue me. I believe now that he knew I had much greater responsibilities ahead of me and that my continued life was imperative. I am grateful now to have been spared, even though it must be said that significant health challenges continued to face me for years after the fact."

His parents were suffering as well. "The most difficult experience for a parent is to watch one's child suffer," Deborah said, "and I have watched my beautiful, kindhearted, brilliant, and talented son walk through hell on earth."

Kevin was admitted to the hospital in Birmingham for two months of intense treatment. He did not return to school but was tutored at home until he recovered. In his early twenties, Kevin again began experiencing bipolar episodes, with especially debilitating and sometimes destructive manic periods. When these periods subsided, he said, "and the pieces lay scattered in front of me, there was no greater anguish than to direct one horrified prayer upward. *God, what have I done?*"

About a year before Kevin left for treatment at the National Institute of Mental Health in Washington, D.C., he had joined the Quaker meeting in Birmingham. This seemed to be a perfect fit for him," his mother said. "Kevin has always been my most spiritual child, and I'm very pleased that he has finally discovered what he has appeared to be seeking since childhood."

Ultimately, a combination of medications and therapy was successful, and Kevin, now in his thirties, has modified his lifestyle to help keep himself on an even keel. He calls himself "Job in remission" and adds, "I hope I don't become Job in an acute state. . . . Having chronic illnesses teaches you to pace yourself and to set realistic long-term plans. And after the experience in earlier life, I never doubt the existence of God. I may not always understand the plan, but I do know that I am still here for a reason."

An active member of Friends Meeting of Washington, D.C., where he now lives, Kevin is involved in young adult organizing and is a member of the meeting's Ministry and Worship Committee. Because psychiatric disability still has a stigma attached to it, he is not always forthcoming about having bipolar disorder. He is more inclined to reveal his disability to other young adult Friends than to older members of the meeting, he says, "but those who I have opened up to have always been very supportive and understanding."

According to Faith Williams, who also serves on the Ministry and Worship Committee, Kevin is a valuable member of the committee and of the meeting. "He comes regularly to committee meetings and participates—he has designed the postcards to send to newcomers. His spoken ministry in meeting for worship is often meaningful for me, as are his contributions to the online community. There is something touchingly honest about him, I think because he's already been through the dark."

This kind of welcoming acceptance is consistent with Friends history, says Jim Dickson, a national disability advocate and activist who uses a guide dog named Pierson. Early adherents of the Religious Society of Friends, founded by George Fox in seventeenth-century England, were dubbed "Quakers" because they often trembled noticeably as a result of the emotional way in which the Spirit spoke through them during worship. Fox—who some modern scholars believe was himself bipolar—was known for recruiting new members by attending staid Church of England services and disrupting worship with loud challenges from the pews to ministers over scriptural interpretation.

There was, Fox believed, "that of God" in everyone, regardless of physical, emotional, or intellectual condition. The Friends meeting that Kevin Camp attends, on Dupont Circle, Dickson says, is accustomed to visitors with a variety of brain disorders, and their participation is seldom considered disruptive. "The meeting welcomes everyone," he says. "We believe in continuing revelation, in that each person has to develop her or his own relationship with God, and the relationship changes all through our lifetime. Whether someone has a learning disability, schizophrenia, depression, or cerebral palsy, our responsibility as believers is to look for 'that of God' in them."

21

Feeling Part of a Community

Ezra Freedman-Harvey

Ezra Freedman-Harvey personifies the word *persistence,* succeeding at many things others thought he shouldn't even attempt. He lives with familial dysautonomia (FD), a rare neurological condition affecting only Jews that was once considered fatal. It can seriously impair mobility, breathing, digestion, the heart, and the kidneys. It can also affect vision. Ezra was born without depth perception and with limited peripheral vision, in addition to an inability to produce tears. With eye surgery and years of eye exercises, he has been able to gain some depth and peripheral vision, and he has learned how to accommodate and navigate in life with low vision.

Ezra has been fortunate in that the survival rate and quality of life for people with FD have improved with recent interventions, and in the devoted care of his parents. His mother, Georgia, is an art curator and consultant. His father, Gary, is a psychologist, and Ezra has an older sister who is not affected by FD. When Georgia and Gary married, and again when Ezra and his sister were each born, the couple made a commitment to raise their children in the Jewish faith, as both of them had been raised.

At Congregation B'nai Tzedek in Orange County, California, a Reform temple where Ezra's family worshiped, the rabbi suggested that Ezra could have a modified bar mitzvah, like those designed by a growing number of Jewish congregations to include adolescents with disabilities. But Ezra, with his parents' support, wanted a full ceremony, with all the preparation it entails. He felt it was his rightful place, as a full participant, to conduct a service. "I wanted to read from the Torah and be able to read the prayers like my classmates," he said.

Because the regular Wednesday afternoon preparation classes were too much for Ezra physically, his parents found a rabbi to tutor him privately. This separated him from his classmates but gave him the opportunity to achieve the goal he set for himself. When the time came, Ezra proudly took his place on the bimah. He read from the Torah in Hebrew and conducted many parts of the service in Hebrew and English, like his peers, and he felt incredibly successful. The experience demonstrated to the rabbi why other young men and women with disabilities would want to do what Ezra had done. It also changed the way the congregation viewed Ezra, and it continued to resonate through his confirmation, at the end of tenth grade.

Starting in kindergarten, Ezra was the first "full inclusion" student in his school district, which meant that he was always in a regular classroom, all the way through twelfth grade. Although full inclusion is now commonplace, it was still a relatively new approach for children with disabilities, just gaining acceptance, when Ezra started school. As he neared the end of middle school, his parents, thinking he would be unable to achieve fully at a large public high school, looked for a small private high school that would better fit his learning style and his desire for total independence. He did well, and in his senior year he began taking classes at a local community college, where he has continued his studies since graduating from high school. As part of his high school studies he also attended two years of Hebrew high school on Sundays to fulfill his language requirement.

Over the years, Ezra and his family have drawn on the resources of all three major branches of Judaism in order to accomplish his goals within his faith. "We have had to face the dilemma of raising a Jewish child versus not giving him experiences that he heard about at religious school," said Ezra's mother, Georgia. "We are often asked which movement in Judaism we follow, but it's not a simple answer. We have taken the approach with our children that it is important to think outside the box at times when trying to accomplish your goals in life."

Ezra's bar mitzvah tutor was an Orthodox rabbi, who respected and prepared him for his service in the family's Reform temple. Ezra attended a Jewish summer camp in New York sponsored by

Chai Lifeline, an international organization that provides services of all sorts to medically compromised Jewish youths and is open to all branches of the faith. His Boy Scout troop was sponsored by Long Beach Chabad, an Orthodox organization. Chabad's generous programs provided Ezra with many opportunities he would not have had otherwise. The Orthodox outreach enabled him to remain connected to Judaism and to have experiences that his peers were having, although these experiences also isolated him from the mainstream at his own synagogue.

Scouting was an activity in which, from the start, Ezra felt he belonged. "From the time I started scouting as a Tiger Scout, I liked being part of a troop," he said. "When I first went from Cub Scouts to Boy Scouts in the fifth grade, I started thinking that I could become an Eagle Scout—and I did achieve that goal."

As with many of the challenges Ezra has taken on, accomplishing that goal wasn't easy. Although the scouting movement makes accommodations for members with disabilities, at times it seemed to him that the program required more from him to prove he was Eagle-ready than it required of someone without a disability—but this only made him more determined to achieve his goal. Ezra designed his Eagle leadership project to benefit Chai Lifeline, the organization that had been so helpful to him over the years, sponsoring his summer camp and offering other resources. He created a "giving library" and an inventory system, with more than six hundred new books for Chai Lifeline to provide to children in hospitals and at home when facing illnesses.

When the time came for Ezra's Eagle examination, however, complications arose. He had just returned from camp, three thousand miles from home, with some health issues that put his appearance before the examining board in doubt. But he was determined not to let this health setback stop him, and that night he faced the three-member panel for his interview. Also present was his scoutmaster, who was there to present the scout to the Eagle board. After deliberations, Ezra, his scoutmaster, and the rest of the Freedman-Harvey family were called back in and informed that Ezra was Long Beach's newest Eagle Scout, a triumph for all of them.

Ezra's next challenge was to enroll in Orange Coast College's hospitality program. He now uses a low-tech magnifying bar with a yellow line through it for reading, eliminating the need to have the print in all his textbooks enlarged. He is looking forward to the day when he will be able to access all his textbooks and assignments on his computer. If there were one thing he could change about living with FD, Ezra said, it would be "that I would be able to see better and write more clearly."

Ezra has always had a natural inner compassion for older adults, a group he would like to work with. At college he has learned to advocate for himself, join clubs, take on leadership roles, and serve as a teaching assistant in several classes. For two years in a row he has been recognized at Honors Night for his service to the community and has been awarded a scholarship. He recently completed his certificate in Leadership Studies. He regrets that there is no Jewish student organization on campus but looks forward to continuing his studies at a four-year university where there is a Hillel chapter.

Despite his many accomplishments, one of Ezra's most difficult struggles has been to learn about death, especially the deaths of friends at early ages. Typically, familial dysautonomia limits a person's life span, and Ezra can now be counted among the older survivors. Under the circumstance, the issue of mortality is one the family grapples with. "We must always juggle how high to set the bar for Ezra," said Georgia. "In this house we made the choice to 'go for broke' and hoped that he did survive. We want every day to be a life filled with possibilities, not one cut off by choices we made for him."

A few years ago, Ezra's best friend, a young woman named Kacie whom he had known since they were both three years old, died of a rare disease. Kacie and Ezra had often talked about being invisible, especially as teens living with a chronic illness. After Kacie's death, her mother and Kacie's mother started a project called Kacie's Kloset, with the goal of helping chronically ill teens feel connected with other teens and not marginalized and isolated. The project continues to grow and reach out to more teens.

Ezra's faith experiences are best described as "feelings of belonging," and he looks forward to joining in congregational services whenever possible. The Freedman-Harvey family now attends a smaller, Conservative congregation, Surf City Synagogue, in Huntington Beach, a synagogue closer to their home. Ezra is a regular congregant. From the start, he has been embraced by the members, who have made him feel welcome and comfortable there, beginning by providing him with large-print prayer books. He is always looking for ways to help other congregants and make visitors feel at home. Ezra says this is a fulfilling experience for him—just being an accepted member of the congregation and being seen as someone who has something to give to it.

Creating a home centered on Jewish values has paid off for the Freedman-Harvey family. At twenty-one, Ezra has been to Israel twice with his family. He continues to identify strongly with his Jewish heritage and faith. He hopes that by having achieved so many goals and milestones, he will encourage other young adults living with ongoing health conditions never to give up but to always keep going and dreaming.

"I've always felt a connection to Judaism, and this is important to me," Ezra said. "By observing the holidays and attending services, Jewish life will always have a place in who I am. My Jewish journey has only made me want to keep being a part of the Jewish community and learning more. One goal of mine is to go on a Birthright trip to Israel." Birthright is a program that provides free trips to Israel for North American Jews under the age of twenty-five.

In 2011, Ezra is aware that discrimination still exists and that he must rise above it. He has already learned some life lessons that few of his peers have had to address. He is open about discussing them and feels more strongly than ever that everyone deserves to be treated with dignity and respect. He hopes that out of his experiences he can facilitate conversations that result in greater respect and compassion for people living with disabilities. "I'd like to teach people how to interact with someone who has an illness, so that they don't feel afraid to get to know people who live with disabilities."

91

22

Sharing Space

The Cleggs Lane Men's Group

Reaching out in the realm of faith and disability is not confined to the western side of the Atlantic, according to the Reverend Kathleen LaCamera, an American graduate of Yale Divinity School and a longtime resident of the northern British industrial city of Manchester. LaCamera, who is affiliated with the United Methodist Church in the United States, is a chaplain with a local mental health trust. She recounts how a chance meeting at a community support center between a Methodist church worker and a government health worker led to a discussion about health improvement and then to an innovative collaboration.

Paul Foster, employed by the government-funded local health service, was starting a men's health group to support people with both physical and mental disabilities. Pat Culpan, a church-funded "community cohesion" worker, was looking for opportunities for area Methodist churches to help people living in one of the most economically depressed areas of Manchester. Culpan knew that a small Methodist chapel there was teetering on the edge of closing its doors, and she had an idea about how to save it.

What grew out of their conversation that day, LaCamera reports, was a partnership in which a church with a tiny, aging membership offered space to a group of self-declared "misfits" in need of refuge. Almost three years on, this relationship between congregation, local government, and support group participants has resulted in nothing short of new life in the neighborhood known as Little Hulton.

Cleggs Lane Methodist Church's pastor, the Reverend Philip Brooks, calls the collaboration between his congregation and what became known as the Men's Health Group a "holistic approach to ministry." The church's investment in the group has made its members a part of the church family, rather than just tenants using church space.

But Brooks is the first to acknowledge that it's been a learning process for everyone involved, and the process hasn't been "completely perfect." Longtime church members were hesitant to open their doors to a ragtag bunch of men with a history of debilitating physical and mental illnesses. Ironically, some members then became annoyed when members of the men's group failed to show up on Sunday mornings. Soon, however, church members and group members came to know and invest in each other, and the relationship started to become mutually beneficial.

Without fail, every Friday morning around ten o'clock, members of the Men's Health Group begin trickling into the church's main hall. They range in age from nineteen to sixty-five and bring with them physical and mental challenges ranging from epilepsy to depression, from addiction to autism.

Foster's determination to start the group, and the church's commitment to supporting it, came from seeing firsthand how few men in the area who were struggling with physical and mental illnesses actually sought out help or medical treatment. Many of them ended up isolated, unemployed, and spiraling into increasingly debilitating ill health. According to the local borough's statistics, Little Hulton suffers from high levels of crime and unemployment and ranks among the most "health-deprived" communities in the United Kingdom.

The Friday meetings quickly spawned a Thursday gardening group, open to both men and women. The land behind the Cleggs Lane Church building was such a mass of weeds, brambles, and trash that people called it "the wilderness." The gardening group spent months painstakingly clearing it and making it ready to grow vegetables and other plants. The Men's Health Group also took it upon themselves do some long overdue upkeep on the church exterior and grounds in general.

"The church has never charged any fees for heat or electricity," Reverend Brooks told LaCamera. "The men in the group started ministering to our elderly congregation right from the start,

doing things around the church." Those "things" include painting, repairing, helping set up for events, and clearing out long-
neglected corners of the building. The men even dug out and
hung up Christmas and other seasonal decorations that older congregation members had been unable to manage for some years.

"The whole experience has opened the church up," the minister said. "Others in this very deprived local community have seen
what's going on and said, 'Here's a church that accepts people
as they are and doesn't want anything in return.' For me this is a
model of service mission."

At the church's annual Harvest service in 2010, the men's
group donated fresh vegetables they had grown to decorate the
altar. During the service, group members talked about what it
had meant to them to grow those vegetables and to be part of
the church's men's group. "It was a great example of the worshiping and practical sides of ministry coming together," said Brooks.
"And if the church had been in a stronger position, if the men
hadn't been in a position of real need, then this wouldn't have
happened."

What might the future hold for this innovative cooperative
venture? Local doctors have begun referring their patients to the
group—"socially prescribing" it—according to LaCamera. They've
seen that men taking part have become less drug dependent, more
self-confident, and less in need of medications. The success of the
Men's Health Group supports a growing understanding among
health care professionals in Britain that social inclusion—through
which people find their way back into the mainstream of society—
is a key to recovery from both physical and mental illness.

Church worker Pat Culpan, who brought the men's group and
Cleggs Lane Church together, has been hard at work getting the
church's newest project off the ground: a once-a-week community
drop-in café at Cleggs Lane. Members of the men's group have
trained in food hygiene and help run the café, which adds to their
experience, marketable skills, and confidence as they make their
way back into the life at the heart, rather than on the margins, of
their community.

Cleggs Lane's student pastor, Alan McGougan, told LaCamera that he had been so "personally transformed" by the experience of working alongside the men's group that he had decided to take a full-time position with a congregation in Scotland that was eager to "take the walls of their church out into the community."

Paul Foster, having set up and facilitated the men's group for several years, has moved on to set up a similar project in another north Manchester neighborhood. Two members of the men's group were recent guest speakers at a regional gathering of church pastors talking about how the group operated at Cleggs Lane and how others might create similar partnerships in their own parishes. Local radio has been out to talk to group members about what they are doing and how it has transformed their lives.

Drawing on the experience at Cleggs Lane, Methodists at another small church down the road have begun working in partnership with the local mental health trust, where LaCamera serves as a community chaplain. They are hosting relaxation sessions for church members, trust patients, and the general public. The sessions are led by LaCamera, who said she hopes the partnership will both add to the life of a local church with dwindling resources and help those struggling with mental health conditions to find their way back into the community.

Looking back at a time when the members of Cleggs Lane Methodist Church actually voted to close their doors, Pastor Brooks marvels at the unexpected road they have traveled together as partners and pilgrims. Paraphrasing the British writer Kester Brewin in his book *The Complex Christ,* Brooks said, "This kind of ministry is all about being prepared to risk a relationship where nobody knows where they are going to end up. That's where God works."

23

A New Way to Share God's Grace

Steve Schoon

While faith and spirituality may not be able to reverse or repair a disability, for many people they can provide support, comfort, and encouragement to cope. Sometimes a congregation can fully embrace a member with a disability and provide for that person's nearly every need, both material and religious.

Steve Schoon was diagnosed nearly twenty years ago with relapsing-remitting multiple sclerosis (MS), a debilitating deterioration of the protective coating around his nerves. Since then he has had numerous, sporadic, short-term relapses involving muscle spasms, fatigue, occasional loss of balance, and emotional anxiety. With rest and the use of a rubber-tipped cane, he was able, for a time after each episode, to resume his normal activities, including driving and managing a business.

As the relapses progressed, however, Schoon had to rely increasingly on his cane, which he has chosen to see in a spiritual way. "Through my cane," he said, "God is irresistibly inviting me to let go of my crutch of self-reliance and walk with Him into spiritual and relational terrains that I have often feared to enter."

At the same time, Schoon has had to rely increasingly on members of his congregation, First Christian Reformed Church in Grand Rapids, Michigan. "My fellow church members have seen me struggle and have watched me learn to rely on my cane," he said. "They surround me with God's grace, unselfishly providing me with 'canes' of spiritual, emotional, and physical support along the way."

One man, a deacon, gently but persistently offered to put together a monthly schedule of two men from the church to exercise Schoon's feet and legs on Tuesday and Thursday nights. The volunteers learned exercises from Schoon's physical therapist to slow the progression of atrophy in his muscles. They listened as Schoon expressed his frustration at being unable to play on the floor with his grandchildren, for fear he couldn't get back up.

As Schoon's ability to maintain his balance diminished, the men from First Church changed ceiling lightbulbs, moved furniture, and shoveled snow from his sidewalks. They did for him, Schoon said, what his own father had done for others all his life. The son wanted to be able to express his faith in the same way, but the MS was destroying his deeply ingrained concept of ministry. Yet his situation taught him humility, weaning him from his self-image as a strong, independent person and helping him see his cane as a new way of sharing God's grace.

During the early stages of his MS, clients at Schoon's auto collision repair shop who had not seen him for a while sometimes asked, upon noticing the cane, whether he had had knee surgery. Schoon would explain that he had MS. If the customer told him it looked as if he were "handling" it well, Schoon would reply, "No, I don't, but God does."

It is not that Schoon has known no periods of doubt. Throughout his journey, and especially in recent years, he has experienced increasing difficulty with mobility, spasticity, fatigue, and stress as medications lost their effectiveness. These symptoms undermined his ability to focus on his business. He was reevaluated, and his diagnosis was changed to secondary progressive multiple sclerosis.

Eventually, Schoon needed to shift from a cane to a walker for support, and before long he began using a wheelchair. He became depressed, thinking he was no longer physically able to extend God's grace to others, as he always had. Throughout his business career he had tried to integrate his faith with his work. "Our business was founded on treating our employees with God's love," he said, "and expressing God's truths to our customers by our integrity and professionalism, and donating to ministries both locally and in other countries."

As Schoon's need for physical care grew and he could no longer go to work, he felt he was losing his identity and his ability to help others spiritually—the MS was robbing him of his spiritual ministry. He believed he was responsible for extending God's grace to others but was no longer capable of doing so.

"When I went on medical disability and gave up my management of the shop, I was taken out of my work environment, where most of my contacts with people outside of the church had been," he said. "The intensity of the MS had stripped me of my opportunity for daily interaction with people." Schoon soon found that most of the people he had interacted with in his business circles drifted back into their own worlds and gave up contact with him. He still had the companionship of his wife, family, some close friends, and church members, but he was experiencing many of the harsh realities of living with a disability.

With his income dissipating and the pain of spasms draining his energy, Schoon found himself sitting at home struggling with depression and thinking that God had removed him from his ministries. In 2008 he was forced to sell his home during the collapse of the local housing market, although, thanks to a caring, Christian real estate broker, he was at least able to find a buyer. His wife's growing need to care for him on top of her own work, together with Schoon's loss of his ministry identity, added to the tension of the change in their marital roles as they endured the six-month waiting period to be approved for Social Security disability income.

After the home sale, Schoon's daughter and son-in-law welcomed Schoon and his wife into their house, not far from the church. His church friends helped renovate a barrier-free apartment in the house, gutting the interior, painting and installing cabinets, and assembling the computer. They gave him a wheelchair when a church friend's father passed away, and the exercise crew kept a close eye on it, making minor adjustments and doing regular maintenance as part of their ministry. One friend designed a strap so that Schoon could lift his leg to put on his slippers, and another built a safety support rail for his bed.

About the time Schoon moved, he remembered a conversation he had had with his closest friend six months earlier, while sitting quietly around a campfire. The two men had enjoyed a relationship for years in which they held each other spiritually and morally accountable. The friend knew that Schoon felt he was no longer able to live his life for God as he thought God wanted. "Steve," the friend said, "you know your ministry is over—what are you going to do?" There was a long pause as they stared at the stars and watched the smoke rise. Schoon replied, "I don't know, but I'm sure that God has a plan for my life."

That divine plan soon became manifest. Schoon found he had the time and faith to study the Bible, pray, and count his blessings. He began a Facebook page on which to write devotionals and faith stories, sharing a few of his writings with a seminary friend, who challenged Schoon to write twelve more devotionals in the coming year. In 2010 Schoon was encouraged by responses from friends and Facebook readers across the country, and he has now written more than one hundred devotionals, intentionally choosing not to place the emphasis on his MS.

The men from church who had earlier exercised Schoon's legs began to drive him to his therapy center and learned the proper physical therapy techniques, which they in turn taught other men. Soon men were coming to Schoon's apartment four nights a week, enabling him to regain some strength and stabilize his condition. The church men designed and built inexpensive exercise equipment specifically to help with Schoon's needs. Naturally, his relationship with these men deepened as they shared their life stories and prayed together. Others from First Church call Schoon or visit, sitting and talking about their lives and faith.

Women from the congregation have also pitched in. One, who is a nurse, put Schoon in contact with a palliative care doctor, who evaluated his condition. The specialist worked with Schoon's physician to develop a medication plan that reduced the frequency and intensity of Schoon's spasms. Other women from the church provided respite care, taking Schoon's wife out for dinner as a break from being his primary caregiver. As more people became involved in Schoon's care, his wife became free to attend a Bible study group at church and a women's retreat, spend time with the couple's grandchildren and her aging mother, and feel less pressure from caregiving.

Concerned about Schoon's feelings of isolation, one couple from church built a ramp into their house so that he could visit. Other members help him transfer in and out of his van at church and drive him to dental and doctor appointments. As Schoon's physical weakness has progressed, church members have readily increased their support by stretching and exercising his body twice a day, four or more days a week. When Schoon and his wife express their thanks, the most frequent reply is, "Thank *you* for allowing us to minister to each other!"

First Church's embrace has gone beyond making it possible for Schoon to attend Sunday services. A group of men affectionately called the "Old Geezers" gathers at the church on Tuesday mornings for coffee, and once a month, one of Schoon's exercise companions picks him up and brings him to the gathering to swap stories. As enjoyable as the experience is, an hour with these storytellers is about all Schoon can handle before he needs to go home to rest. He remains able to participate in First Church's pastoral search team, though, because its members make sure they meet in places that are wheelchair accessible. And when his energy permits, Schoon works with other members for several hours during the week planning worship services.

The consistent compassion and support of a few of Schoon's friends and the ministering members of First Church have allowed Schoon to be a mentor to young men of college and high school age. His depression and the perceived loss of his ministry in business have been replaced by a focus on writing and sharing God's grace through listening, teaching, and praying.

Schoon's experience with weakness has led him to permit others to make him their ministry. "I am not physically cured," he said, "but I am being spiritually healed."

24

A Mass for Everyone

Rosita Kardashian

In 1994 Rosita Kardashian, director of Parents' Place/Club de Padres of Catholic Family and Community Services in the Diocese of Paterson, New Jersey, was inspired to organize a bilingual, Spanish-English "Mass of Inclusion" that would allow for the full participation of people with disabilities. Kardashian's ministry offers services to Latino families who have children with disabilities.

"I've witnessed such simple spirituality and strong faith in so many of the very low-income families who have children with special needs whom we are blessed to serve," said Kardashian, whose family came to the United States from Central America when Rosita was eight. In El Salvador her mother had worked with Archbishop Oscar Romero, who devoted his life to the poor and disenfranchised and who was assassinated in 1980. "My mother's stories inspired me to give those families something I knew would be very special to them," Kardashian said. Seeing their children with special needs participating in the celebration of the holy Mass would be a proud and spiritual moment for the families, she thought.

Two years later, after much planning and preparation, the Mass was celebrated at the Cathedral of St. John the Baptist, and it was something to behold. Nearly fifty young people with developmental disabilities participated in the liturgy in Spanish and English, joined by about six hundred family members and friends. Club de Padres members with disabilities joined the choir. They also acted as lectors, altar servers, and ushers. "It is their right as children of God," Kardashian told the congregation. Catholic churches are inclusive, she said, "but this was the first time in our diocese that a group of young people with disabilities had full participation in the celebration of Mass." She told the worshipers, "You will be witnesses to the many gifts and talents God has given to people with special needs."

Parents' Place members made symbolic offerings to presiding Bishop Frank J. Rodimer. One young man presented a music instrument, representing the center's musical instruction programs. Another offered a medal from the Special Olympics. A third person, who had received vocational training from the center, presented a check from earnings as a bus aide at Catholic Family and Community Services.

The readers were young people with developmental disabilities who had practiced untiringly for their moment to read the Word of God. In subsequent Masses of Inclusion over the years, the group selected young people with many physical and intellectual disabilities to read the lessons. To the congregation, the fact that the readers had disabilities made those moments authentic testimonies to God's love for everyone, not just people who excelled in school, had great jobs, or had natural athletic abilities.

Among the hundreds of people in the crowd at the first Mass of Inclusion, Kardashian was uncertain of how many attended out of support and how many out of curiosity. Most, she was certain, left touched by the love and abilities of the young people. For their part, parents and families sat in awed silence as they watched their sons and daughters move about the altar with the ease of doing something entirely natural to them.

"We who helped them rehearse and practice for those Masses were more nervous than they were," Kardashian said. "We were inspired by how easy it was for all of them to carry out their roles as participants in the celebration of Mass. Our bishop then was Bishop Frank Rodimer, and he never missed an opportunity to celebrate a Mass with this special group. It was always a humbling experience for all of us. God's love transcended all barriers and allowed his children with special needs to bring his love to the hundreds of worshipers who witnessed this spiritual gift."

Recalling that first Mass of Inclusion years later, Kardashian said, "It was something that not only brought hope and pride to all those adults and children who participated but also brought an important message of inclusion to the community at large. I am not a theologian, nor am I a person who knows her Bible very well, but I do know God's love, and I was truly inspired by the natural faith of those families who came to that first Mass of Inclusion and who continue to come to us for help."

Juana Ortiz, who has cerebral palsy, is typical of those whose families benefit from the Parents' Place/Club de Padres and who were moved by their participation in the Mass of Inclusion. She had moved to Paterson from the Dominican Republic in 1988, at the age of fifteen. In the Dominican Republic, her family attended a Catholic church together on Sundays, but Juana never participated in the Mass. Years later, she was invited to celebrate with the bishop at the Mass of Inclusion. "At that moment when I was asked to participate I felt shock," she said. "I couldn't believe it, because never before had I seen a person with a disability participate in a Mass. People with disabilities tend to attend Mass but they are not asked to help lead."

Ortiz found the songs in the service a little challenging, mostly because participants were asked to sing in English and in Spanish, which meant they had to memorize or at least become familiar with the lyrics in both languages. One year, before a Mass of Inclusion, they began practicing in early October and continued through December, working with a church chorus for an hour on weekends.

Ortiz's music teacher recorded all the songs for her in both languages, including "Song of Joy/Himno de la Alegría" and "Lord, When You Came to the Seashore/Pescador de Hombre." "I remember participating in the Mass singing 'Song of Joy' while I was wearing a black skirt and a white blouse, just like a typical chorus member, while the bishop was standing next to the altar," she said. "Celebrating the Mass and seeing the bishop made me feel blessed. It was a great opportunity to show the community that people with disabilities can also celebrate Mass like anybody else."

David Roldan, a native of Paterson, son of Colombian immigrants, and also born with cerebral palsy, had an equally positive experience with the Parents' Place program. "My family has always had a close relationship with the church and a strong faith in our Catholic teachings. As we were growing up they taught us faith in God. They also taught us about all the sacraments of the Catholic Church. They taught us that we had to try to go to Mass on Sundays. They taught us to say a prayer before going to bed and to pray to our guardian angel for protection."

As Roldan was growing up, he began to prepare to receive the sacraments and was included in all the regular religion classes. He made his first Communion at St. Anthony Church in Paterson, and although he used crutches to get around, he remembered feeling no different from anyone else. In confirmation class, he was allowed to take his confirmation test orally. His teacher asked him the questions and wrote down his replies. Roldan said that if he hadn't been allowed to take his test that way, it would have been much harder for him and would have taken him several days to finish.

Roldan was pleased when he learned that he and others with disabilities were to participate in the first annual Mass of Inclusion and that the bishop would preside. "Before this Mass," he said, "I had never participated in a Mass. I can't remember ever being at the altar with a priest before." During the service he read one of the selections from the Gospel. "I had to climb up to the pulpit, and that was a little difficult, but awesome. I really enjoyed it. I was happy. That was the first time I participated in the Mass. I think my mother was happy for me also, because she saw me and heard me reading from our holy book. She was very proud of me. To this day she tells me that."

In subsequent Masses, Roldan participated by offering petitions, singing in the choir, and joining in the procession. The Masses, he said, "showed the community that we were not limited by our disability and we were able to participate with the respect and loyalty that the church deserves."

The club was of particular comfort and support for Roldan and his mother a few days after Christmas 2010, when Roldan's father was kidnapped and murdered in Colombia before the family could respond to the kidnapper's ransom demands. David was close to his father and was devastated by the loss. Kardashian offered him the opportunity to come to the center every day to be with his friends and have something to get out of bed for. He said his deep faith was the only thing that allowed him to begin to accept his father's death.

The Mass of Inclusion in Paterson was not unique. In March of 2011, during a conference on "Faith, Deafness, and Disability," Capuchin Franciscan Father William Gillum led an instructional session for conducting similar Masses. Gillum is the chaplain at McGuire Memorial, a home in Pittsburgh for people with mental and physical disabilities, and the author of *Awakening Spiritual Dimensions: Prayer Services with Persons with Severe Disabilities.* According to a Catholic News Service story by Anna Weaver, Gillum held the session in the light-filled chapel of the Shrine of the Most Blessed Sacrament in Washington, D.C. Classical music played as fifteen parish staffers and caregivers, sitting in a circle, heard the priest demonstrate how to create prayer that is accessible to worshipers with disabilities.

Before the chapel session, Gillum told participants in another workshop that the goal of a successful disability prayer service was to create "a sacred flow of prayer . . . in an uninterrupted, structured, and sequential motion of worship, evoking the divine, leading the participants into contemplative and intuitive moments of communing with God." According to Weaver's Catholic News Service article, he said that the best way to do that was to make use of as many senses as possible and to remain as simple as possible. At his Pittsburgh facility, Gillum said, he found that lighting candles and ringing bells had a calming effect.

During the session, Gillum first passed a priest's stole around the circle, and each person felt it, engaging the sense of touch. He then had one participant help light a candle while others had water poured on their hands, experiencing another tactile sensation. In order to put people with disabilities at ease, Gillum suggested that church members offer a simple greeting: "Welcome to church. Welcome to God's house. We are here together. We are friends."

After a short prayer, Gillum had each person in the circle touch the open pages of the lectionary. Then he offered his own simplified version of a Scripture passage, followed by a brief homily about how God, who created the human body, also makes everyone unique. Finally, holding hands, the group prayed the Our Father together. In a real service for people with disabilities, Gillum said, the priest and members of the congregation would typically do a writing activity, recording their thoughts and reactions to their experiences, and then contemplate a picture of Jesus. As the participants left the session, Gillum addressed each one by name and said, "May Jesus bless you, be with you today, and give you all good things."

Gillum said he had little doubt that such prayer services reach people, because "there are smiles, there are all kinds of indications that they are happy to be there."

PART 2

Ministry by People with Disabilities

In North America, Christian tradition teaches—among many other things—that God helps those who help themselves, and with faith all things are possible. To some extent these messages have become clichés and, worse, excuses not to help or intervene on behalf of people in need. This is troubling, because in this misunderstood fashion, such messages feed into the all too prevalent view of people with disabilities as dependent receivers, objects of pity, even troublemakers or drains on the economy.

Yet people with disabilities, like nearly everyone else, much prefer to help themselves and, when it is possible and practical, others. After all, no one has better insight into the relationship between faith and disability than people of faith *with* disabilities. Often, as the stories in Part 2 illustrate, they are called to—or thrust into—personal ministries, or they find their existing ministries transformed.

But although people of faith with disabilities can be dogged, determined advocates for themselves and others, their personal experiences and expertise do not immunize them from struggle and frustration. The stories in this section are those of both ordinary and extraordinary people who are not naive about their circumstances. They live with disabilities, often in poverty, but somehow find a path, a job, a calling that enables them to use their gifts and abilities in service to others. Many are pastors and have found ministry to be a lifeline; others are lay advocates and activists. Their parents and partners are key elements in their successes.

Pastor Joe Kovitch, a university chaplain who appears in chapter 40, is a good example. He acquired his disability as an adult, after spinal surgery that led to his using a wheelchair. His words are powerful: "The wheelchair has its blessings—it helped me focus my sense of calling. In an odd way, it was liberating . . . a way of connecting to the whole new community, a hidden community. People knew I had been a big athlete, a runner, and I miss running. I wouldn't have chosen this, but I choose to use it."

Episcopal priest Claire Wimbush, born with her disability, has used an electric wheelchair since she was three. She has been comfortable in both her faith and her disability since childhood. As one of her colleagues describes her: "She's not a priest despite her disability. Her disability doesn't limit her priesthood. Her disability is part of God's provision of this priest. That is, her broken body—and her openness in talking about it, coupled with a wicked sense of humor—helps all engage our brokenness and God's promise of healing."

Another ordained leader, the Reverend Susan Gregg-Schroeder, offers hope to everyone who lives with depression. Having hidden her depression from her congregation for years, she now serves others through a theological understanding that came during her darkest days. "Medications may stabilize symptoms," she says, "but it is relationship and love that heal the soul."

A deaf advocate, Mary Heron Dyer, says: "It's time to break the 'silence' about hearing loss and the impact it has on the individual and the loss it presents to churches as newcomers are turned away—or members themselves begin to drop out when the churches do not address this issue by investigating and installing appropriate assistive-listening systems." In her story, too, we see someone with a disability using her insights and gifts to benefit others.

Rabbi Lynne Landsberg, the senior adviser on disability issues for the Religious Action Center of Reform Judaism, has strong words: "Before my brain injury, I belonged to one minority that was strong and articulate—the American Jewish community. Now I belong to a second minority that is the victim of discrimination yet remains powerless and barely heard—people with disabilities."

These five leaders with disabilities and the sixteen others whose stories appear in Part 2 are comfortable in their own skins, open about their disabilities, and without pretense. With their amazing gifts, they break the silence, tell their stories, and set out to change the way people in congregations think, feel, and love.

These leaders do not waste energy pretending to be perfect. Those of us who work hard to hide our self-perceived inadequacies and vulnerabilities have much to learn from them. They have the moral character, the focused strength, to claim their fragilities and disabilities rather than make excuses, denying what exists. Their message to us? We refuse to be ashamed of the way God has made us, and we intend to lead useful, contributing lives.

25

Thrust into Untried Territory

JoAnn Misail

When JoAnn Misail was a little girl, living in a third-floor apartment in Boston, Massachusetts, she wrote a letter to God and threw it out the window, convinced it would reach God. To her, it was that simple and clear. Faith is the thread that has run through her life as a member of the Greek Orthodox Cathedral of the Annunciation. It was in this congregation that she was baptized, went to Sunday school, participated in youth groups, was married, and taught Sunday school herself.

As a young adult, Misail attended Northeastern University and Lesley College, married, and had three children. Then, in 1980, when she was in her late thirties, she manifested tingling up her right leg that continued across her lower body and down her left leg. She was diagnosed with a disease called transverse myelitis, but except for two mild outbreaks, the disease did not affect her daily life for years. Ultimately, though, it was diagnosed as multiple sclerosis (MS).

By late 1995, walking had become difficult for Misail, requiring her to hold onto her husband's arm or use a cane or, for longer distances, a walker or scooter. Misail believed that her disability rendered her ineffective and helpless. She wanted to hide her disability, to protect her image of being "well," while she waited for some miraculous reversal. She became more comfortable in churches where people did not know her. "This challenge in my life drew me even closer to God," she said. "I was constantly thanking God for steps I made that once I took for granted."

The disease complicated Misail's relationships with friends and family, some of whom wrestled harder than she did to reconcile her disability with the concept of a loving God. Although she tried to tell herself that the people close to her were doing their best, it was still hurtful when some ignored her and others spoke to her slowly and loudly, as if she were not intelligent enough to understand them. A few didn't want to be seen in public with her when she used a walker or scooter. Drawing on the faith she had known since childhood, Misail resolved to persevere. "I was not going down in defeat," she said, "for I always held onto God and I knew I could move on only with his strength."

Even before her diagnosis of MS, Misail contacted the National Multiple Sclerosis Society. Through it, she met a woman named Irene who had serious MS symptoms and whom Misail found to be loving, caring, warm, and generous—someone "sent by God." The two made an instant connection. Misail considered Irene a secular humanist, but despite their differences in faith and politics, the women's bond grew stronger as they spent more time together. JoAnn and her husband, Gus, attended concerts with Irene and her husband, John, both at Harvard's Sanders Theatre and at Trinity Church in Boston's Copley Square, where they enjoyed Handel's *Messiah* and a special Christmas candlelight carol service. The two women also attended an adult "MS Vacation Week" in Connecticut, packed with activities not usually associated with people with MS. During the week, the pair led a swarm of scooter riders—unannounced—into a restaurant for lunch, stunning the hostesses.

"If people stared at our unconventional bodies, Irene and I always smiled back," Misail said, "continuing our fabricated tale to each other of our ski accident and the dangerous feats we achieved before the terrible falls." After her friend's death, Misail "thanked God for the multiple sclerosis that brought Irene and me together and for the blessing of the special gift of time Irene and I had together. God gave me strength through Irene and blessed me with a true and beautiful friend."

When a new young priest, Father Dean Panagos, came to the Greek Orthodox Cathedral of the Annunciation, Misail asked him if he would visit her mother—whose immovable faith had so influenced her life—in a rehabilitative institution. The priest suggested she meet him there so they could pray together, and Misail, with her youngest daughter, did so. As they left, the priest asked JoAnn if she would host an informal coffee for him at her home so he could meet his parishioners in her neighborhood.

To this day Misail doesn't know whether the priest recognizes how much his simple request brought her to a better place by offering her the opportunity to let go of her isolation from the church. Being on the giving and offering side gave her a warm feeling and served as a reminder. "I sensed I had lost the opportunity to serve," she said. "Putting me only in the role of the receiver denied half my humanity."

Gradually, a new world began to dawn for Misail. She sensed that her disability, the crucial experience in her life, needed to become the framework of her relationship with God. She was a part of the Greek Orthodox Church and longed to explore the teachings of her faith, yet she felt unable to reveal her disability openly. Reading an article in the weekly newspaper *Hellenic Voice*, Misail felt that the Holy Spirit was moving her toward a home theological study program: the Saint Stephen's Applied Orthodox Theology diploma course offered by the Antiochian House of Studies, an educational program of the Antiochian Orthodox Christian Archdiocese of North America. Misail applied and was accepted into the course, beginning what she called "a humbling, exciting, and a bit fearsome study of the Orthodox faith. My goal was to heighten the Church's awareness about people with disabilities, their vision of their disability, and their need to be integrated into the Church."

As her new world of study opened, Misail no longer felt confined to what she called her "broken body." She was overtaken by the intrinsic meaning of a new universe, one that created a beautiful symmetry blending her strengths with her weaknesses. She looked first for people with disabilities in the Bible and was perplexed to find that all those in the New Testament had been healed. With greater insight, she found that Jesus "included persons with disabilities as a focus of concern in his ministry of healing." It comforted her to believe that the stories of healing in the New Testament were examples of Christ's bringing persons back into the community—a metaphor for the transformation not just of the individual but of the entire community. "Christ intentionally sought out those who were placed outside of the community," she said, "and he chose to use healing to unite them with the rest of the society. Many at that time assumed that those who were disabled had brought their suffering on themselves through sin and banished them from the community. Healing was necessary to their reconciliation."

What Misail hadn't noticed when she applied to the study program was that the final event each year was a one-week residency at the Antiochian Orthodox retreat center in Bolivar, Pennsylvania, about a thousand miles from her home. She had been comfortable studying at home and contacted the director, Father Joseph Allen, in the hope that she would not have to attend, because of her disability. Allen reassured her that the campus was completely handicapped accessible, and JoAnn would be able to use her scooter. A student from Canada who used a wheelchair would be in the same session, he said, which encouraged her. JoAnn's husband, Gus, taking some of his mechanical engineering work with him, drove his wife to the center. "We spent a week in this beautiful place, together with Orthodox students from around the world," she said, "preparing ourselves for fulfilling the ministry that God had given to each of us."

In her third year of study, in order to fulfill the program's annual requirement of a directed study project, Misail proposed that she organize what she called the first Pan-Orthodox Divine Liturgy and Forum, titled "Embracing the Whole Body of Christ." The project came to fruition on June 10, 2006, at the Taxiarchae Greek Orthodox Church in Watertown, Massachusetts. A large audience turned out, among it people both with and without disabilities and representing Orthodox jurisdictions including the Antiochian, Bulgarian, Greek, and Romanian. Misail hoped the liturgy-forum would be not an end in itself but a beginning, and so it proved to be.

Two young people who attended, a man who was blind and the mother of a Down syndrome child, wanted to keep the momentum of the conference alive. "The three of us formed a new small group," Misail said, "called 'Embracing Access,' which included a number of people with disabilities and family members of people with disabilities and which met periodically at my home. We believed an inclusion of persons with disabilities in the church would be a grassroots effort."

In early 2007 Father John Chryssavgis, an ordained deacon of the Greek Orthodox archdiocese and theological adviser to Ecumenical Patriarch Bartholomew, spiritual leader to the world's nearly three hundred million Orthodox Christians, contacted Misail. Earlier, Chryssavgis, whose son has a physical disability, had written a book, *The Body of Christ: A Place of Welcome for People with Disabilities*. "The Church is by definition a place and a process of communion, open to and inviting all people without discrimination," he wrote, "a place of hospitality and welcome. An earthly reflection of the heavenly promise. A community of people with different yet complementary gifts. A vision of wholeness and of healing, of caring and of sharing."

Chryssavgis asked Misail if she would assume responsibility for writing a draft on issues related to disability for a possible official statement on disabilities to be issued by the Standing Conference of Canonical Orthodox Bishops in the Americas. Chryssavgis finalized the statement and presented it to the hierarchs, who approved the document, titled "Disability and Communion," on June 26, 2009.

Misail's MS grew more severe in 2009. "Again I was thrust into untried territory," she said, "where the conditions of my life were drastically modified. I was not alone. I became engaged in exposing my feelings through a constant discourse with God, in levels of fear, confusion, devastation, and exhaustion. Whatever the frightful conditions I encountered, I hoped God would help me continue to go forward in spite of seeming impossibilities. *And he has strengthened me to move on again.*"

Chryssavgis is impressed by Misail's efforts. "I've learned over the years not to presume to represent but to receive from people with disabilities, whether listening to or learning from their experience," he said. "JoAnn is one of those people who can reach out to many others, encouraging and enlightening with sensitivity and compassion."

26

Life over Adversity

Jim Hukill

When Jim Hukill was only twenty months old, doctors told his family that because of his rare, debilitating form of muscular dystrophy, they should expect his life to be greatly limited. The Orlando, Florida, minister, who has used a wheelchair since he was six, has instead made it his life's mission to help strengthen the families of people with disabilities and open the doors of churches to children and adults who live with disabilities.

Over the decades, Hukill has rolled his wheelchair past one barrier after another, despite having slight strength in only one arm and neither of his legs. He earned a bachelor's degree in pastoral ministries from Southwestern Assemblies of God University in Texas and, like his father, became an Assemblies of God minister. He credits his remarkable success to his parents and later his wife, Rhonette, with whom he has founded several ministries devoted to people with and without disabilities.

"My mom was a huge advocate," he said. "My family's leadership in my life gave me tools to understand that with my faith, my determination and vision, I could accomplish whatever I wanted to. I was determined to be a minister myself."

After graduating from seminary, Hukill and a driver took to the road in a van for an itinerant ministry, going from church to church, telling Hukill's story. In 1998, after marrying in 1994, he and Rhonette moved to Orlando to help a friend start a church in the suburban community of Hunter's Creek.

But Hukill had a vision for a new, national ministry that would focus on strengthening families in which a member was disabled. "We began to look at our lives and discovered that there was a real need for a network of people who would help us have a successful life and marriage," he said, considering that so many marriages fail when one person has a disability.

Hukill named the ministry Eleos, a Greek word meaning "mercy." A voice-activated computer and the Internet enabled him to spread his message and counsel throughout the nation. He also produced a half-hour television pilot about people with disabilities. One segment in the magazine-format show was an interview with disability activist Ginny Thornburgh at First Presbyterian Church of Orlando. The pilot was not picked up for further production, but it led to invitations being extended to Hukill to air the show around the country. "It was satisfying to know that the idea was unique and creative enough to gain some interest from some small market networks," he said. "I still believe there is a place and a market for a visual voice for the disability community in media."

Nowadays, Hukill has only enough strength in one hand to operate a computer. Still, he spends much of his time on the road, visiting churches of various denominations, and at summer camps for young people with disabilities. "I preach a message of encouragement, a message that challenges," he said. "We provide insight into how churches can become more accessible for people with disabilities, to help people that have limitations, visible or invisible, to go beyond, to experience a freedom in life. I still have a voice, and that's all it takes."

When Hukill officiates at baptisms, he barely stirs from his wheelchair. Rhonette, who serves as his hands, performs the actual immersion. "It's a great symbol of the unity of marriage," said Hukill. "It shows how two people can work as one."

In 2006 Jim led his organization, Eleos, into a merger with the Christian Council on Persons with Disabilities (CCPD), resulting in a new organization called Lift Disability Network. Combining the legacy of CCPD and the vision of Eleos, Lift has a global mission to elevate life in the disability family. Most recently, Lift has set its sights on conquering what Hukill calls the "Four Great Giants of the Disability Life Story": isolation, fatigue, poverty, and hopelessness. By implementing three life values—"Love, Learn &

Lead"—Hukill and Lift are once again raising the supremacy of life over adversity.

A centerpiece for Lift Disability Network is a practical, heart-warming magazine designed to give the disability family a voice. *Lift* magazine is a platform for people with disabilities and their families to tell their stories. Chief editor Rhonette Hukill said, "We use real stories about real people facing disability." As Jim's partner, Rhonette has her own stories. In addition to her responsibilities in their ministry, she oversees the management of her husband's daily care. Together, they feel they have been empowered by their experiences and the knowledge that disability does not have to rule life.

"The church needs the gifts of people with disabilities, and people with disabilities need an opportunity to give," Jim said of his national ministries. "If it hadn't been for someone who made a house of worship available to me, then I wouldn't have been able to have an expression of my gifts."

Activists cite Hukill as an example of the role religion can play in giving meaning to the lives of people with disabilities. Churches across the country have opened their doors to him and listened to his message. What he really wants is for these congregations to do more than listen. He would like to see them take concrete action to welcome people with disabilities.

Ginny Thornburgh, of the American Association of People with Disabilities, describes Hukill as "an eloquent speaker with a beautiful singing voice." She adds, "He's a remarkable man who demonstrates the theme that is so important to me, that people with disabilities have enormous gifts and talents to bring to their congregations."

27

Civil Rights Begin at Home

Lynne Landsberg

Rabbi Lynne Landsberg was a rising star in Reform Judaism until January 10, 1999, when her Jeep SUV hit a patch of black ice on a Washington, D.C., street and crashed into a tree. Landsberg's son, Jesse, who had just celebrated his eighth birthday and was on the way to religious school, escaped serious physical injury, but Lynne was left with debilitating traumatic brain injury.

An articulate, multitasking graduate of Boston University, Harvard Divinity School, and Hebrew Union College–Jewish Institute of Religion in New York, Landsberg was at the time of the crash overseeing seventy congregations in the eastern United States for the Reform movement, the nation's largest Jewish denomination. Within weeks, she was due to become president of the Harvard Divinity School's Alumni/Alumnae Council. Earlier, she had spent eight years advocating for social justice on the federal level, as the associate director of Reform Judaism's Religious Action Center, and making speeches around the country.

The collision left Landsberg in a coma for six weeks, her prospects for survival uncertain at best. But she did survive, and after four months in the hospital—for much of it relying on breathing and feeding tubes—she returned home, where she spent almost two years under twenty-four-hour care. From that point, with the help of her faith and her Jewish community, Landsberg began the daunting task of trying to relearn everything.

Looking back, some would have thought the experience might have caused her to lose her faith, she told members of the Central Synagogue of Rockville Centre, New York, in a March 18, 2011, sermon. "But no, it in fact strengthened my spiritual core," she said. "What it ultimately did was to define my spiritual mission: that is, to help people of all nationalities and religions understand a fundamental principle of every faith—that we are all created in God's image—all of us, those with disabilities and those without disabilities. Now that has become my spiritual mission—to help everyone understand that we are, all of us, created equally."

Landsberg wrote in a chapter of *Managing Brain Injury: A Guide to Living Well with Brain Injury* that her Judaism provided the resources and support that enabled her to rebuild her life. The three pillars of this support were prayer, visits, and practical help. In this, she writes, her experience offers a model for all religious faiths.

The first element, especially when her life was in the balance, was prayer. In the hours following the crash, rabbis, cantors, and laypeople—some of whom she didn't even know—recited healing prayers and psalms on her behalf in synagogues across the United States and in Israel. Members of congregations she was overseeing came to her hospital room, and one woman from her own Washington congregation, Temple Micah, sang to her. Her temple held a healing service on her behalf. "It was as if the arms of the Jewish community were wrapped around me tightly yet lovingly, keeping me in this world," she wrote. "Visits like these made me later realize that during my entire hospitalization, I was on the receiving end of a core Jewish value that I had become a rabbi to teach."

At the same time, Landsberg is clear-eyed about the role of prayer: "I do not believe that God discriminates by healing those patients who garner the most prayers. Rather, I believe that prayer strengthens those who pray, thereby enabling them to reach out and help the one who is stricken."

Landsberg's friends and family, including her eighty-year-old father, were constantly at her bedside, keeping the hospital room full and lively. One Friday afternoon, members of local congregations brought to the room a loaf of challah bread, an element of the traditional Sabbath meal, which they blessed and shared.

"Each visit diminished my feeling of isolation and affirmed my connection to the world I had known before my brain injury," she recalled. "While I was in the hospital, those who fulfilled this *mitzvah* [positive commandment] of visiting the sick brought the world to me. Once I was settled back home, my visitors brought me to the world."

As Landsberg observed, the practical support and assistance she and her family received from the Jewish community are not particular to her faith. "It is the tradition of all religions that people lend their time and talent to help others. Within my religious community, the 'caring committee' of my congregation, Temple Micah, went into action."

Congregation members and neighbors ran many errands for the family. While Landsberg was still unsteady on her feet and couldn't drive, people came during the week and took her out for meals. Families from the synagogue prepared Friday night meals for Shabbat for Landsberg's father, husband, and son while she was in the hospital. The Sabbath meals kept coming after Landsberg was released, until she felt—with some anxiety—that she was ready to prepare her first Sabbath meal since the accident.

"It would be a crucial step forward," she wrote, "as well as the first sobering realization that I would never again be able to do things as I had done them before the accident." After she had been home for eight months, four women whose children had gone to a Jewish nursery school with Landsberg's son, Jesse, years before began coming over on Sunday mornings to teach Landsberg how to cook, while their children were at religious school.

In 2000 Landsberg's former employer, the director at the Religious Action Center of Reform Judaism (RAC), Rabbi David Saperstein, asked her to return to work when she was able to, giving her a concrete goal. "The possibility of my returning to the RAC with traumatic brain injury seemed inconceivable," she wrote. "Yet the thought of my contributing again to the Jewish community as well as the opportunity to think and learn and become productive was as irresistible as it was frightening." Saperstein asked only that Landsberg do her best, when she was ready. The offer itself was significant because, as Landsberg noted, two-thirds of people with disabilities who want to work are unemployed. For her, returning to productive work was the best therapy. "If it hadn't been for the

RAC—the challenges it offered and the faith they had in me—I would never have made the progress I have."

For all the help provided by her faith and her faith community, Landsberg gives equal credit for her remarkable journey from a near-fatal collision and near-total incapacitation to a lengthy and grueling regimen of therapy and an upbeat outlook. "Improvement from brain injury comes in small steps," she said, "like the first time I smiled in two years, which made my family ecstatic. If you maintain a positive attitude, work hard, and follow therapists' directions, things will get better—but in smidgens."

Still, because of the level of her cognition at the time, Landsberg did not feel ready to return to work, even on a volunteer basis, until six months after Saperstein's invitation. At that point she started back at the office two hours a day, two days a week. She had to make considerable adjustments. Her first assignment was to telephone rabbis around the country and ask them what resources they used and what resources they needed. To do so, she first had to write out a simple, short script to read for each call and then practice it with her speech therapist—a frustrating task for someone who describes herself as a former fast-talking New Yorker.

Ultimately, Landsberg decided it would be most productive to work out of her home office, still on a volunteer basis, because even with the help of an assistant she could work only part-time. Despite having scaled down, almost a decade later she is back on the road, making speeches, appearing on panels, attending conferences, and, to judge from several phone interviews, nearly back to speed in her speech, although she is less articulate than she once was when speaking off the cuff.

Outside the office, Landsberg met something unfamiliar. She realized that she was part of a new minority and experienced discrimination as an American with a disability. "When I walk into meetings, social situations, and commercial establishments with a cane, people often ignore me," she said. "However, when I attend disability-related meetings or activities, people don't even see the cane. They accept Lynne Landsberg as a whole person."

Landsberg often reflects on the great distance she has come since her crash. She sees her long and continuing progress in terms of Judaism's dual concept of healing of the spirit (in Hebrew, *refuat hanefesh*) and healing of the body (*refuat haguuf*).

"For me," she wrote, "the healing of the body has come far more quickly than my doctors had forecast. But my healing of the soul has been much slower. I think of *guuf* as the outer self and the *nefesh* as the thinking, feeling, inner self, and I wonder, what does it take to heal the all-encompassing soul?

"I know that healing of the *nefesh* requires one to accept certain harsh realities. Continued healing is dependent on my emotional ability to mourn the old Lynne Landsberg and to embrace the new Lynne Landsberg. No longer do I measure my successes by comparing them to my former achievements. It cannot be a matter of what I've lost, but what I've gained: an understanding of how much good is in each and every day and each and every person."

Rabbi Landsberg now is the RAC's senior adviser for disability issues and founder and cochair of the Committee on Disability Awareness and Inclusion of the Central Conference of American Rabbis, which means that she represents the denomination in the wider ecumenical community. "Before my brain injury, I belonged to one minority that was strong and articulate—the American Jewish community," she likes to tell groups. "Now, I belong to a second minority that is daily the victim of discrimination yet remains powerless and barely heard—people with disabilities."

Landsberg has strong words for rabbis who say they have no members with disabilities who require special accommodations. "Civil rights begin at home," she wrote in a 2010 op-ed column for the weekly newspaper *Forward*, "in our synagogues and in our communal institutions. We must make conscious efforts to break down the physical, communicative, and attitudinal barriers that separate individuals with disabilities from our community. It is time to come together to help our congregants, indeed all Americans, recognize that people with disabilities are people first—people with unlimited potential, not to be defined by their disabilities."

In a sermon she delivered at her temple on April 16, 2004, she said, "I thank God for my rehabilitation. I thank God for my resilience. And I thank God for my religion." The sermon was in many ways a progress report to everyone who helped in her recovery.

"We Jews need to make sure the severe discrimination suffered by all Americans with disabilities—who number more than fifty million people—is made public," Landsberg said in the sermon. "We need to make sure that those without disabilities understand that things they may say or do, without thinking, can be ego deflating and life or hope shattering to people with disabilities.

"Let us take a hard look as Jews and see who is *not* in our midst. Who is not sitting next to us in a synagogue service or a Jewish community event because they have no way of getting there? Who is not reading our mailings due to the size of the print? Who cannot read our prayer books because synagogues have not purchased large print or Braille prayer books? Who cannot hear our lessons, meetings, or sermons without special equipment or an ASL interpreter? Who is not participating in a family *simcha* [joyous occasion] because they cannot get up to the bimah or the platform or the stage? Who is not attending our religious schools, day schools, or even rabbinical schools because of a physical or learning disability? We would never consciously do it, but are we unconsciously putting a stumbling block before the blind?"

28

Open to Real Experiences

Chris Maxwell

On a mild March day in 1996, the Reverend Chris Maxwell—normally a bundle of confident, focused energy—was feeling unusually tired as he prepared for the week ahead at Orlando's Evangel Assembly of God. Probably the flu, he figured. The next morning he felt worse, so he called in sick, asking the church administrator about the condition of the steeple. That's odd, the administrator thought, our church doesn't have a steeple.

As the day wore on, things went downhill. Maxwell, besieged by the worst headache he had ever experienced, started babbling about pets the family didn't have. By the morning of the third day, he was virtually paralyzed by fatigue, unable to communicate. Most frightening of all for the then thirty-five-year-old pastor, much of his memory was gone.

Maxwell's wife, Debbie, sped Chris to the emergency room at Florida Hospital East, where an MRI confirmed what doctors suspected: Viral encephalitis had devastated his brain's left lobe, site of speech and memory functions. In addition to severe memory loss, the minister would have epilepsy for the rest of his life. Maxwell's immediate response was panic.

But within weeks of the encephalitis attack, determination had displaced fear. Maxwell began intense speech therapy and memory retraining to repair the devastating damage left by the encephalitis. For the most part it was "repetition, repetition, repetition," he said. "Images. Games. Questions. Tests. They would read a story and then ask me questions about it. I felt like a man with a master's degree who had returned to preschool."

"Some moments I caught on, other times circumstances crushed me," he recalled of that time. Still driven, Maxwell tried to return to the pulpit too soon, just weeks after his attack. But he was blocked by leaders of the congregation.

"They didn't know if I was going to have a seizure," he said. "I can remember being very angry. I wanted to be the preacher." He wanted it so much that within two months he was back in the pulpit, after his neurologist assured the congregation that its pastor was ready to return.

Still, much more work lay ahead of him. The years that followed were tough on the whole family—especially the Maxwells' sons. "Growing up, you need a rock in your life that's always there, someone you can always go to," recalled Taylor Maxwell, the oldest of Chris's three sons, who was ten when his dad fell ill. "I felt like I couldn't go to him." Youngest son Graham, six at the time of the illness, has little memory of what his father was like before then. All he can recall of that time was that the family spent a lot of time crying and praying. "I didn't know what was going on, so I started crying, too," he said.

Maxwell turned to technology to help him return to his former life. A Palm Pilot became an extension of his brain for short-term memory as he recorded and stored every bit of information that came his way, including what he liked to order at which restaurant. Each night, Maxwell downloaded the day's events into his home computer. For the first time, the man who once memorized whole books of the Bible used PowerPoint to deliver sermons. Congregation members helped, too, by wearing name tags and prompting him on the Bible verses he groped for during sermons. And they noticed something new about their pastor. Although he was back in church, Maxwell spent less time in the pulpit than he did roaming the aisles, approaching people individually—and astounding the congregation with his comments.

"He had this gift, this insight," the ability to sense the exact problem or crisis a member was struggling with, longtime congregation member Judy Padgett recalled. "It was almost as if he could see right through you. . . . It seems like God made us transparent before him for a period of time."

126

Maxwell soon returned to his traditional preaching style, but unquestionably, Chris Maxwell wasn't the same person. In 2005, sitting in the living room of the family's snug, two-story Orlando home, Debbie Maxwell called Chris her "second husband," because "God switched husbands on me in the fifteenth year of our marriage."

The Maxwells' insurance covered only two months of formal speech therapy, and the second month only after a protracted struggle with the insurance company. So the burden of recovery fell most heavily on Chris himself and on Debbie, who gave up homeschooling the boys to take a teaching job at a local Christian school. Chris read voraciously and tried to retrain the way he used his mind. *Why did my brain seem so dead in particular places?* he asked himself.

Maxwell's saving grace amid the turmoil of his recovery years was one thing the encephalitis had not destroyed: his sense of humor. The MRI machine at Florida Hospital became his "prayer closet" because he spent so much time sequestered in it. At the beach and at ball games, he donned a T-shirt sent by relatives reading, "Insufficient Memory at This Time."

Maxwell's doctors agreed that his will and determination were crucial to his recovery, but in the next breath they described his comeback as "miraculous" and "an act of God," said his neurologist, Hal Pineless. "If you saw his first MRI in the hospital and met him today, you wouldn't believe it was the same person."

Steven Attermann, the primary care physician on duty the day Maxwell was admitted to the hospital, attributed much of Maxwell's recovery to his faith. "Prayer went a long way to help him," Attermann said. "What prayer does for you is that it gives you the inner peace that allows you to get on and fight your other battles. Other stresses go away."

The doctor and the pastor bonded—so much so that one day in Attermann's office, Maxwell asked Attermann to pray with him. An observant Jew, Attermann was briefly taken aback. But something about Maxwell touched him. In the sterile examination room, he joined hands with Maxwell as the pastor read from the Old Testament Psalms.

It is impossible to separate the treatment he got from medical professionals and therapists from the role of religion in his recovery, Maxwell said. Yet things did not always go smoothly at his old church, Evangel Assembly. Pentecostals such as Maxwell believe in faith healing through the "laying on of hands." A few months after his attack, fellow pastors put their hands on Maxwell's head and shoulders and prayed for help for his doctors and for supernatural healing. But his memory and speech were not restored.

Members of his congregation had different reactions when they learned of the experience. "Some believe it saved my life, and that is why I can do the things I am doing these days," he said. "Others argue nothing changed." As a result, some members left the congregation. For others, the problem wasn't lack of faith. "They had trouble with the new Chris," Maxwell said. He had become "a leader looking for help," a wounded spiritual healer.

Inevitably, his disability has become a part of Maxwell's ministry. Previously, as a freelance writer, he had produced curriculums, devotionals, articles, and stories for religious magazines. After his illness, his writing changed focus: He has written three books and edited and ghostwritten ten others. Television and radio hosts have called to interview him, and partly to answer his interviewers' questions, he wrote the book *Changing My Mind: A Journey of Disability and Joy*, dealing with his brain injury and recovery.

Despite Maxwell's tremendous progress, things did not return to where they had been before his illness. He continued to suffer the long-term effects of brain injury, mostly scar tissue in his left temporal lobe and epilepsy. "It's still an adjustment," Debbie Maxwell said in 2005. "It's still not the person I married." She paused, struggling to explain. "He is the same person I married— only more intense and emotional." For Chris, the brain injury has been a different kind of "born-again" experience. Despite his travails, or perhaps as a result of them, the once frenetic pastor exudes serenity.

"The Chris that I know now I can safely say I like better, because he's so much more caring and sincere and compassionate," said Lee Grady, former editor of *Charisma* magazine and a close friend. "Because he was wounded himself, through this process he has a lot more sympathy for wounded people." Another friend, the Reverend Terry A. Smith, pastor of The Life Christian Church in West Orange, New Jersey, agreed.

"No, he's not the same man as the former Chris," said Smith. "He still struggles with his memory and his basic personality has changed. But now he is actually better. Better at leading more people. Better at working as a team player. Better at understanding the struggles of others. And better at depending on God—the One whose strength is made perfect in Chris's weaknesses."

In 2006 Chris Maxwell left the Evangel pulpit and Florida to become campus pastor and director of spiritual life at Emmanuel College in Franklin Springs, Georgia, his alma mater. He continues to write books, host a radio show, and travel around the nation and world, sometimes sponsored by a pharmaceutical company, telling people at churches, hospitals, and conferences his story about living with epilepsy. He has more than four thousand Facebook friends, as well as a Chris Maxwell Facebook Readers Group, and has traded in his Palm Pilot for an iPhone and iPad. "With many people aging and so many soldiers returning from war with partial brain damage, we need as many helpful devices as possible to assist us with our memories," he said.

He added, though, that he relies on "high-touch as much as high-tech." By "high-touch" he means teaming with people who face similar life-changing experiences related to epilepsy and other issues. "We seek to remember we are not alone. People need people."

The "high-tech," he said, "is a reminder that we are living in much better times. Modern antiepileptic medications, pocket PCs, iPhones, text messages, electronic memos, and many other devices assist people with brain damage. By quick and simple access to memory devices we are better able not to risk forgetting important information. Our devices remind us when to take medications, give us music for times of relaxation, and store brief documents as reminders for daily tasks we often forget."

Neither high-tech nor high-touch will re-create the time—or the person—Maxwell was before his illness. "I've learned that my life will never be the same as it was—and that's OK," he said, "because now I know it's full of more love and support than I could have ever imagined. I continue to cherish my family, including my new grandson, and watching my sons grow into wonderful adults. I continue to write, publish, and work on my radio show.

"All I've learned has brought me to a conclusion: We must be open to real experiences, no matter how painful they are. We must process those experiences and, in the end, share them. I tell you my story not just to make you laugh or cry but to allow myself to admit that it's been a hard and complicated road for me and my family, especially for my sons, who suddenly had to deal with a new father.

"I encourage my students at Emmanuel College, in high schools, and at writers and epilepsy conferences to write for the health of it—to get those emotions out—and sometimes I have them write the story of their future. For all of us with epilepsy, I envision a better future with fewer seizures and more understanding, where everyone can be honest about their struggles. I'm sure you've heard that 'the truth shall set you free.' I've been able to explore the truth of who I was, admit the hardships of my experience, and accept the new life I've been given."

29

Purpose in the Pain

Lisa Copen

As a teenager, Lisa Copen read the inspiring book *Joni*, by Joni Eareckson Tada, who had become a quadriplegic in a diving accident at the age of seventeen. Copen was impressed with the strength Tada revealed by sharing not only the things she was able to overcome after the accident but also how weak and vulnerable she felt as a quadriplegic. Tada's influence would remain with Copen for decades. "By reading Joni's story," Copen wrote in *The Transformed Power of Story*, a book to which she contributed a chapter, "I saw firsthand how a much-needed ministry was rooted in the experience of one who had gone through a fire of refinement—accompanied by personal suffering—rather than one who had gone to seminary to follow a calling. It was a memory that would stick with me."

While in college in Oregon, Copen was attracted to social work and volunteered hundreds of hours at a rape crisis network and a home for battered women. Yet something was missing. "Although I could take an unlimited number of classes and volunteer many hours," she later wrote, "I had not experienced what these women had gone through. Of course, I was extremely grateful to the Lord that he had not sent me down these particulars paths of 'education' so that I would be qualified to offer my personal experience; however, I found it difficult to connect on a level that I wished for, in order to offer my best."

Exhausted, Copen left college after four years, without a degree, and took a job in retailing, selling clothes. "I was extremely relieved," she said, "that if I sold a woman a scarf that was not her best color, her life was not at risk because of my advice." Then she fell in love with a man in San Diego. She drove "up and down the coastline, wondering what God's plans were for my life, and singing the worship song 'He who began a good work in me will be faithful to complete it,' with tears streaming down my cheeks."

At the age of twenty-four, while working at a nonprofit organization, Copen awoke one morning to find that one of her wrists felt frozen in place. Within days after she was taken off computer work, the wrist began to heal, but then the other one froze, and pain and swelling began to spread throughout the bones and joints of her body. Within a few weeks of visiting various doctors, she had a diagnosis: rheumatoid arthritis. Nine months later, when medication had failed to put the disease in remission, Copen resigned from her job and returned to college. With the help of her boyfriend, who later became her devoted husband, she was able to graduate and get on with life.

Still, there were difficult times. "I began to grieve the loss of my dreams and my identity, which was ingrained in them," she wrote. "So, as I went into the deepest emotional and physical valley of my illness, simply trying to get dressed before noon and to complete at least one household chore before my husband came home, I asked God, 'What now?'" Copen and her husband made plans to adopt a baby, and she began casting around for a career—or a calling.

Copen spent several years volunteering for the Arthritis Foundation, writing its monthly newsletter, and found it a comforting place. At the same time, she felt frustrated by her inability "to express my faith in Jesus, as well as my spiritual struggles. I was trying to understand how one can completely believe that God will heal, yet at the same time wonder if healing is truly God's will at that time."

"In my experience," she wrote, "the only thing that was going to get me through a life living with chronic disease was to cling to Jesus, and to know that God had a purpose in the pain. I believed my pain would never be wasted, and that though I would struggle with how my life could be defined by this illness, I was still living in God's 'Plan A' and not in God's 'Plan B.' This was the hope I wanted to offer people, but I was restricted in what I could write for this secular organization."

She recalled, "I sought out Christian support for people who lived with chronic illness but was unable to find a support group or ministry specifically reaching out to them. Chronic illness can be anything from diabetes, lupus, fibromyalgia, heart disease, multiple sclerosis, and even cancer, to the lifelong side effects of the treatments.

"I had assumed there was at least one main organization for people who lived with illness, but I could not find it. I remember going to the Christian bookstore after my first appointment with the rheumatologist, and the only books on the shelf in my area of interest were how to 'die with dignity' or how to survive cancer. 'Where are the books for people who live with chronic illness?' I asked a store clerk. She said she couldn't think of any and went to ask other clerks. She came back and said that that was quite an interesting idea; there were a number of people she knew who had illnesses."

So beginning with a simple newsletter, Copen founded a rapidly growing, California-based Christian organization called Rest Ministries that today provides resources for people with chronic illness, pain, and disability. She is also the author of many books and other resources, including the paperback *Beyond Casseroles: 505 Ways to Encourage a Chronically Ill Friend*, a practical book that reminds people to listen, avoid euphemisms, and provide wanted and needed support.

"Based on the lack of Christian resources for those with chronic illness," she wrote, "I could have easily assumed that I was the only one who had not yet been healed, despite my faith. Thankfully, I knew that my pastor had rheumatoid arthritis, and he was one of the first people I went to for advice and encouragement for this unexpected detour in life. I remember him praying with me and asking God to heal me, while lightly grasping my hands with his own hands, which had started to show deformities."

Copen recalled the influence that Joni Eareckson Tada had exerted on her years earlier, and now she had the opportunity to hear her speak. Afterward she stood in a long line, waiting for Tada's autograph and the chance to ask whether Tada knew of any

Christian ministries specifically for people living with chronic illness. Copen was beginning to think this was what God had called her to do, and if such a ministry existed, she wanted to be a part of it. Tada was supportive when Copen told her about her desire to start a chronic illness ministry. She said she knew of nothing like it and agreed that the need was great.

With a single computer, purchased with her husband's job bonus, Copen launched Rest Ministries. The newsletter, ". . . And He Will Give You Rest," was followed by an online group, "Share and Prayer," and then by a community support group called HopeKeepers that met at a local library branch. Because Copen knew of no Bible study curriculum about chronic illness, she wrote her own, a five-lesson curriculum called "When Chronic Illness Enters Your Life." After that, "God took over," Copen said, "and expanded the ministry in ways I never could have imagined. About three hundred HopeKeepers groups are currently active, and our newsletter evolved into a website that is updated daily, including devotionals that have gone out via e-mail for more than ten years."

In 2004 Copen had what she calls a "full circle moment." Joni and Friends ministry called to see if Rest Ministries might be interested in becoming one of its affiliates, specifically for people with illnesses or invisible disabilities. "It's been a joy and an honor to now be a part of Joni's ministry," Copen wrote. "In order to reach out to the many people who live with chronic conditions who do not know Christ, we began National Invisible Chronic Illness Awareness Week. It has grown to become a full virtual conference with twenty speakers giving seminars in a five-day time period over the Internet, where one can 'attend' for free and without ever leaving the comfort of home. Our annual conference has become a well-recognized and respected event by the online patient community, and we've reached hundreds of thousands who would not have previously visited our Christian website."

Copen recognizes, however, that hurdles to inclusion remain. "I often encounter churches that are reluctant to embrace the chronically ill," she wrote, "because there is an unspoken assumption that the church will be weighed down by their needs as well as depressed by the fact that these people are not healed. After all, if church is supposed to be an example to the community on how wonderful life can be if one walks alongside Jesus, what message would be sent if it appeared that some members had given up on the hope of being healed? What are we communicating to our visitors about God's healing power if there is an announcement in the bulletin about a chronic illness group meeting? Won't those people with illness always need something like rides, meals, or childcare?

"Those involved in church leadership may ask, 'Why do those chronically ill people have to be so sensitive? Why do I have to constantly accommodate their needs? Can they not just be grateful that we are doing our best?' The truth of the matter is that people want to be loved and to feel like they are cared for. Most churches believe they are doing this, but those on the receiving end often say that the message or ministry is not being clearly communicated."

There is, Copen insists, a concrete upside to inclusion. "I have found that people who live with chronic illness understand suffering on a daily basis and are the most compassionate and understanding group of people you may ever know. Often it is those who live with illness who are the ones trying to make and deliver meals to others who are only slightly more ill than they are. And if you stand outside a room where a group of people are who have chronic illness but who know Jesus, you'll be pleasantly surprised to hear the joy and laughter that reverberates, even through tears. To live with an illness each day, one can find a sense of humor, true joy in the Lord, and an appreciation for life that was never completely understood before the disease."

30

The Advantages of Disadvantages

Thomas H. Graves

As a boy and as a freshly minted pastor, Thomas Graves had several passing encounters with disability. A beloved grandfather who had lost a leg in an Illinois coal-mining accident played games with young Tom on his wooden prosthetic. A man named John in his suburban church lost his ability to walk and make himself understood as a result of a neurological disease, yet he made himself an admired member of the worship community as a cheerful greeter and a bell ringer.

Graves finished Vanderbilt University and chose a life in ministry and academics, graduating with advanced degrees from Southern Baptist Theological Seminary and Yale Divinity School. He assumed the pulpit at his first church, in rural Shelby County, Kentucky, in the fall of 1973. There he met a congregation member named Eddie who had lost an athletic scholarship to college when he was felled by a progressive muscular disease but who remained active in the church, attending Sunday school and worship services. For a while the man was able, with assistance, to walk from his car to the rear pew, where he sat on Sunday mornings. Later it became too difficult for him to manage on his own, and he had to be carried, but he never stopped coming to church and participating as fully as he could.

In 1983 these brushes with disability ceased being abstract for Graves when he saw a doctor for what he thought would be a routine examination. He had some numbness in his left arm and some clumsiness in his right leg, and he had found himself stumbling while playing a weekly game of tennis. After Graves was hospitalized and underwent a long series of tests, his doctor told him in caring tones that he had multiple sclerosis, and his physical life would change greatly as a result. He would have to make many adjustments and accept that he would need to rely on the help of others.

"I thanked my friend for his skill and wise advice and assured him that I could count on the loving support of my close-knit family," Graves said. "Then I closed our conversation by saying, I also happen to have some pretty good models to guide me along the way. And I remembered Granddad, John, and Eddie, with their humor, love, faithfulness, and joy."

At the time of his diagnosis, Graves was thirty-six and serving on the faculty of Southeastern Baptist Seminary. He shared the news with top officials at the school, whose response was both caring and supportive, which set the tone for the way he would share the news for the remainder of his career. "Though I did not broadcast the news, I did not try to hide it from anyone and took the initiative to tell all future employers of my condition," he later wrote.

Four years later, Graves was called to pastor St. John's Baptist Church in Charlotte, North Carolina. "I presented the pastor search committee with a letter from my doctor describing the benign form of my disease and what could be expected in years to come," he said. "As far as I know that news was never shared with anyone else in the congregation, not even the spouses of the committee members. I informed staff members of my illness, and we made some adjustments to make my functioning a little easier, such as reconfiguring the service of Communion so I would not have to climb stairs. I remember tripping once while serving Communion and almost falling into a deacon's lap. I later explained to him the reason why and then had my wife shorten my ministerial robe by several inches so I could see my feet, because I certainly could not feel them."

Graves was credited with helping to initiate a revitalization of the St. John's spirit, and in 1991 he was invited to become the first president of the new Baptist Theological Seminary in Richmond, Virginia, as well as a professor of the philosophy of religion. Again he shared his medical records with members of the seminary's board of trustees, and he began serving as president with no public display of his MS.

But four years later he suffered his first major setback. Unable to walk, to see clearly, and even to swallow easily, he was frightened that the disease had taken a permanent turn for the worse and he might spend the rest of his life in a wheelchair or bedridden. That time, with a few weeks' recuperation and the administration of steroid drugs, he regained most of his former abilities. But over the years his condition slowly degenerated, and he suffered three more major episodes. Each time he recovered quickly, yet each event left him noticeably weaker.

"There were some advantages for the school in having a disabled president," Graves said. "The school's recruitment practices and operating policies moved from the expected attitude of equality and fairness to one of hospitality and eagerness in dealing with issues of disability. As the school was in the process of facilities renovation, decisions were made to create a model environment that assured accessibility for all persons."

In 2005, with the school in the midst of a major fund-raising effort, Graves's physical condition suddenly emerged as a matter of crucial importance. The trustees could see that he had progressed in a few years from a slight limp to the use of a cane, then a walker, and finally a motorized scooter. Although he suffered no mental lapse because of the MS, it was obvious to Graves that his physical disabilities would in the future prevent him from functioning effectively as president. He could no longer travel by air without accompaniment; he had given up driving; and he had lost the use of his left hand, so he could no longer use a computer keyboard with ease. Even a minimal amount of walking was increasingly difficult. The trustees made adjustments such as getting Graves a chauffeur and having a voice recognition program installed on his computer. Yet it was obvious that a plan of succession needed to be put in place.

In the spring of 2007, Graves stepped down. Since then he has maintained his strong interest not only in the school but also in issues of disability. In 2007–2008, for example, he served as chair of the Association of Theological Schools' Task Force on Disability and Seminary Education. Composed of faculty and staff from seminaries and divinity schools throughout North America, the panel was charged with writing a policy statement that would address disability issues. The thrust of its statement was that theological schools should provide a welcoming, supportive, and enabling environment, ensuring a hospitable community by removing attitudinal as well as physical barriers. The Association of Theological Schools adopted the policy at its biennial meeting in June of 2008.

The Reverend Ron Crawford, who succeeded Graves as president of the Richmond seminary and who has known Graves for twenty-five years as a friend and colleague, remembers that "as a young man he had such a strong, warm presence behind a lectern." Over the years, Crawford watched the disease take more and more of Graves's physical vitality. At the same time, Crawford said, "I'm surprised when people mention Tom is disabled. I have to remind myself, 'Oh yeah, he has MS.' There is nothing disabled about his mind, or spirit, or faith. Tom is a giant of a person who happens to ride around on a scooter."

Crawford finds it interesting—and significant—that Graves's academic discipline is theodicy, which deals with the issue of human suffering and "the problem of evil." Before Crawford succeeded Graves in Richmond, he was pastor of College Park Baptist Church in Orlando, and each winter Graves spoke at Crawford's church. "On one occasion," Crawford said, "he spoke to the congregation about theodicy from a personal perspective. While I don't remember all the points he made, I remember that he was profoundly honest about his own illness, thoughtful in terms of articulating a philosophical perspective that was sensible and practical, and, as always, expressed a deep sense of faith and trust in a God who loves us and desires the best for us. Sitting on a stool with his walker beside him only drove home the power of his words."

Graves preached that sermon, "The Advantages of Disadvantages," from many pulpits, and in the spring of 2011 it appeared as an article in *Christian Ethics Today*. Learning from adversity, Graves wrote, is a complicated matter. While his perspective comes from his personal experience of living with multiple sclerosis, "we all share disadvantages of failure, grief, sorrow, sickness, and frustration. Living with limitations is a universal human experience. It has visited us all.

"I do not want in any way to identify God as the source of the evil that comes upon us. God does not send pain our way so that we may gain something from our difficulties. When we find ourselves in the midst of sorrow and difficulty there are some things we can learn; but that is a far different thing than saying God brings evil upon us in order to teach us a lesson."

What he wanted to address in his sermon, he said, was "my experience that there are some advantages for us when we face difficulty and disadvantage. Particularly in the book of Psalms, we hear of the difficulties of life and the importance of facing hardship with honesty. Sensitivity to sorrow belongs at the very heart of biblical religion. It is interesting how often in our worship we focus on psalms of celebration and order. But the truth is, most of the psalms are not songs of celebration; the largest number of psalms are laments. Let us consider the advantages of disadvantages. Let us begin to see if there are some lessons we can learn.

"It seems to me, one very clear lesson that weakness teaches us is that we are all part of a very fragile human family. Weakness teaches us that life is fragile through and through. Life is defined by our limits; life is defined by finitude. When we confront the created order we find ourselves living in a world with metaphysical limitations."

Rather than asking, "Oh, why *me?*" when we meet difficulties, Graves suggests, we might better ask, "Why *not* me?" In his sermon, he said: "Often we have an idea that as persons of faith a protective shield has been built around our lives and nothing evil is going to happen to us. You know that is not true! Very good people suffer; sometimes they suffer because they are very good people. There is not a Biblical promise that difficulty will never come to the faithful. There is simply the assurance that even in trouble you will not be left alone. You will not be abandoned. . . .

"Disadvantages can lead us to see the failure of self-reliance, recognizing that there are some things we cannot and some things we should not face on our own. It is the most difficult thing, it seems to me, for Americans to grasp, with our inbred rugged individualism. What we can learn from facing disability is to recognize the need to lean on others.

"It may well be that the issue of suffering can be the very thing that brings us to the deepest understanding of Christ and an experience of faith. We have some choices to make as we face difficulty. Faith or unbelief. Anger or creative response. I would hope for each one of us, as we face our disadvantages, that we might learn of some advantages as well."

31

Called to Community

Mark Johnson

Like many children growing up in Charlotte, North Carolina, in the late 1950s and early 1960s, Mark Johnson went to church because that's what his family did, he wrote in his memoir, *I Love Today*, from which this chapter is adapted. His parents were volunteer Sunday school teachers at Sharon Presbyterian Church. His dad served in leadership positions, and his mom sang in the choir and planted flowers and maintained the gardens. Johnson and his brothers attended Sunday school and worship services. They participated in youth group activities and played basketball in the church gym. It was all part of life.

"In the midst of this life, we developed some sense of who God is and what he expects," Johnson recalled. "We learned that God is good and that he likes boys and girls who are good. That meant respecting our parents, doing our chores, and working hard in school. Only now they were coated with theological meaning and injected with an extra powerful shot of motivation, since God, like Santa, could see everything."

Mark realized that fear was not an ingredient in this spiritual recipe. The Johnson boys weren't raised to believe that God would strike them down in a bolt of lightning or otherwise punish them if they were bad. It was just that they didn't want to disappoint God. Somehow, they knew God loved them and wanted the best for them. And much as in the relationship they had with their parents, the thing they feared most was letting God down or being undeserving of his love. They did their best to earn the love of God and their parents, even if it meant sitting quietly through some dry church services.

Everything changed just two weeks before Mark's twentieth birthday, when he sustained a spinal cord injury in a diving accident. Although the Johnson family had endured trying times in the past that had tested their faith, this event brought them to their knees, spiritually speaking. Their church at that time, Carmel Presbyterian, immediately rallied around them. The pastor visited, and church members prayed incessantly for them and sent a steady stream of hot casseroles and pecan pies to fill their stomachs. As Mark's parents sat vigil around his bedside, their friends ran errands, fed the dog, and shuttled news and people back and forth from the hospital.

"Yet in the midst of these outward signs of Christian love and concern, my parents were beginning to lash out at the God they had served for so long," he said, "feeling that he had betrayed them. My dad, in particular, was furious at God. More than anyone, he had believed that if he did everything right and worked hard in the church, God would protect him and his family. My mother's anger was not as concentrated. She knew implicitly that God had not caused—or even allowed—my injury; however, she still wrestled with her sense of loss and grief. Together, they agreed that they would not return to church, at least for now."

While Mark did his best to put on a brave face for his family and friends, during the night, as he lay alone in his hospital bed, he wrestled with his own spiritual questions. He grieved over his injury and a life that was quickly being defined by chilling phrases such as "permanently paralyzed," "confined to a wheelchair," "take him home until you can't take care of him anymore," and "he won't live past forty."

"Like my mom, I knew that God had not caused my injury, but still I wondered where God was during this time," he said. "I was still very much afraid, but gradually I began to have a sense that God was with me. God was starting to become personal."

In 1972 Johnson was still wrestling with his new identity. After five months spent in hospitals, he'd had time to settle in at home and begin to navigate the world as a person with a disability. Not surprisingly, he was starting to feel aimless and restless, wondering what he should do next in life. During that time Billy Graham returned to Charlotte to hold a crusade in his hometown, and the visit piqued Johnson's interest. He asked his father to drop him off at the Ovens Auditorium that Friday evening—the crusade's youth night. As Mark's father drove away, the young man wheeled himself through the entrance and toward the front of the auditorium, where an area had been set aside for people using wheelchairs. After singer George Beverly Shea warmed up the crowd with his renowned baritone voice, Graham began to tell the story of Daniel, a devout Jewish boy who was captured by the Babylonians, taken from his family and homeland, and forced to serve the Babylonian emperor's royal court. Though traumatized, Daniel didn't give up, but instead went on to develop a successful career interpreting dreams. Neither did he give up his faith in God, even when his captors insisted, on pain of death, that he worship their pagan gods.

"As Billy preached, I understood that it was no longer adequate for me to rely on my parents' faith in God," Johnson said. "While they had done a great job raising me in the church, it was time now for me to make my own personal commitment to God. I was being challenged to finish the process that began in those dark nights in the hospital. More so, I recognized that God was with me, not just in the time of my accident but also as I was developing my new sense of self, and that he was calling me to lead a full and active life, with or without a disability."

Within four years of Johnson's accident, his parents had also reconciled with their faith and returned to church—his mother with a sense of peace, and his father with a mixture of wariness and hope. Because Mark was still living with his parents, he attended church with them. The congregation welcomed them warmly and did what they could to accommodate Mark and his wheelchair. Among other things, they built a beautiful ramp for the church's entrance and approved the use of their gym for the local wheelchair basketball team.

At the University of North Carolina at Charlotte, Johnson earned a bachelor's degree in psychology and a master's degree in education, specializing in guidance and counseling. He took a job as a counselor at Charlotte Rehabilitation Hospital, providing support to current and former patients who were also adjusting to life with a disability. Although many of the patients' problems involved physical barriers, which often left them feeling angry and depressed, more fundamental issues arose from social attitudes about disability that supported segregation and promoted paternalism. These attitudes said that having a disability was a negative thing. When couched in spiritual terms, these were the same attitudes that told Johnson he needed to be healed, as if he wasn't good enough for God's love the way he was.

Twice after his accident, Johnson met this frustrating belief face-to-face. The first incident took place on a summer evening a year after his injury. He was lying in bed when a friend visited. "His name was Tommy, and he was here to heal me," Johnson recalled. "Earlier that evening, Tommy had attended a worship service at his church, where a visiting healing preacher was praying over people. After the service, Tommy invited the preacher to accompany him to my house and pray over me, but the preacher declined. Undaunted, Tommy decided that he had the same faith and could do the same things that the healing preacher had done, and he headed directly to my house."

Knowing Tommy to be sincere in his desire to heal him, Johnson agreed to let him try. "I could tell it was important to him. He read a passage of Scripture, prayed over me, and then grabbed my arms and commanded me to stand up. But I didn't. Although I shifted a bit from the force of his actions, my body otherwise continued to rest comfortably on the bed. Tommy was both embarrassed and devastated and quickly retreated from my room, never to come around again."

More than ten years later, after marrying and having a child, Mark was vacationing with his family in Myrtle Beach, South Carolina. His wife and daughter were playing in the water while he sat poolside, watching them and enjoying the warm summer sun. Eventually, a woman approached him. Sitting next to him, she smiled and asked if she could pray for him. "I understood that like Tommy, she was sincere in her offer and thought she was doing a good deed. She may even have thought that she was doing the will of God. I smiled back at her and answered, 'Sure, as long as you know that I'm happy.' I could tell that my response startled her. Her smile vanished, and she awkwardly stood up and walked away without saying anything else."

In retrospect, Johnson thought that his friend Tommy and the woman by the pool represented a lot of people in the church, and to a degree he understood their motivation. Disability is frightening to many people. It generally comes from injury, illness, or aging, and it always means that some part of the body, whether the brain, the legs, arms, eyesight, bodily functions, or a combination of parts—do not work the same way they do in people without disabilities. "In a society that places a high value on ability and being independent, we don't want to think that it's possible that we, too, could lose that," said Johnson. "I understand that, and yet I see, too, how pity is promoted when people focus solely on what a person can't do, rather than what they can. When we do that to people, we miss out on the opportunities to see them as partners in ministry."

Johnson learned this lesson from his friend and mentor Wade Blank, whom he met while living in Denver, Colorado, in the early 1980s. Blank was a Presbyterian minister who had worked in the civil rights movement before dedicating his life to working with people with disabilities. Blank especially singled out people with severe disabilities, and as he did so, he witnessed the ways in which society shunned and pitied them. But the minister saw the value and dignity in each person and treated him or her as a colleague and partner. Blank, Johnson, and others organized a group they called ADAPT and successfully fought for accessible transportation, first at the local level and later at the national level. Working with Blank, Johnson learned how communities are strongest and most effective when every person is valued for his or her contribution.

From Denver, Johnson and his family moved in 1986 to Atlanta, where he began volunteering at Shepherd Center, a private, not-for-profit hospital specializing in medical treatment, research, and rehabilitation for people with spinal cord and brain injuries.

In 1987 he was hired as the facility's advocacy specialist, and later he became its director of advocacy. Over the past twenty years, Johnson has earned more than a dozen state and national awards for his advocacy for people with disabilities.

After Johnson and his wife, Susan, were married, they did not attend church regularly. But like many other couples, they agreed, once their daughter Lindsey was born, that it was time to start going again. They wanted Lindsey to be exposed to the Christian faith and brought up in the church, so they soon joined Alpharetta First Presbyterian Church and began to get involved. The church had all the necessary physical accommodations in place, so Mark was able to be as involved as he wanted to be.

Over time, Lindsey found her own place in the Christian youth group, Young Life, and Susan and Mark began to attend church less frequently. Although they very much believed in God, "we weren't spending much time with him at church beyond Christmas and Easter," Johnson said.

That all changed during a return trip from a Florida vacation in 1996, when Johnson lost his wallet at a roadside fruit stand. Four months later it was returned by mail by a stranger, who had found it and then misplaced it. In his letter accompanying the wallet, the man apologized and included a copy of *The Daily Word*, a booklet of daily devotions that he said he had found to be meaningful. The man wrote that he hoped the devotions might also be useful in Johnson's life. Johnson was touched. He read the devotion for that day and was glad that he had, for it gave him a sense of peace and reinvigorated his faith.

"What was most meaningful was that this Good Samaritan offered this gift without knowing anything about me," Johnson said. "He didn't know who I was, or what I did, or whether I was already a Christian. And more importantly, he didn't know that I had a disability. He offered this gift simply because his love for God compelled him to do so. It was not a gift of pity, but one of pure Christian love."

Over time, reading *The Daily Word* became a vital part of Johnson's morning routine, laying an uplifting foundation for the rest of his day and reminding him continually of God's presence in his life. He later gave copies of the devotional book to his wife, his daughter, and several of his family members and friends. In 2001 Lindsey introduced her parents to North Point Community Church, which they still attend.

Toward the end of 2008, Mark began to feel restless. His work was going well, his family was fine, and he and his wife were learning to slow down and enjoy life. Still, he felt a spiritual uneasiness. Despite all that he had accomplished in his advocacy work, he worried that he wasn't doing what God wanted him to be doing. He wondered if he was losing focus or doing too little. He continued to read his daily devotions and attend church, and he tried harder to listen to God.

The title of the *Daily Word* devotion for Friday, February 13, 2009, was "Healing," and the lead sentence was "Divine love heals and restores me. I am alive, alert, and enthusiastic about life." Mark read the devotion as usual and then began his day. But as the day progressed, he started to feel sick, and Susan took him to the hospital emergency room. His appendix had ruptured, but because of his spinal injury he had been unable to feel the pain. During several periods of nighttime delirium, he experienced a deep sense of awe and peace, as well as a spectrum of visions, some from his early life.

Several days into his recovery, Mark asked his nurse to give him his laptop computer, and with great energy and clarity he began to write about the visions he had just experienced and the messages that seemed to emanate from them. "The word that kept coming to me was 'love,'" he said. "God created us because he loves us and he wants us to love each other." Mark felt that the visions were confirming the work he'd been doing but added a spiritual component that had been missing. "I think God wanted me to see his hand in my work and to share that message with others." This he has done since then, faithfully living out that calling, using a faith that has become personal, he said, "to share the good news that God loves us and calls us to community just the way we are."

32

Everyone Has Some Challenges

Al Mead

Even as a young boy living on Chicago's South Side, Al Mead was a competitor. In 1968, when he was in the third grade, he found himself in a race for his life after a sports accident resulted in a blood clot and gangrene. Doctors were able to save him, but only after amputating one leg above the knee. That experience, he says, "framed the foundation as to who I am today and the journey I was put on, to be an example and an advocate for people with disabilities, particularly in the area of sports."

Mead grew up in a Christian home, and his family's small African American congregation rallied around him after the accident. His personal relationship with Jesus Christ deepened, he said, and helped him in the trials he faced in the months and years that followed. His father was a deacon, the pastor's right hand, and the congregation "embraced me and accommodated me in every aspect. I participated in every event that involved kids; inside or outside the church. I stayed plugged in because the church was so embracing and encouraging. As a result I became the 'encourager' for the church because of my perseverance and action."

The major hurdle Mead faced was that he wanted to continue as an athletic competitor, and prosthetic legs at that time were not designed for use in sports. The boy's life changed when he met an African American prosthetist—one of the first designers of artificial limbs in Chicago—named Mike Lewis, who began designing stronger and faster legs that would allow Mead to compete in high school, intramural, and recreational team sports, from baseball and basketball to ice hockey. He was good at all of them, and not just good for a kid with an artificial leg, which enhanced his confidence.

At Morehouse College in Atlanta, a historically African American institution, Mead studied biology and business and continued his interest in club and intramural sports. He expressed his religious faith mostly through choir singing, both in a local congregation and with the renowned gospel choir of the Atlanta University Center. During his time at Morehouse, Mead made another fortuitous connection, with a prosthetics designer named Larry Rice, a Georgia Tech engineer who wanted to take artificial legs to a higher level.

Equipped with one of Rice's prosthetics, Mead began winning track and field competitions. Indeed, in his first outing with the leg, a regional meet in Statesville, Georgia, in 1982, he broke the world record in the hundred meters for an above-the-knee amputee. He quickly advanced to elite world levels of performance, eventually participating in international Paralympic competitions—which follow the quadrennial Olympics—in events for amputees, using his new leg. In the process, he attracted the interest of sponsors, manufacturers of prosthetics for nonathlete amputees, who could underwrite even more sophisticated limbs. These companies hoped that the attention Mead brought to their products would convince insurance companies to pay for less costly, mass-market versions.

Mead had a breakout performance in 1988 at the Seoul Paralympics, earning a gold medal, and four years later in Barcelona, where he was team co-captain and took home a silver. At the closing ceremonies in Spain he sang "Mighty Spirit." "I wanted to sing a song that was more spiritual, that said a lot about what I am, but also about my spiritual relationship with the Lord. There is a triumph of the human spirit, but without God I wouldn't be here—or have made it this far."

Until he was sidelined by a calf injury, Mead was expected to do equally well before a hometown crowd in Atlanta in 1996. Nonetheless, Mead served as vice-chairman of the Atlanta Paralympic Games, in addition to being a member of the United States Olympic Committee and the President's Council on Physical Fitness and Sports. As his athletic career blossomed, the young man's personal and professional life also prospered. He joined an executive search firm, married, and had two daughters. His limp was hardly noticeable. He became a member of a predominantly white Southern Baptist church in the Atlanta suburbs, where he agreed to become choir director when a sudden vacancy arose, and he helped as the congregation became increasingly multicultural and multiracial. "It was a good fit," he recalled. "I was able to express my faith in the form of worship leading; inspiring and motivating others through music and worship." But Mead felt he was at a spiritual crossroads, with no sense of personal calling.

With his growing worldwide success and visibility in the Paralympics—he broke world records in the hundred meter dash and the long jump—Mead felt that he was being given a platform from which to share his faith. "God was showing me a lot of great success in my life," he said. In 1999, Dan Cathy, president of the Chick-fil-A restaurant chain, prevailed on Mead to join Cathy's megachurch, New Hope Baptist. Mead eventually became a full-time staff member and associate pastor, overseeing a sports ministry and establishing the congregation's cross-cultural ministry and ministry to people with disabilities.

One of the first things Mead did at New Hope Baptist was to open the church's gymnasium and fitness facilities to people from the broader community. He also helped facilitate the start of "Blaze Sports," a program established through the U.S. Disabled Athletes Fund to help people with disabilities. Both, he felt, were the kinds of programs that would have helped him as a young boy after his accident. "It's great to see the many kids who have adaptive needs that we can accommodate," he said. "I'll make sure they are accommodated. My philosophy is, you don't have to be a member of our church to participate in our programs."

Mead continues to speak in communities all over the country. "A big part is speaking at schools, partnering with them," he said. "As an accomplished athlete with a disability who has reached a pinnacle of medals, I can demonstrate that everyone, no matter who you are, is going through some form of challenge. The principles that I try to model are principles that anyone could grab hold of and say: 'I can use these in my life.'"

33

Nourishing Vocation

Jamie Dennis

Jamie Dennis was born with retinitis pigmentosa, an eye condition that causes progressive tunnel vision and sometimes eventual blindness. By the fourth grade, he began learning Braille as a precaution against losing his eyesight entirely. Because his Kentucky farm family wanted him to see as much of the country as he could while he could, his uncle, a long-haul truck driver, arranged to take the grade-schooler on several trips from his home in Caneyville to Southern California and the West so that he could see sights like the Grand Canyon and the Pacific Ocean.

The part of Kentucky where the Dennis family lives was settled during colonial times by English Catholics from Maryland. In the centuries that followed, immigrants trickled in from Ireland, Italy, and eastern Europe, creating a thriving, largely rural Catholic population—including monks at a Trappist monastery known as the Abbey of Gethsemani, where Thomas Merton once lived. At the time Jamie was growing up, there were so many Catholics that the public school system was staffed with Ursuline nuns serving as teachers and administrators. Dennis's mother did not want him to attend a special, residential school for the blind away from home, so he became the only blind boy in the local school system. His mother helped, volunteering to be with him every day.

Much of Dennis's early life centered on the church. He was baptized and made his first Communion, but by the time he reached third grade, the pressure of schoolwork and the lengthy drive to church meant the family attended services less frequently. Something new engaged the boy's interest: "Trains became the main motivation in my life," he recalled. From the time he was six, he preferred to visit the Kentucky Railway Museum in New Haven than attend Mass. By seventh grade, Dennis had become such a mascot of Kentucky train buffs that the Paducah and Louisville Railroad gave him a surplus red caboose, which he and his father, a Tennessee Valley Authority boilermaker, mounted on a section of track and turned into an apartment for Jamie. During middle school, father and son built a short, life-size, narrow-gauge railroad on the family's 120-acre farm, a one-mile stretch of track complete with four stations, which they christened the "Dennis Railroad."

Although he was able to operate his family's locomotive back and forth on its short length of track, Dennis knew that his diminishing vision meant he would never realize his ambition to become an engineer. Instead, he set his sights lower—just to work in the office of a railroad company. But while attending Brescia University in Owensboro, Kentucky, a school founded by Ursuline nuns from Brescia, Italy, Dennis again felt the pull of his Catholic faith. Until then he had been attending church about twice a month, with little real understanding of his faith. At college he took it upon himself to learn more, and he began going to Mass every day. Each night, seeking refuge from cacophonous dorm life, he returned to the chapel and sat alone for an hour or two in a back pew, enjoying the peace and quiet.

"Eventually I started making my way up to the altar," he recalled, "to become more adventurous, sitting in front of the altar." Something then drew him to a little room off the altar, where a box holding Communion materials was kept. He felt great love emanating from the container. "I decided it was time to give myself to God. However, I didn't want to take that big step and think about priesthood. I had to totally give myself to the church in priesthood or totally give myself to a wife and children."

In his junior year at Brescia University, Dennis visited his diocese's director of vocations, Father Andy Garner, to talk about prospects for the priesthood. Garner cautioned him that as soon as he seriously considered such a course, others might make it difficult. Sure enough, Dennis recalled, one professor and several other students told him he didn't have what it took to be a priest, shaking his confidence. His father, too, was shocked, for he hoped that Jamie, a self-described rough-and-tumble farm boy, would one day take over the family spread. His mother wondered at first whether his failing vision might keep him from his calling, but she soon reverted to her lifelong support. Both Jamie's bishop and the college president encouraged his choice.

At the end of his last summer of undergraduate courses, after undergoing a psychological profile, Dennis met with monks at St. Meinrad Archabbey Benedictine Seminary in Spencer County, Indiana. "The seminary was nervous because they had never had a blind person there before," Dennis said. "They didn't know how I would navigate the campus, how I would handle textbooks." Still, Dennis was admitted, and with the help of two voice synthesizers for his laptop, he completed his first year and began his second shortly before our interview.

"The first year a lot of my classmates had never seen a blind person before," he said. "They thought I was so delicate I'd break into a million pieces if they touched me. But I've also had plenty of offers of help. Some people think it's a taboo subject to ask about disability; I disagree. Questions do come up: 'Are you mad at God?' 'Do you ask, Why me?' I say no, I am not mad at God. He allows things to happen for a reason. There is suffering that we go through in life—some more than others. I trust in God. I know if I trust him he will see me through whatever situation I'm in."

One of Dennis's first projects outside class was to join others in a campaign for a Braille edition of the Book of Hours, a daily devotional. The effort involved negotiations with a Catholic Church publishing company and a producer of Braille materials. "I'm not afraid to tell the Church that we need to get with the program," he said, "but you can't make demands. You go through proper channels. The more patient and understanding I can be with people, the better off we all are."

Looking to the future, Dennis has been seeking out older, successful blind priests, including several who are parish pastors, and talking to them by phone. They have been encouraging but caution that he may face difficulties that other seminarians and priests won't. People might look down on him because he is blind, or lack confidence in him. If he returns to his Kentucky diocese, as required, he will need a driver in order to visit parishioners in rural areas. "I will have to rely on the laity a little more—and I'm okay with that—I've been mostly among sighted people all my life." Recently, on a return visit to Brescia University, Dennis helped lead an "Uplifting Mass," which celebrated differences and included blind people, wheelchair and cane users, people with Down syndrome, and some little people. Dennis's former assistant, Jennifer Wayne Byerly, who attended, called it "the most reverent and godly congregation I had ever seen."

Despite his career in seminary, Dennis still hears the siren call of the train whistle. Once, his friend Father Randy Howard asked him why he loved trains so much. The seminarian replied that there was something about the power he feels when he's driving a train, sitting at the engineer's throttle, knowing that he has hundreds of horsepower at his fingertips. At the same time, he knows that power comes with great responsibility, and he has to respect it. Howard said, "Just imagine the power working through you when you're behind the altar one day, changing the bread and wine into the body and blood of Christ."

"That showed me how the railroad hobby had nourished my vocation," Dennis said, "so as time went on I decided to use my train at home for the service of the church." There have been many unusual and innovative vehicles for evangelism, but few can rival the Dennis Railroad, Jamie's one-mile stretch of track. How to use the train for evangelism? "I'm still figuring that out as I go," he said.

During the summer and on weekend trips home from seminary, Dennis dons his engineer's cap, taking members of Catholic youth groups and anyone else who is interested for a ride. "Since the train will mainly be serving the Church, it's only fitting that it have a cross on the front of it," Dennis wrote recently to friends. One of the stations built on the family farm, called Mercy Falls, has a lakeside altar and picnic tables, where Dennis's pastor, Father Randy Howard, has celebrated several Masses so far. Dennis's cherished twenty-three Brailled volumes of the Liturgy of the Hours sits on the shelf of his caboose apartment, where he also keeps his model trains.

Every year on December 12, the feast day of Our Lady of Guadalupe, Dennis organizes a ceremony honoring the patron saint of Mexico, to whom he has built a shrine near the railroad. He invites the many Hispanic agricultural workers in the area to participate in a procession. He begins by transporting a statue of the Virgin Mary on his train to join the procession along a gravel road. His hope is to unite the local Anglo and Hispanic communities.

Sometimes Dennis preaches from the locomotive. Other times, he said, "I evangelize by my attitude, by my actions," looking forward to the day when he can wear both his engineer's cap and his clerical collar.

34

Facing the Abyss without Flinching

Christine Guth

For decades, depression made many of Christine Guth's days in Goshen, Indiana, feel like Ash Wednesday, a time for confessing and lamenting her sin. There were days and months—what felt like a lifetime—when celebrations felt to her like ashes, and death seemed an easy step away. That changed halfway through a decade of part-time study at Associated Mennonite Biblical Seminary, when she began a pastoral internship. A year or so later Guth began treatment for clinical depression. She recalls that her personal therapeutic regimen—learning to survive depression—consumed about as much time, energy, and money as her academics did.

After ten years of study, Guth earned a Master of Divinity degree, and the celebration with her family was a joyous one. But it was not unmixed with poignancy, considering the family's multigenerational history of depression. Guth's grandmother told stories of her own dark spells during the Great Depression, and her mother—a pastor's wife—had struggled during a time when little effective treatment was available.

"I count myself a survivor of depression three times over—my own depression, my mother's, my children's," Guth later wrote. "My own depression fits into a family deeply affected by depression. In my family we pass down depression more faithfully than the family heirlooms, and with it we have passed down the trauma of family life dominated by unnamed, untreated mental illness.

"My mother courageously faced depression most of her life, but treatments available then made little impact. Depression—though unnamed—was considered a character flaw, a spiritual failure, a source of shame, so no one ever talked about my mother's condition, nor mine, when as a teen I too began to experience signs of depression. My parents put on a cheerful face to the churches my dad pastored, out of fear that he might lose his job. I observed the church as a supportive community for others—but not in relation to our miserable family secret."

As Guth moved into her early adult years, she saw herself as emotionally weak, afraid to set goals, unable to count on emotional stability, always on the receiving end of help. Then, at a critical point in her life, with the encouragement of friends who saw gifts in her she could not claim for herself, she cautiously began taking the seminary courses, one at a time. Still, there were setbacks and occasions of doubt.

"If I momentarily gained courage to claim that God was calling me to ministry, I would second guess myself," Guth wrote, "ashamed of my audacity." But her home congregation supported her, contributing a modest amount to her tuition each semester. "The faith in God's capacity to use me in ministry that this support represented was a strong encouragement to persist in my studies."

Midway through her seminary studies Guth started an internship, and as a member of the pastoral team she began to hear how common depression was in the congregation where she was ministering, even though people did not talk about it publicly. With the encouragement of the pastors, she helped form a support group for congregation members with depression that ended up meeting monthly for nearly four years.

"Here at last was a place within the church where those with depression could talk about the suffering we carried privately," she recalled. "Here we could bring to God the pain that dominated our lives, in the company of brothers and sisters. In time we reached out to various groups within the church, sharing our stories and receiving the concern of others. The public silence about depression in our midst that had prevailed was no longer monolithic."

Despite growing feelings of worth and accomplishment, Guth found her mood plummeting during her internship year. The tasks of ministry seemed harder, and she had to force herself to keep at them. More troubling, one of her seminary peers wondered if such depression should not raise a red flag about her ability to engage in ministry.

For years Guth had felt she wasn't worth the money for a psychiatrist. Now, taking a more active role in her care, she found a therapist she liked and had good results with a medication—for about a year. At that point, for unknown reasons, the medication seemed to be failing her. Her psychiatrist suggested two medications that might be helpful in combination. Guth took this advice as an indication that she was "hopeless and disgusting," in need of some pharmaceutical magic bullet. But despite her unwarranted sense of shame, Guth followed her psychiatrist's advice, and, her skepticism notwithstanding, within a few weeks she felt noticeably better.

"As spring arrived that year," she wrote, "it felt like the sun was emerging from the clouds for the first time in many months. After a few more weeks I was feeling incredibly better—better than I ever remembered feeling in my whole life. As this new mood settled in, it dawned on me that I had been living with depression all my adult life—and even before that. I could recall serious depression from my teenage years, and signs of it from as early as age twelve. Until that spring, my life had been a roller coaster of ups and downs, but, I realized, even the best times were colored by depression."

Unfortunately, within a few months of Guth's dramatic improvement, she noticed that depression had begun to affect her adolescent son. For three tumultuous years the family struggled to find medication that would enable him to stay stable for more than a few months at a time. As a divinity student as well as a mother, Christine wrestled with agonizing theological questions:

"Why should a child be suffering so? Who is this God who has made such a world? How can I trust such a God? What is the point of years of life wasted suffering with depression? What about those who suffer around the world with no access to expensive psychotropic meds? How can the world be in God's hands when such senseless misery exists?"

Like many other families who live with disability, Guth and her husband, Bob, have weathered times that taxed the coping abilities of every family member. As her son entered middle school, he began to encounter frequent bullying. The boy, in turn, would pick a fight with his older sister as soon as they got home from school. Fights and arguments continued almost every evening, upsetting their orderly father. Guth's son's depression proved difficult to treat—counseling with four different therapists never took hold. Perpetual crises kept the emotions boiling, and despite her theological and pastoral training, Guth felt that her ability to cope and respond creatively was about to give out. For the sake of her children she approached her pastor at Eighth Street Mennonite Church in Goshen for help. Was there any support the church could provide?

The minister arranged for a group to meet with Guth once a month, but the family's needs went far beyond the support the pastor and the support group could offer. Crises were unfolding daily, and no end to the upheaval was in sight—certainly not within the few months that the pastor had structured the group to meet. Guth tried to accept the help gratefully, but she struggled with its limits, feeling ashamed to ask for more. She judged herself harshly for causing the mess in her family.

One evening, when only one member of the support group, Rachel Johns, remembered to show up for a scheduled meeting, Guth's desperation spilled out. Johns listened thoughtfully to the anguished mother's story and relayed what she had heard to the pastor and others in the group. Through creative thinking and by responding intentionally to what they heard, the support group developed an alternative plan. The new arrangement better met the needs of Guth and her family without placing too great a burden on any one person.

The women in the group took turns checking in with Guth. Each week someone would invite her over for some empathetic listening. This was a great help, because her own depression kept Guth from initiating contact with friends. Johns served as coordinator, relieving the pastor of the responsibility. The revised plan was sustainable and continued over several years, until the needs subsided. Some months into it, another pastor agreed to give Guth and her husband his cell phone number and be on call for times when her son's physical aggression was threatening. During this time, Guth's family also found ways to connect with wider community resources that supplemented the church's support.

From these experiences, Guth learned that even within a busy congregation's practical limits, caring people can be channels of God's grace and love. She watched creative thinking stretch the congregation's limited resources. As a recipient of the church's tangible support and finite resources through times of crisis, she gained a deeper sense of God's care for her family. She learned to direct some of her energy to hurts from her past that needed attention and healing. This brought new opportunities to heal old wounds. She learned that her experiences with mental illness and healing had opened up gifts, which she now shares with a larger community.

As a minister, Guth has worked as a volunteer with the Anabaptist Disabilities Network for more than five years. Currently she serves as program director. She has found that her intense personal and pastoral experiences with mental illness raise difficult theological questions and challenges, but surviving them has equipped her for her present ministry.

"Those of us with mental illness deeply need people who will face the abyss with us without flinching," she said. "Are our churches willing to enter such theological struggles with us? Unfortunately, the stigma of mental illness often keeps us from experiencing the caring of the body of Christ and the tangible love of God embodied in the church. Stigma keeps us isolated in our suffering. Further, it keeps us from accessing treatment that could help. Because it prolongs and intensifies suffering, it is my conviction that stigma against mental illness is sin, a sin for which the church is called to corporate repentance."

Depression, Guth is now convinced, is not a bad habit brought on because of character weakness or moral failure. "We don't get depression from not trusting God enough. This is a truth we need to integrate into the common practices of our congregational life. We don't have to get sucked into making jokes about depression or suggesting that those who turn to psychotropic meds lack faith or moral fiber. When someone has the courage to talk about feelings of hopelessness, let us affirm the courage and extend extra care. I invite churches to reincorporate lament for those who suffer into regular worship patterns. We can make mental illness something we talk about and pray about often in our public worship. In these ways we can embody Christ's love to the many among us who suffer from a mental illness."

35

Contributing Our Talents

Terry Chaney and Marcie Brink-Chaney

It was First Presbyterian's reputation for inclusion and innovation that drew Terry Chaney and Marcie Brink-Chaney to the congregation in Birmingham, Michigan. A married couple who met as students at the Michigan School for the Blind, they found the church to be "a truly warm place into which we have been able to find our way," Terry wrote in the church newsletter. "More important, we have found it to be a place where we are able to contribute our skills and talents."

Terry and Marcie have each been involved in church life in some way since elementary school. Marcie has two master's degrees focused on disability and blindness. She also has an extensive background in amateur music, which was why she was interested in being a part of the church's choir.

Before Terry took early retirement after a thirty-year career in advertising, he began studying to become a certified lay pastor, so he has a good feel for what being a Presbyterian is all about. He is also enrolled in the Master of Arts program at Ecumenical Theological Seminary in Detroit, where—thanks to an educational grant from his church—he is studying how to better include people with disabilities in congregational life. This training has enabled the church's pastoral associate to be confident in inviting Terry to fill in for him at Wednesday night services when he is unavailable, and Terry often serves as a congregational greeter. Both Terry and Marcie are active in monthly "Rejoicing Spirits" services (see chapter 13) on Saturday evenings, designed to celebrate and include people of all ages with disabilities.

The Chaneys have been fortunate, too, in having the financial resources to purchase electronic hardware and software that equip them to participate in church life. When leading worship and preparing sermons and meditations, Terry uses a variety of technologies, including software programs, synthesized speech, and digital text that he types into his computer. This can be transformed into Braille for him to use in the pulpit.

"If I am preaching or leading worship, what you would see is me and a notebook with Braille in it," Terry said. But for all the help this technology has been, the point he prefers to make is that his blindness "is only a part of who I am—and not the key to everything."

36

God's Great and Fiery Compassion

Claire Wimbush

Claire Wimbush describes the medical name of her birth disability—spastic quadriplegic cerebral palsy—as "a fancy clinical way of saying that my muscles don't speak the same dialect as my brain." Because walking was never going to be a practical way for her to navigate the world, her parents decided they had better come up with a good alternative, and Wimbush has used electric wheelchairs since she was three. Starting with a bright red "turbo" model, she became a tiny child strapped into a power chair roughly the size of a small tank. "I could go anywhere," she recalled. "I could chase my brother. I could spin in circles like a ballerina. I was filled with glee—and likely to bang into every solid object within fifty yards. I don't think I have ever looked back."

Growing up, she said during a May 18, 2010, talk to the Duke Institute on Care at the End of Life, her body "was a fact of my environment, like the weather: One adjusted to it and moved on. It hardly crossed my mind that life in a wheelchair could teach me anything. It certainly never occurred to me that the stories I heard in church had anything to do with me and my broken body."

Wimbush was baptized as a kindergartner at Emmaus Kirche in Munich, Germany, a mission congregation of the Episcopal Church. Her family was living in Munich at the time while her father was director of Radio Free Europe/Radio Liberty. Although Claire's mother was a Methodist and her father not a churchgoer, they attended Emmaus Kirche because it was the nearest church offering services in English. At church Claire instantly conceived a fierce desire to play Mary in the annual Christmas pageant. "I *wanted* to hold that plastic baby doll Jesus with all the yearning of my five-year-old heart. My mother sighed, squared her shoulders, and argued with the woman organizing the pageant (and all the other parents) to let me. They said, 'We can't have a Mary in a wheelchair,' she told me. 'And I said, "Why not?"' So the determined little girl became the first Mary in the congregation's memory to arrive at the manger by power chair. "I still remember how awed and thrilled I felt that night, processing down the long aisle with my vision half obscured by one of my mom's blue silk scarves, trying desperately not to drop Jesus."

For Wimbush, it is tempting to say that her call to the priesthood took root in that moment, as she carried the Christ child through the congregation. But the reality was far less romantic. She didn't understand what it meant to be called to be a priest in God's church—much less begin to investigate what it meant to be a priest with a disability—until she was a student at the College of William and Mary, a beautiful but largely handicapped-inaccessible campus. There, where she first began to rely on nonfamily caregivers, she fell in love with the local Episcopal campus ministry. The student group met in the Wren Chapel, built three centuries before anyone dreamed of the Americans with Disabilities Act. To get into the chapel, Wimbush used an outdoor lift that raised her wheelchair up a flight of steps.

On the Thursday of Holy Week one year, she used the lift to get to the late-night service of foot washing. When she came out, the lift creaked down about six inches and stopped dead. It was 10:45 at night, and she was stuck on a floating metal platform with no way to get down. She and her friends scratched their heads for a bit, and then someone said: "Well, we'll just ditch your chair and lift you." They did. "So there I was, in the dark of the night before Good Friday, spread-eagled six feet above a brick pavement while someone held my shoulders and someone held my legs and someone else held my Book of Common Prayer—we were good Episcopalians, after all—and I thought: *We really need theology for this.* And then I thought: *Now we are the body of Christ and individually members of it.*"

After graduating from William and Mary, Wimbush attended Duke Divinity School on a merit scholarship. Jo Bailey Wells, an ordained minister and director of Duke's Anglican Episcopal House of Studies, who taught Wimbush at the Divinity School, was extremely impressed with her student. One Ash Wednesday while at Duke, Wimbush was among the ministers in the Divinity School's Goodson Chapel, applying ashes to the foreheads of fellow students and faculty. She dipped her shaky finger in the bowl and applied the sign of the cross, saying: "Remember, you are dust, and to dust you shall return. Turn away from sin and be faithful to Christ."

As Wells recalled, "You can imagine that hearing such words from Claire—someone who knows only too well what it is for her body to be fading—reinforces the reality of our mortal nature, yet at the same time the hope that is in Christ alone. I went away filled with tears yet full of joy."

Despite her degree, Wimbush went unemployed for two years, but on January 9, 2010, at Bruton Parish Church in Williamsburg, Virginia, she was ordained a deacon, a step toward the priesthood. She served as a transitional deacon—an ordained deacon preparing for the priesthood—at St. Martin's Episcopal Church, also in Williamsburg, thanks to a six-month grant from the bishop of her home diocese in southern Virginia. Wells, who was also Wimbush's first-year adviser at Duke, preached the sermon at the ordination. "Claire has the rare ability to cut to the chase with the incisiveness of a legal mind," Wells told the congregation.

When Wimbush celebrates the Eucharist, Wells said later, she presides with authority and the help of one or two good deacons or acolytes. That is, it takes a team effort. She doesn't apologize for this, but delights in it. To her, it demonstrates what the priesthood of all believers really means—together, we function as a priest.

Wimbush also has the gift of pastoral counseling, Wells said. "Claire's ability to sit still has to do with her ability to focus attention, to listen, to think before she speaks, her receptivity. She is never burdened by a pile of books or 'stuff,' apart from the odd treat for her service dog, Willa, in the back of her chair. She has learned to travel light—which is just what Jesus worked to teach the disciples when he sent them out. That is, to depend on others for food and drink, not presuming to know what the day will hold or the needs will be. Her baggage is internal, not external.

"That makes her very economical. With words she cuts to the chase, but she does so with immense humor and delight. In preaching, for example, she uses no notes but prepares it all in her head. So it comes from deep inside her, yet with a freshness and lightness of touch. One may say she has to do it this way, but certainly she has learned how to make force of circumstance become a gift. She transforms fate into destiny."

"She's not a priest *despite* her disability," Wells continued. "Her disability doesn't limit her priesthood. Her disability is a part of God's provision of this priest. That is, her broken body—and her openness in talking about it, coupled with a wicked sense of humor—helps us all engage our brokenness and God's promise of healing."

Wimbush was ordained a priest on April 10, 2011, at St. Stephen's Episcopal Church in Durham, North Carolina, where she had been working. The eight-year ordination experience brought everything that had come before sharply into focus for Wimbush. "Now it's my broken body that consecrates the broken body of Christ for God's hungry people," she said. "God's tenderness flows through my body and into theirs. This is so glorious and intimate and humbling that I have trouble finding the right words for it.

"But it has not been easy to come to this place. All through my ordination process, I have argued and persuaded and cajoled folks who thought that a person with a severe disability couldn't possibly be called to serve in any sustained ministry, let alone the priesthood. They wonder, how will she manage? There's an unreflective assumption current in my denomination—and in most other denominations, too, I suspect—that those who serve and lead are to be able-bodied. People with disabilities don't minister; we get ministered to. Church habit supports this—not to mention church architecture. We have hallowed the altar step and the altar rail. So a young priest who uses a wheelchair must become something of an architectural iconoclast, whether she wants to or

not. I have gotten really good at holding my mother's kind of conversation: When someone tells me, 'We can't put a portable ramp
on our altar,' I square my shoulders, grin wickedly, and inquire,
'Why not?'"

For every person Wimbush has met who asks, "How can you
manage?" she has met another who says, "Oh, look what an in-
genious and graceful thing God is doing. Let's get creative." She
says she is able to minister because she has been fed, taught, challenged, and blessed by the church and by a whole community of
wise people—including a bishop who told her, sorrowfully, that
southern Virginia wasn't ready for a wheelchair-using parish priest.
"It's simply that my body challenges our paradigm of priesthood—
and particularly priesthood acted out in the parish setting," she
said. Whatever sorrow and frustration she experiences—and she
does have sad and furious days—her experiences in becoming a
pastor, she believes, show the work God is doing with the church
and with her. She has seen as much generosity and comic grace as
she has observed short-sightedness and complacency.

In all, Wimbush spent fourteen months as a transitional deacon, instead of the usual six. The Episcopal Church ordains only
priests who have placements in which to serve, and Wimbush
couldn't find a congregation in Virginia that was both willing and
able to accept a priest with a disability. So she moved to North
Carolina and spent a year serving as a resident chaplain at the
local veterans hospital. In that ministry, her wheelchair was an ad-
vantage, because most of her patients used wheelchairs, too. They
were more likely to trust a chaplain who could sit with them literally eye to eye. When Wimbush was not working at the hospital,
she preached, celebrated Communion, and offered pastoral care
at a local Episcopal church. Neither of her two ministries, however, paid a salary.

Occasionally, after Wimbush's graduation from Duke Divinity
School, unique ministry opportunities arose. For example, she
served on the Access Committee of the Episcopal Diocese of
North Carolina in Raleigh, and in that capacity she spoke at North
Carolina and Virginia Episcopal churches about challenges to

consumers of home health care, as well as her understanding of a "theology of disability."

Recently, in what she called a happy ending, Wimbush was offered and accepted a full-time position as curate for Christian education at St. Thomas' Episcopal Church in Rochester, New York. There she has a congregation to love and serve after all, not to mention a salary. "To be hired to do the work I have been called and trained and ordained to do feels like incredible grace," she said.

The theology of disability that Wimbush tries to live and teach springs from St. Paul's startling insight, so fundamental to Christian theology, that believers are Christ's body in the world. "And Christ's body becomes, in a gracious mystery we call Holy Communion, part of our own," she said. "We take Christ's broken body into our own when we eat the broken bread at Communion. *This is my body, broken for you. Take and eat it.* And at the same time, we are woven into Christ's own body, the church community.

"If you are a person living in the world as a disabled body, all this means something astonishing. It means that my broken body becomes a part of something stronger and more holy, a family of blessed bodies. It also means that Christ's broken body touches and transforms my own. God's strength carries my weakness; my weakness gets infused with God's strength. This is, of course, true for all Christians, able-bodied and disabled alike. This is what it means to share in the community of Christ's body."

This is also what being a Christian means for Wimbush: "In practice, it means my body is not my own personal property. I am not sufficient unto myself. None of us are. Jesus shares his body with us so that we can go out and offer our own bodies to help and care for others. And so that we can receive care from their bodies, when we need it. This is what my friends did for me: They joined their bodies to support mine. I can't climb steps on my own, but I can borrow someone else's strength. And I can offer my own time and joy in return. We are woven into community together, body to body, trying to do with our bodies the things Jesus did with his: touching and healing and comforting and blessing.

Proclaiming, with every breath and every gesture, God's great and fiery compassion."

Wimbush rejects the "virtue-through-suffering argument, as if we ought to welcome pain because it will make us better and holier people. Nor am I trying to minimize the pain, anger, tiredness, fear, and loneliness that often shadow life with disabilities. Not to mention the other worries—financial uncertainty among them. Living as a broken body is hard work, Lord knows, and it's often not much fun. There are times when we don't want to hear pretty words about wisdom and blessing. There are times when we just want to be healthy and strong and well. But life with a disability can open us to knowledge that we would not otherwise have gathered."

37

Letting Go of Victim Vanity

John Alex Lowell

On March 23, 2001, John Alex Lowell was jogging on a sidewalk in San Francisco, toward an intersection, thinking of anything but religion, when a minivan ran a red light and struck him, sending him twenty feet into the air. Trauma surgeons told Lowell's parents that the damage to his skull was so severe that if he survived, he likely would remain in a persistent vegetative state. Instead, after strenuous and lengthy mental and physical rehabilitation, the former IT specialist with two undergraduate degrees from UC Berkeley found himself called by God to be a United Church of Christ minister. He graduated from the Pacific School of Religion, where he founded the Differently Abled Student Union. Although tangible reminders of the crash linger, Lowell is again physically active. He rides his bicycle, jogs, and swims.

Before the accident, Lowell said, he had no strong faith life. "I believed there was a God, I had basic understanding of the Trinity," he recalled. He had been attending San Francisco's eclectic Glide Memorial United Methodist Church, and after the collision he rejoined the congregation—and its choir—when he was well enough. The chief attractions for him were a personal sense of belonging and Glide's widely celebrated affirming ministries for many diverse groups. Still, Lowell found that he did not feel God's presence when he sang in the choir at services, and although San Francisco has a reputation for inclusiveness, the community can also be very appearance conscious, he said. Lowell's skull deformation—which was later repaired—drew stares from the congregation. "I felt a little like the Elephant Man," he said.

It was not until one particular Sunday service at Glide, on February 22, 2004, that Lowell had a poignant moment that led to his spiritual awakening. For some reason, that morning he left his customary seat in the choir loft and sat in the pews to hear the message preached by Glide's associate pastor, Karen Junker. Her sermon was about how people who have been forgiven are required to forgive others, based on Matthew 18:33 NRSV: "Should you not have had mercy on your fellow slave, as I had mercy on you?"

Until then, Lowell said, he suffered from what he called "victim vanity," which led him to discover and worship the victim within. "Why can't those who have been forgiven, forgive?" Junker asked the congregation. The sermon was an eye-opener for Lowell, especially because Junker's brother, too, had suffered brain injury. "I decided to forgive the driver of the minivan, who in general I hated," Lowell said. He found that when he let go of his victim vanity, "the grace of God came upon me." This awakening, Lowell said, was the first of three calls to ministry that he experienced. His disabling head injury "not only cracked open my cranium but also cracked open the laissez-faire shell in which I felt encased."

His second vocational experience came during a brain tumor seminar in 2006, in the form of an observation made by the English writer Dame Edith Sitwell about the poet William Blake: "He was cracked, but through the cracks came the lights." In these words Lowell felt a calling from God to minister to anyone who suffered spiritually. He felt that the accident in 2001, caused by both his and the driver's error, led him to feel "the ever-present love from God shining through the cracks in my own wall of indifference." Lowell said he felt that the shining love from God "embodied in Jesus Christ was to be shared with people of any ability."

Lowell's third spiritual call to ministry happened ten days later at a family gathering on a beach near Santa Cruz. His mother had given him a copy of *Open Christianity: Home by Another Road*, a progressive Christian book by Reverend Jim Burklo, which included stories of ministry to the homeless. The book's central message, that the Holy Spirit is within everyone who is suffering, inspired Lowell to think about ministry as a vocation. He enrolled at Pacific School of Religion in 2006, as much to test his intellectual capabilities as his calling. From the first week at the seminary, he was certain he had made the right choice. At one gathering, Lowell asked whether the seminar had any groups for students with disabilities. The response was, "No, why don't you start one?" Which he did in his creation of the Differently Abled Student Union.

In one class during his trial semester at Pacific School of Religion, in a critical examination of Scriptures, Lowell interpreted the passage 1 Corinthians 12:12–26 as applying directly to disability and Christianity. In the passage, the apostle Paul, who had a spiritual awakening after what might be considered a traumatic experience while on the road to vanity and power in Damascus, talked about how all gathered believers are like organs of the body of Christ. Some are weak and some strong, but all are interdependent, as Lowell understood it: "You don't need to praise the strong, because they don't need it; you need to praise the weak, because functionally they need it." Or as the text put it, "If one member suffers, all suffer together with it; if one member is honored, all rejoice together with it" (v. 26, NRSV). When Lowell read that section in class, he said, "I seized on it."

Since 2005, Lowell's faith home has been First Congregational Church of San Francisco, United Church of Christ—established at the time of the 1849 gold rush. In his initial lay ministry in the church, Lowell found that people with disabilities were not included in the list of groups specifically invited to worship and join the congregation. He proposed an amendment to the church's constitution that incorporated his broader approach to disability by naming many more sociodemographic groups who were welcome at the church. These days, when not ministering at First Congregational Church of San Francisco, Lowell organizes and attends disability conferences for religious organizations and seminaries. Since 2006 Lowell has held a position on San Francisco's Pedestrian Safety Advisory Committee. He does all he can to keep others from going through what he has experienced. "I do have a passion to prevent it from happening to others," he told a reporter for the *San Francisco Chronicle*.

38

The Gift of Hope

Susan Gregg-Schroeder

The Reverend Susan Gregg-Schroeder's depression began in 1991, while she was in her third year of ministry at a large, urban Methodist church. She was enjoying her career and the many opportunities it offered for serving others. The pastor liked being part of a large staff and had no doubt that she had made the right decision to answer her call and leave her teaching career to become an ordained minister. She gave little thought to depression.

"Whereas secular society is finally talking more openly about mental illness," she said, "our religious communities are mostly in the dark ages when it comes to understanding mental disorders as treatable illnesses. Many faith leaders are also keeping silent about their mental illnesses. I know this because I am one of those persons," she said in one of her frequent talks.

Despite her experience in pastoral counseling, Gregg-Schroeder did not recognize or understand what was happening to her. That fall, she recalled, "a series of events hit me like waves, until I felt totally overwhelmed with despair. I had all the symptoms of major depression. I felt disoriented and disconnected from my feelings and myself. I couldn't eat or sleep. Nothing brought me pleasure. I was simply going through the motions. I couldn't stand to be around others and isolated myself from everyone. I felt so hopeless that I wanted to end my life and actually developed an elaborate plan."

One of Gregg-Schroeder's colleagues sent her to a psychiatrist, who happened to be a member of her church. She found the experience to be "one of the most humbling experiences of my life, as I was enveloped with guilt and shame." The psychiatrist wanted to admit her immediately to a psychiatric hospital. After several days of denial, and because her husband could not continue to stay home from work to be with her, she agreed and found herself in the same hospital where she had conducted worship services when she was doing her clinical pastoral education. Since then, the small chapel had been converted into a barber shop.

Few people at Gregg-Schroeder's church knew about her depression and hospitalization, and for two years she suffered in silence, hiding her condition from the church community for fear of losing her job. But her senior pastor stood by her, believing in grace and believing in her. With his support, she finally decided to acknowledge her depression openly. She wrote an article for the church newsletter entitled "The Burden of Silence." The senior pastor wrote an accompanying article about the ignorance surrounding mental illness. A nurse who was a church member set up an informational meeting on depression, and a turn-away crowd of more than 130 people showed up. Seeing such a great need, the church started a depression support group led by a professional counselor.

With the urging—and, she acknowledges, the arm-twisting—of a colleague, Gregg-Schroeder agreed to speak at a bishops' convocation. The stories her colleagues shared with her behind those closed doors, she said, "made me realize that I was being called to speak out about mental illness in the church. I was especially concerned about my colleagues from various ethnic groups where there is fear that such a disclosure may bring shame to the family, not to mention the effects such a disclosure could have on a person's future in the ministry."

Gregg-Schroeder has had subsequent hospitalizations and a variety of diagnoses, including a type of bipolarity that has changed over the years. "But you cannot put a label on the human spirit," she said. "I know that I need to continue to have my medication monitored, maintain a good support system, and practice good self-care as well as preventive care at those times when I feel most vulnerable. I've learned coping skills and have developed inner resources. I relate to the words of Louisa May Alcott, who wrote, "I am not afraid of storms, for I am learning how to sail my ship."

One in four people sitting in the pews has a family member struggling with mental health issues, Gregg-Schroeder said. Sixty percent of those experiencing a mental health issue go first to a spiritual leader for help. Yet clergy often are ineffective in providing appropriate support and referral information. People with mental health issues are significantly less likely to receive the same level of pastoral care as those with physical illnesses, Gregg-Schroeder believes. "People often visit others with physical illness, bring them meals, and provide other helpful services. Mental illness has been called the 'no casserole illness' and 'modern-day leprosy.'"

This is both baffling and counterintuitive to the role of the faith community in modern North American life, Gregg-Schroeder said. "Nearly every person has been touched in some way by mental illness. And yet individuals and families continue to suffer in silence or stop coming to worship because they are not receiving the support they so desperately need. They become detached from their faith community and their spirituality, which can be an important source of healing, wholeness, and hope in times of personal darkness."

For Gregg-Schroeder, hope in the future was a gift that grew out of her relationship with her therapist, who is also a pastoral counselor. The relationship began in the traditional form of therapist and client, but over time it evolved into a relationship of trust, respect, and mutual sharing of life experiences. The two became companions in their respective spiritual journeys. "In sharing our stories," Gregg-Schroeder said, "I was empowered to make responsible life choices based on my inner wisdom."

"My deepest and most profound experience of the Holy One or the Divine Mystery came to me in my descent into the deepest darkness of my depression," Gregg-Schroeder said. "Like the psalmist in Psalm 88, I felt abandoned by everyone. Like Job, I felt stripped of everything in my life that had given my life meaning and purpose. I lost all sense of who I was. I lost all sense of worth."

At that moment, she said, several people stepped in to "rescue" her. She feels fortunate to have a loving husband who wanted to help; access to good medical care; and a competent and compassionate psychiatrist as her doctor since her first hospital admission.

For all her psychiatric and family support, Gregg-Schroeder found at least as much value in the presence of the holy revealed to her by her initial pastoral counselor. While everyone else was trying to "fix" her in some way, her counselor accepted her as she was. While others were looking for a cure, her pastoral friend offered care. He was, she said, vulnerable enough to enter into her dark place without judgment. "He modeled for me an image of a God who surrounds us and holds us in a caring presence. He modeled an unconditional acceptance that I had never felt. In my feelings of worthlessness, he held onto a faith that I was loved as a child of God, just as I was. He became a lifeline to hope."

Gregg-Schroeder now preaches the importance of "being in relationship with other people and with our faith community," which she perceives as "one of the gifts that allowed me to gradually emerge from my deepest darkness and discover the most important gift of the shadow—the gift of hope. Medications may stabilize symptoms, but it is relationship and love that heal the soul."

As part of her mission, Gregg-Schroeder has founded Mental Health Ministries, an interfaith organization that provides educational resources to help erase the stigma of mental illness in faith communities. Mental Health Ministries produces media and print resources that address mental health issues from a spiritual perspective.

"I look back and I realize that I was not alone in my deepest darkness," she said. "I also realize that I persevered, and with the help of others I was able to *choose life*. I have found hope in listening to and reading stories of healing and wholeness restored in the lives of other people who have struggled with this illness. The gift of hope, like all gifts of the shadow, is not linear. Hope is not wishful thinking or escapism. Hope is grounded in the steadfastness of God, who has acted in our past, is acting in our present, and will continue to act in our future."

39

Breaking the Silence

Mary Heron Dyer

Three days after the Reverend Mary Heron Dyer, a recently retired Unity Church minister, had knee surgery in 2008, she woke
up anticipating going home that day. But something was very
wrong—she couldn't hear anything. Panicked, she pushed the
call button and told a nurse she was deaf and asked someone to
call her spouse. Nothing had been mentioned during Dyer's pre-
surgery consultation about deafness as a possible complication.
As the day wore on and a succession of specialists appeared at her
bedside, Dyer's mood grew increasingly dark, to the point that she
was placed on suicide watch.

Although she was first put on an antiviral drug and steroids
and then underwent a succession of alternative treatments, as the
months wore on it became clear that Dyer was permanently and
irrevocably deaf. Six months later she received a cochlear implant,
which allows her to "visit" the land of the hearing, managing one-
on-one exchanges but having difficulty in groups when more than
one person is speaking. Dyer finds it ironic that churches are some
of the worst offenders in not responding to the needs of the hearing impaired. Hearing loss, she points out, unlike other physical
disabilities, is mostly invisible, marked by no wheelchair ramp or
wheelchair-accessible bathroom.

"It's time to break the silence about hearing loss," she said,
"and the impact it has on the individual and the loss it presents
to churches as newcomers are turned away—or members themselves begin to drop out when the churches do not address this
issue by investigating and installing appropriate assistive-listening
systems."

"I thought I was pretty knowledgeable about disabilities and a
vocal advocate for those groups I knew about," she said, "but I was

blown out of the water about my ignorance after I became deaf. I thought hearing and deafness were dichotomous and that it could be 'fixed' by having an ASL interpreter at services. Boy, was I surprised! And dismayed. And saddened. Not a day goes by that I do not have to self-advocate in one form or another."

Fortunately for Dyer and her spouse, Sheryl Butler, the church they began attending in Council Bluffs, Iowa—Broadway Christian, a midsized church of more than four hundred members—responded to her needs with grace and compassion. The first Sunday the two went, they arrived early to see whether the church had an assistive listening system, such as one that transmits sound via an FM radio signal to a user's individual receiving unit with headset. The church, it turned out, had only a standard sound amplifier. Evidently, Dyer was the first person to show up at the church with hearing loss.

Instead of a headset, which Dyer is unable to use because of her cochlear implant, she uses a flexible loop receiver that she wears like a necklace. The minister at Broadway Christian Church, Reverend Jann Osborn, and her husband, Kim, who was handling audiovisual that day, looked over their sound equipment to see if it included a jack into which Dyer could plug her loop, so that she could use her own sound processor. Unfortunately, Dyer had forgotten or misplaced the extension cord, so for that first service she was tethered to the equipment in the back row of the church, unable to move much or even stand up.

As Dyer and Butler, a Disciples of Christ minister as well as a retired electrical engineer, began to see this church as their spiritual home, they continued educating people around hearing loss, its prevalence, its concomitant isolation, and its remediation through assistive listening technology. The few churches that have considered this issue usually have FM systems with pocket receivers, but more often than not these are not advertised, easily accessible, or checked to see if they are working. They may not even be used by those who would benefit from them, because they are so obvious and because many people who have hearing loss, especially older adults, try to hide it. Such systems also break down and need repair, and sometimes they walk out the door with distracted users.

Butler, who worked for eighteen years as a systems engineer for the Kellogg Company, has been instrumental in learning about hearing assistive technology, and together the couple began investigating what are called induction loops, wires that are run around the area to be used and then connected to an amplifier plugged into an existing audio system. As word began to spread at Broadway Christian that this technology was being considered, one woman shared with the pastor the information that she had stopped coming to church because she could no longer understand enough to make it worth her while. She wanted to know when the project would be finished so she could return and fully participate.

For just over a thousand dollars—a special allocation made by the board of trustees after a presentation by Dyer and Butler—Broadway Christian installed another kind of audio loop in both the sanctuary and the fellowship hall. The system runs a wire around the rooms, connected to an amplifier that sends signals from the audio system directly to individual hearing aids and cochlear implants, eliminating ambient noise. For those with lesser hearing loss, the church provides receivers and headsets. Installing the system at Broadway Christian took only about three hundred feet of wire, a professional-quality amplifier, and some sweat equity. By Easter of 2011, Dyer and most other people with hearing challenges at Broadway Christian were able to sit anywhere they wished in the sanctuary and hear.

"I look forward to a day when all churches are 'looped,'" said Dyer, "including signage, advertising, training of greeters, announcements, making the congregations understand how so many of us have been unnecessarily sidelined, excluded." With modern technology and the commitment of the church, "there are simple and affordable solutions to help the great majority of those with hearing loss 'hear.'"

Today, Dyer and Butler joke about God's divine sense of humor, saying that rather than having found their ministry, the ministry found them. On the day Mary became deaf, she joined nearly forty million other people in the United States alone who have significant hearing loss. To reach out to them, the couple established the "Ephphatha Ministry," named for the incident described in Mark 7:31–37, in which Jesus heals a deaf mute, saying to the man, "'Eph'phatha,' that is 'Be opened.' And his ears were opened." The ministry's website offers links to articles about hearing loss and assistive listening technologies, as well as a PowerPoint presentation that Dyer put together, taking congregations step-by-step through the process of providing easy and affordable hearing assistive technology—from education and commitment through consultation, installation, and follow-up. At one Disciples church in Omaha, Dyer and Butler set up a demonstration induction loop in the sanctuary for several people who had hearing aids that could receive the signal, to give it a try.

"If I come to your church to visit in the coming year," Dyer asks members of other congregations, "can you 'hear' the voices of those who have been excluded from fellowship because you have not begun to think about or to address how to make your congregation more inclusive to those with hearing loss? If you want to take the first step, we will be willing to come to you, to meet with you, to educate you, to give you information on appropriate technologies for your congregation."

40

Rolling Back into Ministry

Joe Kovitch

The Reverend Joseph Kovitch, who likes to be called "Pastor Joe," is an ecumenical minister serving both Lutherans and Episcopalians. A chaplain to students, he works mostly with young people at Cleveland State University and Case Western Reserve University and also teaches classes. Kovitch is partially paralyzed, the result of spinal surgery he underwent in 2006 to remove a tumor. Married and the father of three children, he uses a wheelchair but can stand for short stretches and is able to drive.

After his surgery, Kovitch recalled, "I rolled right back into ministry. The chair has its blessings—it helped focus my sense of calling. In an odd way, it was liberating. It gave me permission to use the wheelchair as a way of connecting to a whole new community, a hidden community. People knew I had been a big athlete, a runner, and I miss running. I wouldn't have chosen this, but I choose to use it; there is a purpose in everything.

"The chair allows me to connect to the disability community in powerful ways, to an invisible community in our society. It has opened so many doors and enabled me to connect." The chair, he said, has allowed him to deepen his ministry, opening lines of communication to people with what he calls "hidden disabilities." Kovitch's own disability "speaks before I do. It says, 'I know suffering, I know diminishment.' When I wear my clerical collar (which I do more often) and connect it to ministry, it starts a lot more conversations—emotionally and spiritually—and initiates prayers. It takes you right to people's hurts; the chair becomes a tool."

The greatest disability he encounters, Kovitch said, "is people's apathy and attitude toward people who are disabled. My chair enables me to break through that ignorance; I definitely throw myself out there. My disability does not define who I am, unless

I allow it to. A lot of what defines me theologically or spiritually, I have found through suffering. We're all broken. When I first broke the Communion bread after my surgery, I saw everyone in that room in their brokenness."

On campus, Kovitch uses his chair as an extension of his work as both a counselor and a teacher. It is, he said, a metaphor for students' "inner wheelchair." They look at him and think, "This guy knows adversity. This guy knows struggle." It can ease their invisible anxiety about the future as they emerge as adult personalities.

Kovitch lectures both standing up and in his chair. For students wrestling with who they are, he said, the chair disables preconceived notions and any initial suspicion they might hold about him and his situation. If young people can name their own disabilities, he finds, they can learn what it is they are afraid of.

At the same time, Kovitch levels with the students. "I've embraced the chair as I've embraced running. It sucks to be in the chair, but how do you embrace the chair as part of who you are? Make it work *for* you, rather than against you? You teach other people, because we have an obligation to teach 'able-bodied' people. And not just be the victim. We can have a disability without being disabled, and be in touch with our vulnerability."

Off campus, Kovitch is often asked to consult with congregations that are "broken" and in crisis. He sees this work as "healing communities that are disabled." The chair, he said, often disarms the antagonisms and personal politics and allows congregations at least to listen to him with open minds. "I can roll in and climb into their pulpit and say, 'You don't have to have your brokenness define your community. Let me name your disability and not let painful relationships and broken communication define you.'" Then, without even mentioning his chair, Kovitch tries to be a healing presence. People in the pews think, if he's not letting his brokenness define him, why should we?

41

Listening for Justice

Nancy Eiesland

Nancy Eiesland, best known as the author of *The Disabled God: Toward a Liberatory Theology of Disability*, died in 2009, at the age of forty-four, but no book about faith, disability, and inclusion would be complete without her. In addition to her books, articles, and university lectures, she traveled the world on behalf of the United Nations Convention on the Rights of Persons with Disabilities and for agencies of the European Union.

Eiesland was born into a North Dakota farm family, with a congenital bone defect in her hips that necessitated a full set of leg braces and crutches by the time she was seven. She once wrote that her father observed—as she emerged from the prosthetics workshop of the Crippled Children's School in Jamestown, North Dakota—that she would need a job that kept her off her feet, ruling out work as a checkout clerk.

"His advice and prediction were apt and accurate, but the specifics of my life's trajectory were inconceivable to him and me," Eiesland wrote in *Impact*, the newsletter of the University of Minnesota's Institute of Community Integration. "The life I have now as a professor, theological advocate, wife, and mother would have been unthinkable then, as it was generally assumed that I would need my parents' financial and medical support all my life. I realized that folks thought I was unlikely to marry and still less likely to have a child."

At Wolford Elementary School, Eiesland recalled, "I became a 'poster child' for a national organization seeking to prevent the 'tragedy' of my body. As a spokesperson I processed through classrooms asking children to give their dimes and nickels so that one day there would be no more folks like me. The poise I learned in telling my story served me well as I later began my life as an educator and advocate, but it also often came at substantial personal cost as my body became the lesson, and the words I was schooled to say were uncomfortable beliefs about me." By the time she was thirteen, Eiesland had had eleven operations to correct her hips and treat spinal scoliosis, and Pentecostal preachers had prayed for her healing.

Eiesland briefly attended the University of North Dakota, but after her sister's tragic death in a car crash she transferred to the Assemblies of God's Central Bible College in Springfield, Missouri, where her family had relocated. In 1986 she graduated as valedictorian and within a year was ordained as an Assemblies of God minister. After a few years, though, her ideas as a woman with a disability pushed her beyond her denomination's orthodoxy, and she began what she thought would be her life's work as a hospital chaplain.

Eiesland earned her Master of Divinity degree at Candler School of Theology in Atlanta. As part of the program she did an intensive unit of clinical pastoral education at Georgia Baptist Hospital (now Atlanta Medical Center). While at the hospital she met another chaplain, an Assemblies of God pastor and ex-military man, who set her professional life on a different course. "My time as a chaplain-in-training taught me many things," she wrote, "but ultimately I decided not to be a chaplain because God could use my early life in the hospital for many more things than I could imagine."

Her master's thesis at Candler became the basis for *The Disabled God*, published in 1994, although she barely mentioned her own story there. "The work seemed so deeply personal that even sharing it with my professors made me anxious beyond words. Yet as I showed my account to other people with physical disabilities, in particular, they often found much that resonated with their own experience."

In the book, Eiesland pointed to the scene in Luke 24:36–39, in which Jesus, returned from the dead, invites his disciples to touch his crucifixion wounds. "In presenting his impaired body to his startled friends, the resurrected Jesus is revealed as the disabled

God," she wrote. The lesson is that Jesus is not cured in the sense that he is made whole. The nail holes are a part of him, and not a divine punishment or an opportunity for healing. The lesson demonstrates, Eiesland said, that God remains a God with whom people with disabilities can identify.

Eiesland went on to earn a Ph.D. in the sociology of religion in 1995 and was immediately hired by Candler School of Theology, where she later earned tenure. She married and the couple adopted a daughter. Four years before Eiesland's death, an accident on the job—a chair collapsed beneath her—caused a back injury that left her with a mass of hairline fractures and a swollen spinal cord.

In her later years, Eiesland continued "to work out implications of being a disabled woman in Christian circles." In her own words: "As I have journeyed from Ireland to India and many places beyond—listening to accounts that both resound with familiarity and yet are culturally and theologically distinctive—I have learned an academic and more a spiritual habit of 'just listening'— listening for the claims of justice that are made in everyday life. I've learned that those people whose verbal communicative skills are underdeveloped nevertheless claim me, letting me know that I am one of God's children."

"As she strove to define new religious symbols," *The New York Times* observed in its obituary, "Eiesland's metaphors were startlingly incisive. She envisioned God puttering about in a 'puff' wheelchair, the kind quadriplegics drive with their breath."

42

Off the Pillow of Self-Pity

Angela Victoria Lundy

Angela Victoria Lundy was born into the disability family as the daughter of blind parents in St. Petersburg, Florida. Her mother and father provided a nurturing environment of music and Christian ministry, focused on their family. They were determined to be independent and successful and passed that spirit on to Angela, their only surviving child. In order to improve their economic situation, the family migrated to the Philadelphia area, where Angela attended high school and college and developed her vocal talent at the Settlement Music School. She was ordained by the Missionary Baptist Church and served as a local elder in the Seventh-Day Adventist Church. While working for a decade as an administrator at the Pennsylvania College of Optometry, she married. She raised three children and has six grandchildren.

In 1995, at the age of forty-nine, Lundy was stricken with meningitis, along with two strokes, which left her in a coma for several weeks. When she woke she was profoundly deaf, unable to speak or walk, and had extensive memory loss and Bell's palsy, which distorted her face. Lundy spent months in a rehabilitation center, where she often visited the chapel, asking God why this had happened to her and what she should do for the rest of her life. The answer came in the form of a Bible verse, Deuteronomy 31:8 KJV. "And the LORD, he it is that doth go before thee; he will be with thee, he will not fail thee, neither forsake thee: fear not, neither be dismayed." Lundy's strong faith and the Twenty-third Psalm kept her from feeling dejection, depression, despair, and defeat.

Lundy struggled to regain her memory and to reestablish herself through writing and interviewing the people who visited her in the hospital."These professionals, laypeople, religious associates, and family drew me to sanity in an insane situation, given the sudden change in my life," she said. Still, it wasn't easy. The sudden deafness brought on tinnitus, an extremely distracting condition in which Lundy heard screeching noises inside her head. Yet her faith and her childhood memories sustained her. Prayer reduced the noises, transforming them into hymns and spirituals. Prayer partners and devotions written by former pastors, as well as letters of encouragement, transformed her sadness and shock into joy.

"Living in the segregated South," said Lundy, an African American, "my parents befriended all races and did anything they were determined to do. They seemed to have no fear or pride, asking for the help they needed domestically, socioeconomically, and with my education. They gave the Lord thanks for everything, be it good or something that seemingly was not so good for a season. This has become my pattern as well, and I've learned to wait till change comes if something appears to be an unscaleable mountain."

Sufficiently recovered physically, although still profoundly deaf, Lundy threw herself into work to help others with disabilities. "My commitment to disability advocacy was a direct result of the independent living movement, which gave me purpose," she said. "I saw how differently abled persons were helping others, which encouraged me to get off the pillow of self-pity, change my attitude, and start making a difference."

As a result of writing her visionary autobiography, *Uphill Journey*, Lundy founded Interfaith Specialty Services, Inc. (ISS), an incorporated public charity. The organization is a faith-based community outreach program uniquely serving people with disabilities by assisting churches, theological seminaries, and organizations, ministering especially but not exclusively to the African American community.

The organization's motto is "Fitted and Working Together as One—Stretching Out on Faith." Some of the people it serves are gifted but overlooked and isolated by society because of their mental, sensory, physical, or combined challenges, and Lundy seeks to bridge the gap by promoting inclusion. She also helps programs that assist patients without medical insurance by giving them free, used rehabilitation equipment.

Beginning on her sixtieth birthday, Lundy was called to serve as pastor of a new, multiple-denomination ministry focused on disability, called PEACE (Physically Enabled and Cognitively Empowered). It is a movement of grassroots churches and community groups with a vision for improving access to places of worship for people with various disabilities. Fifteen congregations are now in the PEACE family, providing services to people with disabilities in Pennsylvania, New Jersey, and Delaware. "In a world of chaos and confusion, with a shaky economy, severe budget cuts, and mostly everyone concentrating only on their own needs, we are in a decline in caring for the well-being of others," said Lundy.

Lundy has been recognized and honored by numerous local and national groups for her work. In memory of her parents, she created the "Enabler Award," which is presented to people who give service to others despite having their own challenges. As what she calls a "Christ-centered advocate for disability rights," Lundy has found contentment traveling the country, interacting with other concerned people, and focusing on freedom of religion and inclusion for all.

"I overcome challenges and maintain a positive, self-encouraging outlook in all situations," Lundy wrote. "God allows all things for a reason, and I am steadfastly centered in his will."

43

Serving Communion

Jo D'Archangelis

Being a specialist in faith and disability confers on a person no immunity from either committing or being on the receiving end of unintended gaffes during worship, even in a caring and familiar congregation.

Jo D'Archangelis lives with spinal muscular atrophy, a neuromuscular condition in which the muscles are progressively weakened over time. She also edits *Wings*, "A Faithletter for United Methodists with Disabilities and Those Who Care about Them." A graduate of the University of California–Los Angeles with two master's degrees, she now serves as "a one-person, self-appointed task force on disability accessibility" at Fallbrook United Methodist Church, north of San Diego.

While D'Archangelis was taking Communion at the church one Sunday morning, a server approached her in her wheelchair, tore off a piece of bread from the loaf he carried, and offered it to her to take. D'Archangelis indicated, with a kind of "floppy wrist" motion, that she couldn't take the bread in her hand, and he needed to bring it to her mouth. So the server dipped the piece of bread in the cup of grape juice and attempted to place it in her mouth.

Unfortunately, D'Archangelis couldn't open her mouth wide enough to accommodate what seemed to her to be a golf-ball-sized chunk of bread. Without a word the Communion server, obviously untrained for the situation and not knowing what to do, turned around and returned to the chancel, the fate of the soggy piece of bread a mystery. D'Archangelis sat in stunned silence as the singing of the final hymn filled the sanctuary.

"When the server had tried unsuccessfully to push the bread past my front teeth into my mouth, I had been embarrassed for both of us," the disability ministries advocate later wrote in *Wings*. "Now I was feeling totally devastated: Communion had been offered to me and then it had been taken away, and it was all because of my disability. Tears began to well up in my eyes, and by the time the pastor said the benediction, I was in full-blown sobbing mode—sobbing quietly to be sure, but still sobbing."

As other congregation members streamed out of the sanctuary, D'Archangelis heard a friend's voice behind her, asking what had happened. The friend knelt down beside her and put her arm around her shoulders. Between sobs and apologies for what D'Archangelis self-consciously felt was her unseemly behavior, she described to the concerned friend what she would later refer to as "The Case of the Disappearing Communion." The friend immediately dispatched her husband to speak to the pastor, who was greeting people as they departed through the sanctuary's front door. The minister returned a few minutes later with bread and grape juice in hand, repeated the words about the body and blood of Christ that are part of the rite of Communion, dipped a pecan-sized piece of bread into the juice, and placed it in her mouth. She slowly chewed and swallowed it. There were smiles all around.

On reflection, D'Archangelis wrote, she realized that the whole fiasco could have been avoided, and she shouldn't blame the Communion server. After all, situations like that aren't covered in "Communion Serving 101," and it is human nature to retreat from an unexpectedly embarrassing situation as quickly as possible. Like many other people with disabilities, D'Archangelis felt that if it was anyone's fault, it was hers.

"I simply had no business assuming that everyone automatically knew the do's and don'ts of dealing with me and my disability in church," she wrote. "When Communion is served in my church, normally the first Sunday of each month, I'm usually sitting next to someone who knows how to assist me. This particular Sunday, however, I was sitting next to someone who had not helped me before. For some reason, I didn't say anything to her, or to the Communion server when he approached me, about any reasonable (or unreasonable) accommodations I might require. I just

took it all for granted—much to the resulting dismay and confusion of everyone concerned."

Up to that point, D'Archangelis had taken Communion itself
largely for granted, participating in the rite hundreds of times during her life. Like other religious rituals that are regularly repeated,
Communion had become sometimes more a dutiful habit than a
meaningful experience. From then on, however, D'Archangelis
vowed, "Whenever I am blessed to be able to participate in a
Communion service, I'll try to fully appreciate what those ancient
words and that bit of bread soaked in grape juice say to me about
the love that God has in Christ for each one of us. Even after the
bread and juice have been consumed and the words float off into
the air, I know that love will not be taken from me."

This story, with its disastrous beginning, had a happy ending.
A month after the calamitous Communion, D'Archangelis was sitting next to the same church friend who had sat next to her when
things went awry. This time, before the service, they discussed how
the friend could best provide assistance: "Take the bread from the
server for me," D'Archangelis instructed. "If it's too big, tear it in
half. Dip it into the juice and put it in my mouth. Do it with your
left hand because it's kind of awkward to put something in my
mouth with your right hand when you're sitting on my left. Okay?
Okay."

The two friends watched and listened intently as the pastor
went through the Communion ritual he had gone through so
many times before—reciting the words of confession, forgiveness, and thanksgiving; washing and drying the hands of the servers; and distributing the cups and loaves among them. But this
time, as soon as he finished, the pastor took a loaf of bread and,
beckoning one of the cupbearers to accompany him, made a bee-
line toward D'Archangelis and served her Communion first. No
problem.

D'Archangelis's account of her Communion in her *Wings* column, "From Where I Sit," provoked a resonant memory from
Richard Daggett, a post-polio survivor who uses a power chair and
a respirator and is a member of the United Methodist Church

in Downey, California. At his home church, Daggett has several people who sit near him to help with Communion, which has recently been given in the pews. The bread is served first, and then the grape juice in small, individual plastic cups. One of Daggett's Communion helpers keeps a supply of short drinking straws to help him with the liquid, a gesture she made without Daggett's asking and which he greatly appreciates.

During a visit with a friend to a non-Methodist church that was celebrating an anniversary, Communion didn't go so smoothly for Daggett. The minister explained to visitors that everyone was invited to partake of Communion if he or she was "in a right relationship with the Lord." The implication of the preacher's words was clear: If you weren't in a right relationship, you should take a pass on Communion.

Daggett was sitting in the middle of the center aisle, the only space available for his wheelchair, four rows behind his friend, who was sitting with her family. As the ushers passed the elements, Daggett's friend stayed in her seat, accepting the elements without a thought. When the usher got to Daggett's location, he extended his little tray, expecting Daggett to reach over and pick up the elements. Because Daggett can neither reach nor pick up, he tried to gesture in a way that indicated he needed help, but without success. He wrote later that he wasn't about to shout out in the middle of a church service, "Hey, I need some help here."

The usher quickly retracted his offering of the elements, with an expression of concern—not concern that Daggett couldn't physically handle the elements by himself, but concern that the visitor in the wheelchair was not in "a right relationship with the Lord." As the usher walked back down the aisle after finishing his Communion duties, he whispered to Daggett, "I'll keep you in my prayers."

44

Realizing a Dream

Elsie Vander Weit

Moving into an assisted living facility need not mean the end of an active faith life for people with disabilities. In some cases, it can be a beginning, as it has been for Elsie Vander Weit of Midland Park, New Jersey.

Born with cerebral palsy in a small town in the Netherlands more than sixty years ago, Vander Weit has struggled to make her way in the world—in leg braces, on crutches, and in a wheelchair. Her parents, people of modest means and education, were determined to treat her no differently from her sisters and brother. But traveling to the United States on an ocean liner from Amsterdam, her father kept the five-year-old girl in her cabin in order not to draw attention to her disability.

Arriving in this country with just $200, half a dozen blankets, and a clock, the family settled in northern New Jersey, where Vander Weit's father served as church custodian at two congregations over the years. This enabled the family to live on the church grounds or close by and to practice their faith at the Cedar Hill Christian Reformed Church, whose roots lie in their Dutch homeland. Still, the family was too poor to afford a wheelchair for their daughter. Vander Weit was carried in a baby carriage until she was twelve, when a neighbor lost a child to a brain tumor and donated the child's wheelchair to the family. Lack of a wheelchair, though, did not keep Vander Weit's parents from including her in all family vacations around the country.

"I'm thankful I had the kind of parents I did, Vander Weit said. "They treated me normally"—although Calvinist households at the time were strict, and normal meant going to church, doing for others, and learning her lessons. "Things have changed, but if I wasn't brought up the way I was, I don't think I would have turned out the way I did."

Despite suggestions that her parents send Elsie away to a residential facility, they insisted that their home was *her* home. A taxi took her to a school for young people with cerebral palsy, where she studied until she was twenty, completing the equivalent of sixth grade. Her education took so long, she said, because in those days instruction was very slow-paced, following the conventional wisdom that people with disabilities could not understand instruction well. The school had club meetings and extracurricular activities, but Vander Weit did not participate, taking what she said was her "first stand." She told her teachers and schoolmates, "Don't expect to include me, because Sunday is for the Lord."

She loved church, was baptized, and at the age of twelve joined the choir. In Sunday school she prided herself on being able to win class competitions to locate a particular passage in the Bible. Members of the congregation often brought her gifts while she was recuperating from her numerous operations.

Once, as a child, Vander Weit became curious about how it would feel to take a step, in her leg braces but without her crutches. When she tried, she fell, but that did not deter her from trying to walk again—or anything else, for that matter. She finished her schooling and for decades commuted to a job at a sheltered workshop that handled medical supplies, sponsored by the Elks and Lions clubs.

Later, Vander Weit wondered whether her life might have been different had she been born in more recent times, when greater opportunities exist and expectations are higher for young people with disabilities. Might she have gone to college or even to a seminary, once her traditional Christian Reformed Church had accepted women pastors?

"I would have loved that, I loved the thought of it," she said, but her denomination didn't ordain women or allow them to serve as elders or deacons until the 1990s. "Out of respect for the Christian Reformed Church I kept my distance. I decided to be myself and to let God guide me, let him make it work the way he wanted."

As an adult, Vander Weit had a recurring, puzzling dream of a figure in a white gown, surrounded by people. Vander Weit couldn't see the figure's face, "as if God didn't want me to see it." She had a feeling that the dream might have had something to do with her desire to help others, but she didn't know what to do about it. In 1994, her prayers were answered. A group from the Eastern Christian Children's Retreat, the assisted living facility to which she moved after her father died, was invited to a service and luncheon at the First Reformed Church of Ridgewood, New Jersey, part of a denomination similar to her own.

The Ridgewood congregation is unique. Once a thriving church, over the years First Reformed–Ridgewood shrank to twenty aging members and then to just seven by the time the Reverend Judy Broeker became interim pastor in the mid-1990s. Broeker founded a "Friends to Friends" outreach ministry for people with disabilities, the elderly, their friends and families, and residents of area group homes and assisted living facilities. The church now involves 120 to 130 people in some activity, such as choir or Bible study. About seventy-five attend regular Sunday evening services.

"As a longtime member of the Christian Reformed Church, Elsie was clearly taken aback at our first meeting," Broeker recalled. "To find a female minister pastoring a church at that point in her life was unheard of."

Vander Weit's vision seemed to become manifest at the church when she met Broeker, the first woman minister from a sister denomination that she had ever seen. "My heart just about stopped," she recalled, as she instantly recognized the figure from her dream. "I was shaking like a leaf."

Months later, Broeker asked Vander Weit to lead a group prayer, but she was so dumbstruck she could not answer. "God was so close to me," she said. "All these years, he kept my mind sharp. He said to me, 'I'm here with you. I have something I want you to do. Don't be afraid. You're going to make a difference for people with disabilities. Please accept my will for you.'"

Confused by the experience, Vander Weit told Broeker what had happened, and the minister said it was a gift from God to be used for God's glory. Inspired, Vander Weit became active in Broeker's church as well as her own congregation in Wyckoff, New Jersey, attending services at one church on Sunday mornings and the other on Sunday evenings. She helped with Communion and led Bible readings, seated at a table next to the pulpit at Broeker's church.

"I think in many ways this excited her, and she wanted to become more of a leader in the Christian community," Broeker said. "She became involved with Friends to Friends, exploring ways to serve this ministry. While being here, Elsie has been introduced to a number of opportunities that I believe have helped in her own spiritual growth, as well as helping her to move past some of her fears as she has worked in support of this mission. Many would say that Elsie has been truly a blessing to our work here at Friends to Friends."

For Vander Weit, this new, more active involvement has felt "unbelievably beautiful. It's everything I ever wanted. It's like God opened that door for me. Otherwise God wouldn't have guided me in that direction. He knows what I needed." Ultimately, Broeker encouraged Vander Weit to start a disability advocacy program at her own church in Wyckoff, which she did.

Vander Weit was one of the first residents the Reverend Susan Dorward met when she began her chaplaincy internship at the Eastern Christian Children's Retreat, the organization that operates the group home where Vander Weit lives. Dorward was immediately impressed. "I wanted to know what it felt like to be in a wheelchair, to have a disability, and to need people to help with basic needs. She was very helpful in shedding light on the feelings some of our residents might have," Dorward said, since most of the residents are nonverbal.

"Although I had no experience with people with developmental disabilities coming into ministry," Dorward said, "I'm now determined for people with disabilities to be considered as individuals with needs and desires just like the rest of the world's population. I just wish more people would take the time to get to know people with disabilities."

Ultimately, the pastor of Vander Weit's church in Wyckoff asked Elsie to start another disability ministry in another church in a nearby town. From her group home, Vander Weit became an advocate and a speaker for people with disabilities in local congregations. And in 2001 she ran into Liz Avanzato, who was visiting her mother at the home and trying to find a place for her sister, who also had a disability. "Elsie and I had a connection right away that both of us felt," Avanzato recalled.

"When I first started to visit Elsie, I really didn't have any experience with the disabled other than my own family," Avanzato said. "So situations came up like, whether to offer to help a person to their car, or whether a person would be upset if asked about their disability."

As a result of their experiences and friendship, the two women became regional consultants for disability concerns for their denomination, the Christian Reformed Church, one of the few denominations of its size to have a full-time director of disability concerns. Avanzato and Vander Weit "gave presentations at church," said Avanzato, "to show how the blind can eat, how they know what's on their plate and where on their plate the food is. How they know how much liquid is in their glass. All things that we take for granted. We also gave presentations to show the congregation all the things people with disabilities can do and have done in church."

"Elsie has helped me in so many ways," Avanzato said. "When I have a concern with a person with a disability, I go to Elsie. She is able to tell me how the person may be feeling or give me some advice on how to help the person."

One of the most important things Vander Weit has discovered is that ministers have to learn what people with disabilities need and how to be comfortable with them, which can be a significant learning process. But helping them achieve it is a mission she loves. "I'm thankful for how the Lord has provided direction for me in my life," she said.

"Elsie is a loving and caring woman who has experienced many challenges in her life," said Dorward, who has traveled with Vander

Weit to disability workshops. "She is sharp and will speak her mind when she needs to. She will ask for help and tell you exactly how to meet her needs. These character traits are what make her a good advocate and consultant."

45

Mental Health Matters

Barbara Meyers

Looking back—and notwithstanding all logic and science to the contrary—Barbara Meyers cannot separate her serious, debilitating mental illness from a feeling that she was living a life with no healthy spiritual outlet.

"I was trying to be perfect at everything and living my life by the principles of science alone," she remembers. She had a Ph.D. in computer science from the University of California–Los Angeles and had worked for twenty-five years as a software engineer for IBM. "I loved my job and the work I did, and IBM is a great company to work for. But while I was working I had a psychotic episode and was hospitalized."

Whether or not the absence of a spiritual outlet contributed to her illness, Meyers' commitment and involvement in her faith played a clear role in her recovery. "As I recovered, it was my involvement with a church that helped me balance my life and see that there was something more to life than rationality and logic. I felt that God was calling me to do something else with my life."

New possibilities opened up for her as she helped found Mission Peak Unitarian Universalist Congregation in her hometown, Fremont, California. At an early worship service at the new church, Meyers gave her spiritual autobiography—what some other faiths call "testimony"—which, she said, was basically her "coming out" as a person who had mental health problems.

The congregation received Meyers' sermon so positively that she launched a depression support group at the church. After the group had been going for a couple of years, she began to think she might be more effective if she had some formal training in pastoral counseling. Starr King School for the Ministry, the Unitarian Universalist seminary in Berkeley, California, agreed to let her take a pastoral counseling class there as a special student. About halfway through the class, Meyers realized that this work was where her life was leading. By the end of the semester she had decided to retire from IBM and submitted her application to the seminary. After four years in seminary she began a community ministry to focus on people with mental health problems, formally affiliating with her congregation in Fremont as one of its ministers.

"Having a mental illness has been an invaluable asset to me in working with others with mental illnesses," Meyers said. "There is something about being with someone who has had similar experiences that is very powerful. Peers can often reach people when the medical establishment and families haven't been able to. This is especially powerful when a peer can see you as being able to live a successful life. Just by your presence, you convey that there is hope for them."

One Sunday morning, as Meyers and her husband were walking to church, they encountered a woman named Frances, whom Meyers had met before, begging on the sidewalk. The woman had been diagnosed with paranoid schizophrenia and had been in and out of mental hospitals and jails for years. Frances recognized Meyers right away and smiled.

"Frances wanted to talk to me that morning about an experience that she had recently saying confession to a priest," Meyers said. "She had gone to confession and told the priest that she was in despair and didn't know what to do. The priest told her, 'God never despairs of reaching you because he loves you.'

"She said that this simple assurance that God loved her was worth all the psychiatric medications, hospitalizations, being harassed and jailed by police because of her mental illness, the social workers who lost patience and yelled at her, and the psychiatrists and therapists who didn't understand her. She said most psychiatrists and doctors didn't know anything about religion and how important it can be to people.

"She said that God can do miracles, because knowing that God loved her had made her feel so good. In the medical sense she wasn't 'cured' and probably never would be, because she still has symptoms of schizophrenia, but in an important sense she was healed. This kind of healing brings one a sense of inner freedom, joy, compassion, and spontaneity."

Meyers told her husband that it didn't matter what was said in church that morning, because she had just heard her sermon for the day. To others, Frances might have looked like a worthless vagrant sitting on the street that Sunday morning, yet as tears filled the minister's eyes, she saw the woman as she was: a person of inherent worth who had just delivered a message that Meyers needed to hear. Frances validated Meyers's ministry to people with mental problems, the direction that her life had taken.

Another woman, named Dorothy, whom Meyers counseled had been diagnosed with a psychotic disorder and was hospitalized three or four times a year. Usually, when the woman's illness became unmanageable, someone would call the police, who would take her to the hospital for involuntary commitment. One day, as Dorothy was again reaching the end of her rope, she met with Meyers. They talked about hospitalization, and the minister asked if it would be all right for her to take Dorothy to the hospital. Dorothy agreed. Meyers drove her to the hospital and sat with her, holding her hand, in the emergency room until she was seen and admitted for a stay that lasted a couple of weeks.

A month or so after her release, Dorothy took the minister aside and said she had something to confide. The woman said she kept remembering the time Meyers sat with her, holding her hand, and that sometimes the thought that someone cared enough to do that was what helped her make it through the day. Three years later, Dorothy has not needed to be hospitalized again.

Based on these and other experiences, Meyers wrote a curriculum, "The Caring Congregation Handbook," for use in training faith communities to be more intentionally inclusive and welcoming of people with mental disorders and their families. The curriculum includes stories from various sources to help describe what people with mental disorders go through. A piece called "Coffee Hour Skit" is made up entirely of things overheard during coffee hour conversations at Meyers' own church by the parishioner who wrote the script.

One major project of Meyers' ministry is producing a monthly public-access television program called "Mental Health Matters." Each episode focuses on an aspect of mental health, and Meyers invites guests who have experienced mental health problems, their family members, and mental health professionals with expertise in the relevant area. The overarching goal of the show is to give people hope.

"I almost always have a guest who has suffered from what we are discussing and who has now come to terms with it," she said. "Their very presence is what gives hope—it speaks louder than anything any 'expert' could say."

Meyers recently won a community achievement award for her work. Accepting the recognition, she said, "I had all the advantages: a loving and supportive family, a beautiful home, a good job, a mental illness that was fairly easily dealt with, excellent mental health care, no money problems, good physical health. Many of the people I work with don't have these advantages; in fact some have none of them. Yet they still come back day after day, struggling the best they can, sometimes in the face of ridicule and prejudice, to help out their friends. They are my heroes, mentors, and role models. Their courage is what sustains me."

PART 3

Family Members in Ministry

Few more powerful motivations exist for ministering to people with disabilities than having an immediate family member affected by one. Mothers, fathers, siblings, spouses, grandparents, and even more distant relatives can all become tenacious advocates for loved ones with disabilities. Having a strong religious faith can help, but no one pretends that the role of caregiver for someone with a severe disability is easy.

The role's frustrations—and even the way it can lead to a questioning of one's religious beliefs—come through poignantly in a 2011 Internet blog post by Dilshad D. Ali, managing editor of the Muslim Portal at Patheos, a website. Ali wrote of the despair she felt that year at the onset of Islam's holy month of Ramadan, when the faithful fast during daylight, pray, reflect, and give to charity. Ali's nine-year-old son, Daanish, has autism, and "Ramadan is an especially trying time" for the two of them, she wrote. Just as Ali was preparing the traditional sundown meal to break the fast, Daanish returned home from an outing with his therapist, in the middle of a sensory-induced tantrum.

It took Ali, with the help of her husband, mother-in-law, and other children, forty-five minutes to calm Daanish down enough to be able to eat. Then Ali prayed, as she has for all of her son's life, for him to be able to manage his autism, have peace, communicate, and one day become independent. She also asked Allah to give her the strength to keep going.

Prayer, at home and at the mosque, gives Ali comfort. "But much more often," she wrote, "like today, I wonder, what will it take? How much suffering will Daanish endure? How much longer can I take watching him go through this? Will my prayers ever be answered the way I want them to be answered? Do I believe that Allah will grant me what I desire?"

Sometimes the struggle overwhelms her, she said, and "I question Allah." On nights like this one, she wrote, "I still believe in fasting, I believe in making my five daily prayers, I believe in keeping it together for my family. But I don't believe that it will get easier, that it will get better, and that my prayers will be answered. I beseech God and get angry." And she thinks to herself, "Maybe because I don't believe strongly enough—that is why Daanish continues to have nights like this."

Family members across the belief spectrum at times share Ali's frustration and doubts. Still, as the stories in Part 3 demonstrate, with the support of their faith communities, they can find great hope and relief. Children and adults with disabilities—physical, sensory, psychiatric, and intellectual—have gifts and talents to bring to their congregations. Are those gifts being used? Are they being honored? If so, this attention may blossom and multiply into ministry.

Family members believe strongly that children and adults with disabilities have a right to a full life of faith, including worship, study of sacred Scriptures, and the joy of serving others rather than always being on the receiving end. People with disabilities can participate in leadership—everything from being an ordained member of the clergy to being a greeter; from singing a solo during a worship service to being the person who smiles at everyone he or she meets. All are needed and enriched in the house of God. Both leaders and members of a congregation can come to understand that a child, husband, mother, or sibling with a disability is not a "tragedy" or a burden but a unique human being made in God's image, who brings great joy to others. And, yes, great worry and heartache.

As much as any disability advocate or activist in North America, Ginny Thornburgh knows this firsthand. Thornburgh, who tells her story in the foreword to this book, is the mother of an adult son named Peter who has both intellectual and physical disabilities as a result of severe brain injury sustained in a car accident when he was an infant. From Peter's childhood, Thornburgh said, "it was clear that he was a child of faith—he loved going to church. Everything about church pleased him: the routine, the stories, the friendly people, and the fact that we attended as a family."

But it soon became equally clear that "although lay and ordained leaders of the church were kind to Peter and to our family, they had no comprehensive understanding of disability and kept looking to us for guidance. Initially, there was very little literature available for a congregation determined to transform itself into a place of welcome for children and adults with disabilities; no religious curriculum for children who learn in different ways; no denominational statements on the rights of members and visitors with disabilities; and no low-interest loans or grants for congregations determined to eliminate architectural barriers."

Helping to remedy this situation became Thornburgh's calling: "to work with children and adults with all types of disabilities and their family members so they could access a full life of faith, and to work with congregations and seminaries as they identified and removed barriers of architecture, communications, and attitude." She became a determined and effective advocate for people with disabilities and currently serves as director of the Interfaith Initiative of the American Association of People with Disabilities.

As the stories in this section unfold, more parents like Ginny Thornburgh appear—parents who have been spurred into a volunteer or paid profession by a child's disability—as well as parents whose responsibility is so enormous that they have no time or energy left for anything but caring for their child. Among the parents fortunate enough to have had the opportunity to take action, some have written books about their experiences or started Internet discussion groups as a way to share insights and resources. Others have attended seminary and deepened their understanding of God's will in disability situations, and several have started community-wide organizations that work directly with children and adults with disabilities and their congregations. Out of many of the stories of parenting a child with a disability—despite pain, grief, struggle, isolation, expense, and marital stress—come new horizons, new methods, new activities, and new hope.

Four of the stories in Part 3 are about siblings and their journeys beside brothers with disabilities. It is not easy being the sibling of someone with a disability. Feelings of relief over having been spared such a difficult life may be accompanied by feelings of guilt: Why him, why her, and not me? The brother or sister's behavior might arouse feelings of embarrassment, which again can raise guilt. Most siblings, too, receive less parental attention than their brother or sister with a disability and consequently can experience anxiety and anger.

Often unstated is the expectation by parents that siblings will care for their brother or sister with a disability when the parents are no longer around. This responsibility can be a burden, or it can bring devotion and purpose—as it did in the case of Monica Masiko, who appears in chapter 58 with her brother, Mark, who has a cognitive disability. Monica is studying for a Master of Divinity degree and says that her "theology and vision for the church are shaped by the fact Mark is my brother."

Part 3 also includes two stories about husbands and wives in strong marriages. Karen Miller, married to David, speaks about living with multiple sclerosis and wonders how "people without faith" can handle the disease. Sue Odena, whose husband, Fred, has Alzheimer's disease, asks, "How can I argue with God?" And yet, she acknowledges, "this is a bitter cup we have been given."

Families, and the ties that bind members to each other, are important to everyone blessed to be a part of one. For people with disabilities they are the first—and most enduring—circle of support, strengthened by faith.

46

Traveling from Grief to Joy

Kathleen Deyer Bolduc

From the time Kathleen Deyer Bolduc was a child, one of her greatest desires was to be a writer. In a way she admittedly would never have wished for, that calling as a writer has enabled her to cope with and understand her son Joel's intellectual disabilities and autism—part of a long spiritual journey toward coming to accept his disability. "Living with Joel has been an incredible journey in patience, trust, and obedience, and most of all, in the assurance of the Lord's presence: within me, above me, and in front of me, every step of the way," she said.

In the process, Bolduc began writing books and articles that have helped other parents in similar circumstances. "The Lord honored that journey," Bolduc said. "What had been a wasteland of grief became rivers in a desert. The blessings Joel brought to my life began to spread and bless other people." This, Bolduc believes, was no accident.

"God uses many people throughout the span of our lifetimes to shape and transform us. He sent me one of the most important spiritual teachers of my life on February 27, 1985, the day of my third son's birth." Joel's birth had complications, which doctors at the time said would result in developmental delays for the boy. As he grew to be a toddler in the family's Cincinnati, Ohio, home, the diagnosis was changed to moderate mental retardation, and then in early adolescence, to increasingly severe autism. Throughout this period—the time when Bolduc began to write—she passed through stages familiar to parents of children with disabilities: chronic grief, long-term denial, anger, self-blame, and depression. But she never lost her faith.

"Through this grieving process, which lasted several years, I never stopped calling out to God. Even on my darkest days," she said. "When my mind was too numb to form a prayer, I repeated four words over and over: 'Hear my prayer, Lord. Hear my prayer.' The grief itself became my prayer."

Bolduc went back to school and earned a master's degree in religious studies with an emphasis on the effects of disability on family systems. This helped her understand that her family was not dysfunctional—it was simply experiencing the stresses and strains known to all families who live with disability. Bolduc had several articles published, then a book, another book, and then another. Churches and autism agencies began to ask her to speak, to lead workshops and retreats, and to teach. At first, she said, she was petrified, never having done any of this before, but she felt the Lord kept pouring his waters into the empty, scared places within her.

In her books *His Name Is Joel: Searching for God in a Son's Disability* and *Autism and Alleluias*, Bolduc introduced her son and described the many gifts he had given her family, including his delightful sense of humor and his insistence on being himself, never putting on a mask to impress or manipulate others. She wrote *A Place Called Acceptance: Ministry with Families of Children with Disabilities* as a manual for churches that are looking for ways to become more welcoming and inclusive of people with disabilities.

Despite the gifts Joel brought, Bolduc wrote, life with him was demanding, given his combination of intellectual disabilities and autism. His sensory difficulties made it hard for him to be in large groups of people and to tolerate certain noises. Family members had to deal with his myriad taxing behaviors, the worst being tantrums, hair pulling, and pulling eyeglasses off people's faces. His cognitive disability made learning the easiest of tasks difficult. Joel would never learn to read or write, and in his mid-twenties, he still depends on others to help him dress, tie his shoes, and zip his coat. He needs constant supervision for his safety.

When Joel was eleven, Bolduc told an interviewer for public radio's *Interfaith Voices* in 2010, the family withdrew him from their Presbyterian congregation's Sunday school because of his behavior. But one Communion Sunday they brought Joel with them and sat in the front pew so he couldn't kick anyone sitting in front of them or pull their hair. After the pastor explained the elements of the sacrament to the congregation—that Jesus had died for them—Joel suddenly stood up, faced the whole sanctuary, and patted his chest. "For me! For me!" he said, with a heart-melting smile. To Bolduc, "the love of God was just glimmering on his face." Joel relates to God spiritually rather than cognitively, she said. "God loves Joel for who he is."

Still, Bolduc said, "you might understand why there are days when I shout at God—*enough!* As the parent of a child with a disability, I travel a rocky road. A road that has brought me to my knees in prayer. It is a winding road, and its curves surprise me one day with anger, the next with joy.

"Somewhere along this road, in the struggle to put my son's disability into perspective with a loving God, I had to let go and trust. I began to trust Jesus Christ to tell me what it means to be a child of God, rather than accept society's definition of personhood. I began to trust Jesus to tell me the worth of my son Joel, as well as my worth as Joel's mother. The only other choice I had was to allow the perfection-crazed culture in which we live to define both Joel and myself."

Over the years, Bolduc said, she has learned many lessons from Joel—in her words, an "unlikely teacher"—through both his personal interactions and his experiences in congregational settings.

One snowy Saturday when Joel was fifteen, Bolduc and her son bundled up to visit an old school friend of hers named Janet, just home from the hospital. Janet had undergone a serious brush with death but had miraculously recovered. Because Janet had lived outside of Cincinnati while Joel was growing up, Joel didn't really know her. Still, during the eight weeks Janet had been in the hospital, struggling for her life, Joel had insisted, "Let's pray for Janet." That day, as they prepared to take a comfort meal of beef stew and biscuits to the friend's house, Joel said, "Let's take flowers to Janet," adding, "We need to pray for her."

Bolduc paused, thanking God again for the miracle of her son, disabilities and all, and for his tender concern for those less fortunate than himself. "And I pray for the biggest miracle of all:

that our eyes would be open to the God-breathed miracle of life—all life, no matter its outward manifestations." Although once an atheist, Janet believes Joel's prayers, along with the grace of God, gave her a second chance at life.

Another of the many lessons Joel has taught his family happened not long ago when they were "church shopping" for a new faith community for Joel. He had moved several months before from their home to Safe Haven Farms, outside Cincinnati. For the second week in a row in one particular church, Joel was a jack-in-the-box, jumping up and down every couple of minutes, with an emphatic pronouncement every time he left the pew: "Bathroom!" "Church is over!" "Time to go!"

Each time, his father, Wally, took him out of the sanctuary for a few minutes, then gently guided him back into the pew. No one in the congregation frowned, whispered, or shook his head as this up-and-down routine continued. Still, Bolduc was uncomfortable to the point of irritability. "Why are we here?" she wondered. "None of this really matters to him. It's just one more place he feels anxious. Why do we keep forcing him into new situations?" And then the real source of her irritability arose: "What about *my* worship time?"

Midway through the service the pastor invited people forward to the kneeling rail for prayer. Joel watched with interest as a few men and women walked to the front of the sanctuary to kneel. He watched, wide-eyed, as his father kneeled down beside their pew, bowing his head. A stillness fell over the sanctuary as the pastor prayed, "Lord, we love you. We know you are here, Lord. We know you are waiting to meet us, wherever we are on our journey."

Bolduc glanced sideways at Joel, who was sitting perfectly still, facing the front, his face shining. "Joel loves Jesus," he whispered. "Joel loves Jesus." He paused, looking intently at the front of the sanctuary, where people were kneeling below the cross. He smiled. "And Jesus loves Joel!" He turned, met his mother's eye, grinned, and pointed his hand toward the heavens. "Jesus loves Joel!"

"Peace and joy surged through my bloodstream, washing away discomfort, irritability, and selfishness," Bolduc said. "Once again, my son transcended his disability and became wise sage and teacher to his tired and overwhelmed mother. Just one more reason I am able to say today that Joel—this handsome, blue-eyed twenty-six-year-old who happens to have autism and intellectual disabilities—ranks among the greatest spiritual teachers of my life."

As a near full-time advocate for including people with disabilities in faith communities, Bolduc always recommends starting small. First, the congregation needs to meet the family, she wrote in *A Place Called Acceptance*, and hear their story. If members and clergy seem receptive, they might name a group of buddies to take turns accompanying the person with disabilities to Sunday school.

Looking back on her experiences with her son through a theological lens, Bolduc said, has taught her even more. "The pain I experienced as I grieved Joel's disability broke open the Scriptures for me. I came to understand that Jesus turns the cultural belief— that brokenness is to be avoided at all costs—upside down. Christ challenges me to face and embrace my brokenness, as well as Joel's brokenness, so that God's power might be released within both of us. I came to a gut-level understanding of the Lord's words to Paul in 2 Corinthians 12:9 NRSV: 'My grace is sufficient for you, for power is made perfect in weakness.'"

Over the years, said Bolduc, "I've grown to view Joel with the eyes of my heart rather than with my physical eyes. There are so many reasons to rejoice: Joel's infectious grin, his silly jokes, his compassion for people who are hurting, his spontaneity and unconditional love, his evident joy in worship, the people God has brought into our life through him—caregivers and therapists and doctors, some of whom have become lifelong friends."

47

God's Plan

Linda Starnes

For some reason—perhaps providence—Linda Starnes prepared herself for a life she never expected. A native of Knoxville, Tennessee, and a woman of strong faith, she had no personal experience with disability while growing up. Yet she majored in special and elementary education at the University of Tennessee and taught children with special needs in her state. Later, when her husband (and childhood sweetheart), Tom, a fellow UT graduate, found a job with Procter & Gamble in Dallas, Texas, in 1983, Linda taught special education in schools there.

In 1987 the couple moved to Cambridge, Massachusetts, where Tom entered Harvard University's prestigious MBA program. But the state of Massachusetts would not accept Linda's special education teaching credentials from Tennessee and Texas, so she went looking for a job. She found a position as an assistant to former Pennsylvania governor Dick Thornburgh, then the director of Harvard's Institute of Politics. Through her new boss, she met his wife, Ginny Thornburgh, and their son Peter, who has intellectual and physical disabilities as the result of a traumatic brain injury.

The Starneses' association with the Thornburghs was a continuation of Linda's preparation for what was to come. Ginny, who became her friend, was well on her way to becoming an outspoken advocate for people with disabilities, with an emphasis on the faith dimension. Through Dick, Linda was exposed to an insider's view of practical politics and how to navigate bureaucracies.

After Tom Starnes finished his Harvard business program and Dick Thornburgh was appointed U.S. attorney general under President Ronald Reagan, the Starneses followed the Thornburghs to Washington, D.C. Tom found a job in commercial real estate, and Linda became Dick's executive assistant. Later, after Dick ran for U.S. Senate in 1991, Linda shifted to the Department of Education, where she became a special assistant with the office of Secretary of Education Lamar Alexander. Meanwhile, Ginny Thornburgh had founded the Religion and Disability Program of the National Organization on Disability (NOD) in 1989, working at the intersection of religion and disability. Also during this period, Linda watched as both Ginny and Dick became deeply involved in the drive to pass the Americans with Disabilities Act, which was signed into law on July 26, 1990.

For Linda, the issue of disability suddenly became personal in 1993, when the Starneses' first child, Emily, was born with Asperger syndrome, a form of autism, and a rare genetic condition called Sotos syndrome, which caused a mild developmental disability. Two years later, their son James—called "Mac"—was born with an even rarer medical condition, resulting in a mild cerebral palsy along with significant breathing and feeding issues that required him to be placed on a ventilator and use a feeding tube. Some of their doctors urged the Starneses to let Mac die, arguing that he would never be an aware, feeling being.

Mac's parents, however, were convinced otherwise and, guided by their faith, used all the skills they had developed to convince their doctors and insurers that inside their infant's struggling body was a person. Linda saw something that hinted at the indomitable and irrepressible person he would become, if given a chance: "a bright little twinkle in his eyes" and a left foot that kicked whenever she came by to see him. For two years Mac required round-the-clock care, including a home ventilator, but he survived the challenge.

Linda felt she was well equipped to meet the challenge, too. "If God blessed us with a child who had special needs," she remembers telling a family member years before her children's birth, "I knew I could handle that. It wasn't a wish—I don't know what prompted me to say that."

After moving to Washington, the Starneses worshiped at McLean Bible Church in northern Virginia, a politically connected, nondenominational congregation then on the way to becoming a megachurch. It would also become a favorite of Republican U.S. senators, cabinet members, executives, and bankers. The congregation's dynamic pastor was Lon Solomon, and it was to him that the Starneses turned for help. Their request ultimately launched a program called "Access Ministry," focused on supporting and including persons with disabilities and their families in the congregation.

"We began with several concerned congregants asking for help," Linda recalled, referring to herself and Tom and a few others like them. "We started small, but just like a mustard seed, the inclusive program grew into a vibrant and integral part of the church. Changing minds and attitudes takes some time. You have to help a church staff realize that more inclusive efforts on their part can be as easy as finding a volunteer buddy to go to Sunday school with a child while the parents go to church service." Linda and the church adopted as a motto the line from the Kevin Costner movie *Field of Dreams*: "If you build it, he will come."

The hands at work at McLean Bible Church were both seen and unseen. "Tom and I will never forget the first day Mac was able to attend church with us, when he was about eight months old. It just happened to be a service devoted to baby dedication. Although Mac wasn't on the list to be a part of this event, the staff quickly worked it out to have him presented that morning by Pastor Lon to his church family—with tubes, wires, beeping monitors, and nurse in tow."

Linda and Tom worked with another parent and friend, Diane Anderson, a mom with five kids and a big heart, to launch the first Sunday school class for children with disabilities at McLean. Together they met with Lon Solomon about starting a program for people with disabilities, and as would be her habit, Linda brought a stack of paperwork containing a host of ideas about how the church could welcome, provide support for, and include children and adults with disabilities. "Wisely," she recalled, "Lon said we should start small, execute with excellence, and grow from there." Thus the first Sunday school class at McLean for children with disabilities was born, and Diane and her husband became its lead volunteers.

In 1992, a year after Emily was born and before Access Ministry was formally launched, Pastor Lon Solomon's daughter Jill was born and soon afterward developed a severe, debilitating seizure disorder. Lon and his wife, Brenda, had quietly been dealing with issues similar to the Starnses'. In later years, Pastor Solomon said that until he and his wife had Jill, they were unaware of the level of need and challenge families like theirs faced each day. Jill's life put the Solomons on a new path that prepared them for the day Linda and Diane met with Lon to discuss the start of a disability ministry. As Ginny Thornburgh came to know Pastor Solomon and watched subsequent events at the church unfold, she observed, "Because of that change in Lon, all sorts of good has happened."

As a part of the developing Access Ministry, Mac Starnes attended his first Sunday school class with some fun, loving, and creative teachers—along with a nurse and a red wagon hauling eighty pounds of medical equipment, including a ventilator, a backup battery, an apnea monitor, an oxygen tank, and a suction machine. At the same time, Emily was supported by a buddy in her classroom with other three-year-olds.

"My teachers," Emily recalled, "made me feel like I was their daughter. The preschool program was really accessible. I felt I was just a normal girl learning about God, interacting with other kids my age." Still, although church became a significant part of her life, she was in fourth grade before she made her first close friend in the congregation.

Despite the encouraging first steps, creating a larger program of inclusion at McLean took work. "It sounds odd to think that many of our places of worship don't think about accessibility and inclusion," Linda said. "So you have to use some public relations and diplomacy skills with church staff to build understanding of the importance for including those with disabilities."

With the backing of the Solomons, the efforts of the Starneses, the Andersons, and other family members took root at the church, and its efforts toward accessibility accelerated. Linda and Diane developed and hosted the first Access Summit about a year later. One of the first keynote speakers was Ginny Thornburgh, who addressed a gathering of about three hundred people from the region.

Both of the Starnes children were part of the Sunday school program, which enabled Linda and Tom to worship in the sanctuary. The couple was part of a new parent support group, and Linda was a member of Access Ministry's "Mom's group." Supported by ministry volunteers, Mac and Emily and many other children with disabilities were included in vacation Bible school and summer camp and participated in Friday night and Saturday morning respite activities at the church. "As young children, both Emily and Mac came to know Jesus as their Lord and Savior under the guidance of Pastor Lon and their many caring Sunday school teachers, including Sue and Gordy Langley," said Linda.

McLean Bible Church now includes social events and outings for adults with developmental and intellectual disabilities; a deaf ministry; respite care programs for family members; and a multimillion-dollar center on church grounds for children with disabilities. Access Ministry, under the full-time directorship of Jackie Mills-Fernald, has grown to become one of the largest disability-related ministries in the country. In 2010 the congregation opened a separate, state-of-the-art respite care center next to the church, called Jill's House, named after the Solomons' daughter.

Access Ministry was flourishing by the time the Starnes family moved to central Florida in 2002 to follow a business opportunity for Tom. At Northland Church in suburban Orlando, Linda had to start over again, but her experiences at McLean Bible Church served her well. She had come to "know and learn from many other people in the faith and disability arena," she said. "It provided the foundation for us to be able to come to Florida and be a part of faith and disability activities here.

"It takes some time to build awareness, understanding, and the need for including those with disabilities within a congregation.

But it's worth the effort to keep knocking at the door. Northland started small and built what is now a full ministry, with new families from the disability community coming each week."

Northland's pastor, the Reverend Joel Hunter, was an early and enthusiastic convert. "The local church can be significantly expanded in its ministry by one strong advocacy family," he said. "The Starneses have been that family for Northland's transition into engaging people with disabilities, and for those peoples' ministry to our congregation."

Hunter has taken a particular interest in Mac and the rest of the Starnes family. "Mac has such strong nonverbal communication skills that I once asked him to come forward in the middle of a sermon to show the congregation how much could be conveyed beyond words," Hunter recalled. "He doesn't just pantomime a message—he takes it to places beyond the observer's expectations. He more than holds up his end of the conversation!"

Economies of scale apply in ministries just as in economics. Like regional high schools and big-box retailers, megachurches such as McLean and Northland have the resources to offer comprehensive ministries for people with disabilities. "Most religious communities are struggling with maintenance issues rather than spiritual maturity issues," Hunter said. "We don't become spiritually mature until we can care for those who are ignored or avoided by others. That takes extra work, and in most cases extra staff and volunteers, but it yields great meaning and surprising abilities are discovered in those supposedly 'disabled.'"

One of the first things the Starneses did to contribute to the effort was to adapt their home swimming pool for safe access, which enabled Mac—and later, other members of the congregation with physical disabilities—to be safely baptized. At first Mac attended kids' church and listened to Bible stories on tape, but by the time he was in middle school he joined worship in Northland's enormous main sanctuary with the rest of his family. And although his speech is greatly affected by his disability, he sings along and reads the Bible verses projected on the screen. Like his sister, Mac attends public school, but the first thing he asked his home tutor, in American Sign Language (ASL), was, "Do you believe in Jesus?" (The answer was yes.) Providing a required self-introduction for one of his high school classes, Mac described himself by saying, "I am a miracle created by God."

Now in his mid-teens, Mac still requires breathing and feeding tubes and has undergone more than thirty surgeries and medical procedures ("Jesus kept me from dying," he texts). Nevertheless, he plays percussion in his high school marching band, and with the use of an application for his iPod called Proloquo2Go, which synthesizes voice from text, he no longer relies solely on ASL. He gives short lectures about adaptive technology at county school system meetings and to groups including university classes.

Mac told one interviewer that he wants to be a preacher when he grows up, in particular "a pastor who travels around the world and spreads the word of God." What, he was asked, would be his message? "God will be with you always, even in the hard times."

Emily Starnes has an insight and grace about her life and her disability well beyond her years. "I have asked God why I have this," she said. "I want to fit in so bad. I should accept my disability as a gift from God, but at the same time it's like some obstacle I always have to tackle that is here one day, gone the next, and sprouts up again."

Looking back at her experiences as a young adult—her college studies, her years as a special education teacher, her time with the Thornburghs—Linda Starnes said that "God couldn't have placed Emily and Mac in a better situation."

"The great aspect of ministry with people who have more obvious disabilities is that they transform us into more Christlike people," said Reverend Hunter. "Some people started to get to know the Starnes kids and others with disabilities and found themselves less noticing the limitations and more in love with the people. We started out with compassion and we ended up with a sense of awe for people made in the image of God."

48

Daughter of the Commandments

Hannah Ruth Greenblatt Eppinette

In June of 1995, at Temple Beth Or in Raleigh, North Carolina, twelve-year-old Hannah Ruth Greenblatt Eppinette had her bat mitzvah, the traditional rite of passage to Jewish adulthood. Despite severe mental disabilities, Hannah prepared for the day for months, attending classes three afternoons a week. She was unable to read portions of the Torah and the Prophets or to recite the blessings in Hebrew or English, as is customary. Her parents' simple, fervent hope was that she would be able to sit and stand on the pulpit at the right moments, help open the ark, and take the velvet cover off the holy scrolls.

The morning of Hannah's big day began with a breakfast of her mother's honey cake and apple juice, and then a fancy dress and a barrette in her brown hair, according to a heartfelt account of the service in the Raleigh *News & Observer* by Lisa Pollak, a future Pulitzer Prize winner at *The Baltimore Sun*. Hannah's father, Chuck Eppinette, and her mother, Debbie Greenblatt, told their only child not to worry.

Among the three hundred people waiting in the pews that Saturday morning were Hannah's extended family, friends, speech therapists, special education teachers, and classmates from East Cary Middle School. Up at the pulpit, Rabbi Lucy Dinner told her, "If you have a heart and you have faith within that heart, you can accomplish anything." As a friend read the portion of the Torah on her behalf, Hannah held onto the silver pointer called the *yad* and followed along. Few in the crowded sanctuary were unaffected. Gale Touger, a choir member, recalled it as "one of the most moving services I ever sang for. It was amazing to see the congregation embracing her and her family."

Pollak described what came next: "They sang for Hannah, and in her own way she sang back. She swayed and smiled. She clapped her hands, and she waved her arms. She gazed around the room, sometimes with a smile, other times with a look of awe.

"And then, when the songs had been sung and the prayers completed, Hannah's parents, in front of all those people, told her that they were proud of her.

"Hannah's father leaned over her and stroked her hair. 'This temple is the one place in your life that you've always been welcomed and accepted with no conditions put on you,' he told her. 'Daddy's always worried about what's going to happen to you when Mommy and Daddy are gone. But the love and acceptance that this congregation has shown makes me feel secure that when we're gone, there'll always be a voice for you, and you'll always be loved.'

"Hannah's mother hugged and kissed her. 'You are a person who spreads love and joy and kindness wherever you go,' she said. 'There's nothing more that a mother would want.'

"Then the rabbi, the tall woman in the blue dress, knelt down beside the bench where Hannah was sitting, legs crossed like a lady, making her mother and father proud. 'Hannah, we've been working on this bat mitzvah a long time,' she said. 'I hope that each and every day you think of this place, and that you know that your faith in God and your relation to your heritage makes you always a daughter of the commandments, a woman in the house of Israel, a person who takes her place among us.'"

Hannah's parents were able to share that day the knowledge that Hannah belonged to the Jewish community. Debbie's own mother had died of cancer when Debbie was sixteen. Before she died, she made Debbie promise that all her grandchildren would have a bat or bar mitzvah, a pledge Debbie recalled on the morning of Hannah's ceremony.

Debbie's father, Carl, who had died a few years before Hannah's bat mitzvah, was another matter. He had been angry with God about Hannah's developmental disabilities—something that can happen even among people of faith. At the bat mitzvah, when

Debbie spoke to Hannah, she said, "I want to talk to you about your grandfather Carl, who loved you very much and who worried about you some. . . . I later found out from your uncle that he had some questions for God about you, and I am just sorry that he is not here to see some of the answers to those questions."

"What I remember is not the weather outside but the pure joy everyone experienced within the sanctuary," said Gale Touger, the choir member. "Hannah's bat mitzvah was such a gift to the congregation. We did much of the service in music, because Hannah loved to hear the singing and guitars of 'Mishpacha,' the band I was in. We chose melodies for the prayers that we knew Hannah enjoyed, to help her stay connected to the service. She watched, listened, smiled, and moved to the music. It was a complete service with a classmate reading the Torah portion on Hannah's behalf. Her grandfather, Chuck's dad, had to stay out of her sight until close to the end, because she loves being with him so much that his presence would have been a distraction.

"I felt so honored to sing for Hannah, Chuck, Debbie, and her family, to contribute a part of what gave the morning meaning to Hannah. We all had many tearful moments. After the service, as folks walked into the social hall for the Kiddush luncheon, each person wanted to have a moment with Hannah, to look her in the eye and speak to her—to thank her, praise her, and let her know how much she is loved."

After the bat mitzvah, Debbie's brother Fred told Chuck that the family had flown out from Denver thinking it was going to be a bittersweet moment that might be painful to watch, but they wanted to support Debbie. They were moved that the event had been one of the most uplifting and joyful bat mitzvahs they had ever seen, a special day.

Years later, Rabbi Dinner, too, recalled the service warmly: "It was such a gift. It was emotional. Hannah was so clearly filled with joy. She knew it, she felt it at the level she was. She understood she was becoming a bat mitzvah." The connection between Debbie and Hannah was "a beautiful, spiritual moment, to see the love between them. Everyone felt how remarkable this was—there were lots of tears, leavened with joy, but no pity. People felt really good about it."

Today, Temple Beth Or remains committed to inclusion. Recently, Dinner officiated at the bar mitzvahs of twin boys, both with autism, who were able to read the Torah portion and recite the blessings. For their mitzvah project—a good deed—they worked with autism therapists and less functioning young people to help them communicate and function.

The bat mitzvah had a special poignancy for Debbie, an attorney with a strong social conscience. Even before her daughter's birth, she had led the fight in North Carolina for the rights of people with developmental disabilities and mental illness. According to a 2003 profile in a magazine from the Duke Law School, one of her class action cases established the rights of all people with mental disabilities, who until then had been inappropriately warehoused with psychotic patients, to be allowed to learn skills and live independently. A legal order in the case mandated improved professional standards and increased funding of the North Carolina mental health system by millions of dollars.

Asked by the magazine what drew her to the cause of defending the rights of people with intellectual disabilities, she replied, "I love this work because it is a real opportunity to speak the truth about people with disabilities—to the public, to the courts, to policy makers—and it is an opportunity to make an impact on people's lives."

Within a year of Hannah's 1995 bat mitzvah, Debbie was diagnosed with cancer, and she died in 2005. Upon her death, the North Carolina Bar Association, Legal Aid, and an organization known as The Arc each named awards for her. The North Carolina legislature named a bill that she was responsible for getting passed, which protected special education children from seclusion and restraint, the "Deborah Greenblatt Act." On the day of her funeral, the Raleigh *News & Observer* mentioned her work.

"To this day Hannah's bat mitzvah is still one of the happiest days of my life," said Hannah's father, Chuck. "When you are a parent of a child with a developmental disability, you are always told what your child cannot do, and you battle to have your child included, even marginally, in events in the community. Because of Temple Beth Or and Rabbi Dinner, Hannah had a bat mitzvah—not because Debbie and I forced them to do it; they did it because it was the right thing to do. And the congregation did not focus on what Hannah could not do; they celebrated what she could do. Debbie, who so often had to be in the role of an attorney fighting for the rights of people with developmental disabilities, got to sit back and just be a parent, proud of what her daughter had accomplished. It was truly a blessing."

49

The Greatest Is Love

Karen and David Miller

Karen Miller was a typical overachiever. She finished college in three years and went on to graduate from Georgetown and Harvard law schools. She sprinted into a career as a corporate attorney in Boston and then opened up her law firm's office in London. Her idea of slowing down was to teach legal ethics, first in London and then, after moving back to the United States, at the New York University and University of Miami law schools, commuting back and forth between the two.

Karen's husband, David—the two have known each other since they were both eleven—is equally an achiever. After graduating from Bucknell University, he became an international businessman and investment banker and later a second-career doctoral student at Princeton Theological Seminary. Author of the book *God at Work*, he is now on the faculty of Princeton University, where he teaches business ethics and directs the Princeton Faith and Work Initiative.

For the Millers, everything seemed to stop on December 12, 1996, when a series of seemingly unrelated symptoms Karen had been experiencing, including debilitating vertigo, was diagnosed as multiple sclerosis. From that day onward, dealing with MS became her new job. "I don't know why, at age thirty-nine, I was diagnosed with multiple sclerosis," she said, "forcing me to change my life from that of a highly functioning law professor to a person with physical and cognitive limits and challenges. MS is not a curse. MS is not a blessing. MS is not my fault. MS is nothing that anyone could have caused or prevented, and MS is not an excuse. Perhaps, most importantly, MS is not the end of my ability to live and love. But MS is hard, interrupting and altering life. I do not know how people without faith can handle MS. Faith enters into my life as a disabled person in many ways, some not dissimilar to that of pre-MS life. It helps as a source of comfort, decision making, understanding, and hope."

Some people with MS find the loss of physical capabilities to be the most challenging and frustrating. For Karen, it is the loss of cognitive functioning. "I used to be smart," she said. "When I try to barter with God about my MS, I offer walking in exchange for memory. When I get sad, angry, depressed, or frustrated with MS, it is usually about my 'cognitives.' When I want my pre-MS self back, it is my intelligence I long for."

One of the things that changed for the couple was church attendance. They had always been regular churchgoers, but with MS it became difficult for Karen. She found the frequent standing and sitting, the communal reading and singing, holding books, and even sitting still to be taxing, physically and cognitively. Being part of worship was easier for her in some churches than in others, because of varying degrees of understanding by parishioners and clergy. Being a disability-friendly church, she said, goes beyond having access ramps.

"We try to balance our accommodating to the church and asking the church to become accommodating to disability," Karen said. Some churches have made visible efforts toward inclusion, such as adding asterisks in the bulletin to points in the service at which people may stand or not, "as they are able." "We have had some people tell us they are relieved when not all stand, as it gives them 'permission' to stay seated."

At church, as in other social situations, well-meaning people often look at her and say to each other, or to her, "I would never know you had MS, you look so good." Sometimes a visible disability can be easier for others to accept or understand than an unseen one. On one hand, such a comment is flattering, because Karen and others work hard to function and have no desire to draw attention to themselves. On the other hand, such remarks can be frustrating to hear, because the person offering the compliment may have no idea how hard it is simply to perform everyday tasks—sitting up, brushing teeth, getting dressed—much less to attend church.

"Many times, despite good intentions and efforts when we wake up on Sunday morning," Karen said of herself and David, "we are unable to attend a service 'live,' but do so instead by listening to taped sermons, watching webcasts or televised services, and playing DVDs of pastors such as John Stott and Rob Bell. Though we miss being part of a physical community, this has been a growth experience where we are forced to worship in new ways, hearing from people we might not otherwise be exposed or open to. I sometimes laugh out loud that a Presbyterian Yankee in her PJs is worshiping at home in bed watching a Southern Baptist revivalist."

Even church accommodations can have missteps and pitfalls. Once, the Millers' Presbyterian church—a progressive congregation known for being welcoming and inclusive—decided to add healing oil to the Communion service, which is not usual for a mainline Protestant denomination. Presbyterians form committees and discuss things carefully, attempting to do all things "decently and in order." Karen recalled that countless meetings took place about whether and how to add healing oil to the service, and what the reasons were. "At the first service where the healing oil was to be offered, after the pastor offered a lengthy description of the ancient church's long practice of healing, the issues of illness of all sorts, and the decision to add the oil to the service, the minister invited all to come forward for Communion. And if one also wanted a healing prayer and oil, we were instructed to come forward, and after receiving Communion, to go to the side for a deacon to administer oil to one's forehead."

"The glitch was I could not go forward," she said. "My legs had gotten stiff from sitting and I couldn't get up. We were seated near the back of the church. As I sat helplessly watching row after row go forward and receive Communion and the healing touch I so desperately wanted, I felt alone. I knew my husband, David, who is ordained, would bring me Communion bread and wine, which he lovingly did. It was my sister Lisa who, without my asking or sharing my desire for the oil, came back to our pew and without a word rubbed her forehead against mine. That and our mingled tears were healing."

Karen Miller has had a considerable effect in helping others with MS. "Karen is an exceptionally intelligent, altruistic, caring woman," said William A. Sheremata, author of *100 Questions and Answers about Multiple Sclerosis* and an internationally renowned MS neurologist and researcher. He asked Karen to write the "patient perspective" portion of the book, answering thirty questions on the basis of her and her husband's experiences. Normally a private person, Karen found writing about her experiences as an MS patient "very vulnerable and emotionally difficult." "With the help of her family," Sheremata said, "she has accepted her diagnosis and adjusted her life in response to the limitations of MS, interrupting her flourishing and gifted legal career to focus on MS."

Karen and David are a formidable team, drawing on both their talents. Together they helped lead a grassroots effort to return Karen's MS drug to the market after it had been withdrawn because of concerns about side effects. David rallied friends from churches and synagogues around the country to petition the U.S. Food and Drug Administration. He wrote countless e-mails and letters and made calls to every official, chief executive officer, and board member he knew to pressure, cajole, reason with, and persuade them to return this highly efficacious drug to the market and let informed patients and their physicians decide the future of their well-being. Karen has a favorite line from a letter her husband wrote to one pharmaceutical CEO as part of the campaign. David ended the letter with the sentence, "I will not give up. I love my wife too much."

Theologically, David seeks to understand how health and illness fit together in God's created order. While some might ask, "Why my wife?" David asks, "Why not me?" He ponders and looks for God's presence in pain and suffering. Inside their wedding bands, Karen and David each have inscribed the characters "1C26." The bands were too small to take the full inscription: 1 Corinthians 13:13 NIV—"And now these three remain: faith, hope, and love. But the greatest of these is love."

50

The Gospel in Action

Stephanie Hubach

In 1992 Stephanie Hubach's life changed when the pediatrician announced, after the birth of her youngest son, "We believe Timothy has a chromosomal abnormality"—Down syndrome. "As an economics instructor at the college level, my passion was for academia, and now I had a newborn son who had an intellectual disability," Hubach recalled. "What did that say about him? And about me? Timmy's entrance into my life caused me to reevaluate my yardstick of human value."

In 2006 Hubach chronicled and distilled her experiences in her book *Same Lake, Different Boat: Coming Alongside People Touched by Disability*, from which—along with several magazine articles she has written—this account is drawn. The idea behind the book and her subsequent articles and interviews is that "as human beings, we're essentially the same but experientially different. So identifying with each other is a choice—a choice that can have tremendous blessings."

Hubach and her husband, Fred, were not entirely unprepared for what their lives would be like after their pediatrician's words. Before Timmy's birth the couple had been closely involved with friends whose two sons had both been born with disabling conditions. Yet Timmy's arrival opened their eyes to a whole new dimension of life with a disability, which they entered with the help of Stephanie's faith community, Reformed Presbyterian Church (PCA) of Ephrata, Pennsylvania.

"Suddenly," Stephanie told *byFaith* magazine in 2007, "we were personally immersed in the 'disability world'—including all the caseworkers, specialists, therapists, and hospitalizations that go along with that. As I became increasingly involved in parent groups and disability advocacy organizations, I saw firsthand the depth and breadth of the challenges facing families affected by disability: spiritually, emotionally, physically, relationally, psychologically, and financially. In amazement, I realized that a significant number of them were 'going it alone'—in many cases unsupported by family or friends—and the vast majority were unchurched.

"I began to ask myself, *Where in the world is the Church?* Having experienced firsthand the blessings of a supportive church when Timmy was born, I knew that the Church has just what families touched by disability need—the restorative power of the gospel for their lives in word and deed. As we grew in wonder of and appreciation for Timmy as a person, I also realized that families with a disabled family member have just what the Church needs—the precious image of God packaged in incredibly diverse ways that can benefit the entire body of Christ. But in order to experience this blessing, the Church has to choose to enter, with intentionality, into the lives of individuals and families touched by disability."

Hubach's church learned from and grew with her family and others. For example, over time the congregation became accustomed to the quiet, methodical hissing of Ben Zell's ventilator in the sanctuary on Sunday mornings. The boy had been diagnosed with an inoperable brain tumor at the age of four, and seven years later, during what was expected to be "routine" brain surgery, he suffered a stroke, resulting in significant paralysis and dependency on a ventilator. Until Ben's death at thirteen, members of the congregation walked side by side with his family. With his passing, Hubach recalled, "the silence was deafening." Still, "Ben left a legacy of faith and a congregation changed forever by what we had seen and experienced as a covenant family."

Hubach continued: "While Ben's experiences were perhaps the most dramatic among us, he was not alone as an individual with disabilities in our midst. Over the years, God has captured our church's attention on disability through numerous covenant children and adult members who have special needs. They have been a precious gift. How have we responded to this gift? What have our relationships with these individuals and their families taught us?"

Some of the answers to Hubach's questions have come directly from people with disabilities, such as Ben Zell. Another "teacher" in Hubach's church has been Jon McFarland, an adult member of the congregation who was born with spina bifida, uses a wheelchair, and requires assistance for many activities of daily living. In the midst of his challenges, McFarland has cultivated a positive attitude and a warm sense of humor. His faith and patience, Hubach wrote, enable him to outshine many of his "able-bodied" peers in many ways. "I just focus on living one day at a time, taking each day for what it brings," McFarland explained at a Sanctity of Human Life service at Reformed Presbyterian Church. "And God will just lead me through. Whatever I face, I'll face with him."

What is instructive is that McFarland was able to attend Hubach's church only after the congregation completed a building program making the entire facility handicapped accessible. As often happens, some grumbling arose over the additional expenses required for an elevator, a mechanical lift, and a twenty-one-foot ramp to the pulpit area. Yet in retrospect, Senior Pastor Tom Nicholas recalled, "We had to repent when, on Sanctity of Human Life Sunday, Jon McFarland was wheeled up that ramp and led us in our call to worship from Isaiah 61. Without knowing it, we had set a captive free" and opened "avenues of grace." As Nicholas put it, "Disability ministry is not a nice thing we do. It is the gospel in action."

The church's mission statement says, "Reformed Presbyterian Church exists to be a stream of God's refreshing grace for people from all walks of life." Members understand that "all walks of life" includes people with differing abilities. "Genuinely inclusive relationships are inherently respectful relationships," Hubach said.

Reformed Presbyterian formalized its commitment to respond to people with disabilities by developing 'Covenant Care Groups' for families. Each group is defined as "a covenantal relationship between a family in exceptionally difficult circumstances and a small group of church members who commit to assisting the family in the meeting of legitimate needs." Their purpose is to mobilize the congregation to provide emotional, physical, and spiritual support. Over the years, the church has started Covenant Care Groups for more than ten families. The focus of the groups, Hubach explained, is not on programs but on relationships. Wherever programs are put in place, they are intentionally designed as vehicles to facilitate relationships. Through Reformed Presbyterian's Special Needs Ministry, the congregation fosters a deeper commitment to these "respect-based relationships."

The first recipients of Covenant Care Group assistance, Patty and Roger Coiner, became leaders of this ministry. In 1988, their first son, Douglas, was born with multiple, significant medical issues. When Douglas was twenty-two months old—still on oxygen and tube-fed—the couple's second son was diagnosed in utero with even more complex medical challenges.

"Samuel Roger Coiner was born November 24, 1990," Patty recounted. "Everyone from our Covenant Care Group was at the hospital with us. My husband and I were in considerable emotional pain and grief when our son lay dying in our arms. I can still feel his head lying softly snuggled against my shoulder as Roger and I lay in the two hospital beds that our Covenant Care Group had lovingly pulled together so we could share Samuel's last breaths. He died twelve hours later. No miracle occurred in Samuel's physical body that night, but a miracle did take place in the form of God's grace, faithfulness, and almighty wisdom enveloping us."

"Covenant Care Groups become the hands of Jesus, touching the lives of those in our congregation who find themselves in extreme circumstances," said Hubach.

In 2000, forty-four-year-old church member Tom Heisey was diagnosed with Pick's disease, a form of dementia. Heisey, a devoted husband and father of four children, had been a leader of the congregation and the community, a deacon, and vice president of the local bank. Tom's wife, Pam, described Pick's disease as "characterized by all those things we most dread: It's incurable, untreatable, terminal, and causes dementia." After Heisey's diagnosis, members of the congregation met with Tom, Pam, and representatives of the local Alzheimer's Association chapter.

"Hi," Heisey said to them. "I'm Tom. I'm still Tom." Even as Pick's disease was diminishing his gentle, intelligent personality, Hubach observed, Tom instinctively knew that those characteristics that give him value and identity could never be taken away. Throughout his illness, eight men from the church faithfully rotated through a visitation schedule at the nursing home where Tom was being cared for. The men's goal was to "honor what's left instead of what's lost." Although Tom could no longer speak to them, their visits spoke volumes to him, Hubach said. Tom passed away in February 2010, at fifty-three.

In Hubach's congregation, the adults with intellectual disabilities are often the ones who patiently extend grace to everyone else, she said. "It is noticeable, because they find it necessary to keep re-teaching us the same things." Keith Laudermilch is one of these tolerant persons. "Keith, an adult member of Reformed Presbyterian with Down syndrome, is a man with a mission—one that he executes with determination and grace," Hubach wrote. "One evening the session, the governing body of the church, was meeting in a glassed-in room in our church narthex. Keith saw [the elders] through the windows and walked right into the middle of the meeting. Looking each elder in the eye, Keith asked them his favorite question: 'Do you love Jesus?' After hearing their replies in the affirmative, Keith reminded them, 'Jesus is coming again.' Then he left.

Reflecting on the incident, Pastor Nicholas remarked, 'Now, you can look at that as an interruption, or you can look at that as prophecy. God sent him to the elders of our church just to give us a check. He comes in and says the most profound thing that could ever enter into a session meeting: 'Do you love Jesus? Is he the center of your life? Do you have the hope of his coming again?'" Our adults with developmental disabilities at Reformed Presbyterian Church regularly remind us how to reflect the life of Jesus, full of grace and truth."

Another of the adult members with developmental disabilities, Kandi Shultz, has found many opportunities for service to the congregation, from assisting in the kitchen and stuffing envelopes in the office to raising money for worthwhile causes and helping with youth activities. Every Wednesday night Schulz finds a ride to Reformed Presbyterian and watches the children in the nursery. "If there are extra events, she wants to come and help," said Sharon Fasnacht, leader of the children's ministry. "She has such a special heart for the kids in the nursery. She holds them, feeds them, rocks them, plays with them—just loves being a mother to them." Through Shultz, Hubach said, "we are learning to value the Spirit at work in her life, for the common good."

Hubach believes congregations need to take several steps to become as supportive as her own, beginning by identifying with people with disabilities. "Identification starts by simply acknowledging the reality of disability in our world. In Western culture, we've been pretty effective at attempting to sanitize our lives of any association with difficulty or discomfort. If we're honest, we don't like to deal with people who have disabilities, because it reminds us of our own vulnerabilities.

"We need to enter into people's lives—with or without a disability—from a posture of respect. Even as Christians, we often operate more from positions of power and control than we're willing to admit. We like to see ourselves as the strong ones who minister to others in their weaknesses. But Christlike, respectful relationships are built on two pillars: grace and the image of God. Grace levels the playing field. In grace, we identify with the shared difficulty and brokenness in each other's lives—regardless of how that manifests itself. On the basis of the image of God, we identify with the shared value of every life as a life worthy of celebration—regardless of how that life is 'packaged.'"

Sometimes, said Hubach, showing equal concern for one another means "rolling up our sleeves and learning how to care for a child with autism, or spina bifida, or cerebral palsy, so that their parents can enjoy an uninterrupted worship experience. Sometimes adapting means that we all learn to accept 'distractions' in the Sunday morning service so that a person with developmental disabilities can do what all of us were created to do: to worship God in spirit and in truth."

Hubach emphasizes that expanding one's comfort zone with regard to disability is an ongoing process. As her congregation's former associate pastor once stated, "I think I always had compassion and respect for people with disabilities, but I didn't know how to feel comfortable around them—especially people with intellectual disabilities. Exposure and ministry opportunities have changed this for me. I have learned that we are all unique individuals and therefore uniquely different. But we are all more alike than different."

51

A Mother's Letter

Amy Julia Becker

Two major life experiences have shaped the faith and writing of Amy Julia Becker, a graduate of Princeton Theological Seminary who lives in Lawrenceville, New Jersey. She cared for her mother-in-law as she battled cancer, and she welcomed into the world her daughter Penny, who was diagnosed at birth with Down syndrome. These experiences expanded and enriched Becker's understanding of what it means to be human and to receive each and every person as a gift. Becker has written two books, *Penelope Ayers: A Memoir* and *A Good and Perfect Gift: Faith, Expectations, and a Little Girl Named Penny.*

As a protective parent, Becker understands that even among caring, believing people, intervention is sometimes necessary to ease the way for children with disabilities. In a letter written to a Sunday school teacher at Penny's nondenominational church, Amy Julia introduced herself and her three-year-old daughter, anticipating that the teacher might have questions or concerns about teaching a child with Down syndrome. Amy Julia wanted to begin the conversation "in hopes that Penny's presence in your class will be a blessing to her and to the other three-year-olds as well.

"You may remember when Penny was born, as many people in the church were praying for us. It was December 30th, 2005. The doctors told us Penny had Down syndrome a few hours after her birth. I spoke with our pastor the next day. He cried with me on the phone. There was so much fear—*Was there anything wrong with her heart? Would her little body (she was only five pounds) be able to stay warm? Would she be able to nurse?* But just two days later she was home, healthy and putting on weight. Those immediate fears had been addressed.

"It took longer to overcome our grief. Grief for the child we thought we deserved. Grief for an image of ourselves and our family that had been shattered. It was an ugly grief. It brought up all my insecurities, the value I wrongly placed upon ability and intelligence, the value I wrongly placed upon conventional beauty.

"I'm thankful to say that the grief seems to be over. In fact, I sometimes look back and can't understand that sadness, sadness so thick and strong I thought it would pull me out to sea and drown me. Now, I don't see Down syndrome anymore when I look at her. I see Penny. Cute, mischievous, funny, with those big green eyes and pudgy cheeks. I think of her saying, 'Watch this move, Mom,' and striking a pose. Or looking sternly at her younger brother when he is trying to take a toy from her, and then, in her best imitation of a teacher at school: 'Please stop, William.' I no longer have fears about her future that keep me up at night. I no longer have reason to cry. In fact, I go to sleep most days with reason to celebrate.

"I tell you these things because I think it is hard, upon first meeting Penny, to recognize who she is as an individual. It was hard for me. It was as if Penny's character had been stamped with red capital letters that said, 'DOWN SYNDROME.' I couldn't read the writing underneath, because I was so distracted by the stamp. But now, as I read those words, I find I am eternally grateful for what they say.

"I'm sorry if all this background information is unnecessary. There are plenty of people within our congregation who have embraced Penny, and celebrated her life, without preamble. When she was in the hospital last year, dozens of people called to tell us they were praying. And we are grateful that our church has a history of including people with disabilities.

"But Penny's participation in Sunday school hasn't always been easy. In a general sense, the Sunday school hour is difficult for families of children with disabilities. Part of the trouble is that it only happens once a week. And the teachers are volunteers, many of whom have no training in special education. For instance, when Penny was in the one-year-old class, she used sign language to communicate. By the time she was two, Penny knew over one hundred signs. But for all her teachers knew, her communication was limited to a handful of words. I'm not sure there was a solution to the problem. I didn't expect her teachers to learn sign language, and yet I longed for some way to overcome that communication gap.

"Or, there was the miscommunication that happened when Penny was invited to move from the nursery into the one-year-old class. I was told she would enter with an aide. As far as I could tell, Penny had been singled out, not on the basis of her behavior or abilities, but on the assumption that she wouldn't be able to handle class without one-on-one assistance. I envisioned Penny, forever aided by an adult. Not interacting with peers. Not having to abide by the same rules. Seen by the teachers, and the other kids, and their parents, as different. I told the director of children's ministries that I would rather Penny not have an aide, unless her teacher requested it.

"There was one day when her teacher said, 'Penny paid attention just like the other children during the lesson today!'

"I probably shouldn't even admit what went through my head. I wanted to say, 'Really? At home, she just sits in the corner and drools.'

"Of course, one thing these stories demonstrate is my own defensiveness. I later learned that the director wanted Penny to have an aide because she felt she had failed families in the past by not providing a similar resource. I later saw Penny's teacher as a gentle, kind, loving woman who, yes, had prejudged Penny's intelligence, but who also wanted the best for Penny and wanted to encourage me as a mother. I suppose I need to remember that we are all in this together. Just as God is teaching me, God is teaching the Sunday school teachers, other children, parents, the whole community of faith.

"That's the thing about having a child with a disability. Penny serves as a magnifying glass. Flaws in my own character, flaws in the world around me, become bigger than they were before, more obvious. Because of Penny, I have been forced to recognize the way

I rank and judge people based on external attributes rather than their intrinsic value as humans created in the image of God. I suspect something similar is true within the church. Having children with disabilities in our Sunday school classes forces us to address the question of what we believe about humanity and community.

"When Penny was first born, someone referenced a story from Mark's Gospel: Jesus sat down, called the twelve disciples, and said to them, 'Whoever wants to be first must be last of all and servant of all.' Then he took a little child and put it among them, and taking it in his arms, he said to them, 'Whoever welcomes one such child in my name welcomes me, and whoever welcomes me welcomes not me but the one who sent me' (Mark 9:35–37 NRSV). It's easy to say we want to welcome all children, and yet children like Penny—whether they are children with Down syndrome or autism or an undiagnosed condition—are sometimes harder to welcome. How do we welcome the child who has tantrums? the child who has trouble understanding the lesson? the child who just can't sit still? And yet I believe that if we can figure out how to welcome all, we will figure out what it means to invite Jesus into our classrooms, into our relationships.

"From your years of service, I have every reason to believe that you care deeply about welcoming every child who walks through your door. My hope is that together we can find ways to make it easier to welcome the children with disabilities. I've talked with the director about some practical ways to address these issues. You may be planning to attend the upcoming Sunday School teachers' workshop, which will offer a session on caring for children with special needs. We've also talked about finding a member of the congregation with special needs training and asking her to serve as a liaison between teacher and parent.

"Finally, it can be so frenetic on a Sunday morning, especially in the midst of the happy chatter of toddlers, and I imagine it must be hard when we all deposit our children at your doorstep and rush off to worship. The director and I spoke about the possibility of a Sunday school open house, in which lines of communication between parents and teachers can be established, where teachers might have a little more time to hear about the kids in their classes, and where we as parents might get a better sense of how we can encourage our children to learn and grow in faith.

"Penny came home from Sunday school last year singing, 'My God is so big!' with emphatic hand motions. What a gift it has been to our whole family for her to begin to participate in the life of the church. Now, she reminds us to bless the food at dinner-time. She initiates prayer for other people. She asks to read the Bible. She has started to love Jesus. I know she will be blessed by being in your class. My hope, however, is that she will not only be blessed, but that she will also be a blessing. That's my hope for all of us. That we might recognize each other as individuals who are needy and who nonetheless have something to offer. That we all might give, and that we all might receive."

It is difficult to imagine anyone charged with instructing young children, religious or secular, who would not be moved and well guided in teaching a student with a disability after reading such a letter.

52

Invited In

Fran Jarratt

Like most latecomers to Sunday morning worship at St. Andrew Presbyterian Church in Albuquerque, New Mexico, Fran Jarratt and her brother Rob were welcomed by an usher and given a bulletin, a hymnal open to the right page, a hello, and a smile. They stayed for the service but declined to come into the sanctuary, preferring to stay in the back, behind the glass window looking in from the church's narthex.

"I was apprehensive that we really wouldn't be welcomed, both because we were late—and because of Rob," Fran said. At the age of three her brother had suffered serious brain damage following a reaction to a vaccine, and he later developed diabetes. As an adult, he walked with an ungainly gait, was sometimes difficult to understand, and had some problems with impulse control.

The brother and sister had been turned away from three other area churches, but this time—on the recommendation of another of Rob's sisters, a professor at the University of New Mexico—they made the right choice. In the 1950s St. Andrew wrote into its charter that part of its mission was to serve people then known as "the handicapped." In more recent times the congregation established a ministry called "Comfort ye, my people," for people with long-term mental illnesses.

"When Fran brought her brother Rob to worship, we were happy that St. Andrew Presbyterian Church provides easy access to folks with physical challenges," said the congregation's senior pastor, Frank Yates. "Our church is all one level, and there are no steps anywhere in the facility. Other folks had come to St. Andrew for the same reason—easy access."

During the "passing of the peace"—an embrace or handshake signifying the unity of all Christians—at that first service, the church's director of family life, Deborah Huggins; its pastor, Frank Yates; and some ten other worshipers approached the siblings, welcomed them again, and invited them to come into the sanctuary. Fran explained that it was difficult for Rob to worship in the sanctuary because of his behavioral disability, and she was concerned that he might be disruptive. Rob sometimes became agitated with all the sensory input, and he would vocalize his anxiety. "I wasn't sure how the congregation would react to his singing," recalled Jarratt, "because he sang with his whole heart, and recited the prayers with great fervor."

The members assured the newcomers that there would be no problem, and Fran's initial reaction was positive. People shook Rob's hand and didn't speak over or through him. "The people were very friendly, and we were invited to come back," Jarrett said. "They invited us to stay for fellowship after the service," the first time that had ever happened.

Over time, Fran shared her family's story with the congregation. She is the oldest of six children, and her parents were Presbyterian missionaries, stationed much of the time in central Africa. Rob, the youngest child, developed seizures while the family was living in what was then the Belgian Congo. At first he could neither walk nor talk, but during a recuperative stay in rural Arkansas, Rob's devoted mother found a school for him to attend, and he learned to speak and walk, although he was sometimes unsteady on his feet. The boy was welcomed in the local country church, which provided much comfort. Later, back at the family's African mission, Rob became close to a caretaker, who nurtured in the boy a love of gardening, which became a lifelong passion.

Because Fran remained uncertain about how her brother would be received at St. Andrew, the siblings worshiped on the other side of the glass for weeks. "Rob wanted to go right on in, but I wasn't sure how it would be if we crossed over." Then, gradually, other members of the congregation began to join them in the narthex for the service, which they could watch through the window and hear over a loudspeaker. "Fran and Rob didn't want to 'bother the congregation,'" said Yates, but "slowly they began to feel more comfortable as people welcomed them and showed that we were genuinely glad they were worshiping with us."

One Sunday Fran felt comfortable enough to bring Rob to the back row of the sanctuary for worship. "Great step, I thought to myself," said Yates. "Then they moved halfway down the row of pews. Finally, grace upon grace, Rob wanted to sit in the front row. What a day it was when Fran and Rob moved to the front and announced with their action, 'We feel love and accepted.'"

The move was a good one. "The front proved to be easier for Rob to manage," said Deborah Huggins, whose ministry includes people with disabilities, "since he sometimes used a wheelchair, and so he worshiped with us in the front row after that."

Rob was a man of deep faith, and he loved to participate in worship services, robustly singing the old hymns, reciting the Apostles' Creed and the Doxology, and saying the Lord's Prayer— the older, King James Version he had learned from his parents. Reverend Yates took Rob's contribution to the worship service in stride.

"From the front row Rob would blow me kisses every time I got to the pulpit to deliver my sermons," said Yates. "What better way to know you are loved and appreciated by a church member than to have them blow kisses your way as you begin to preach? What a blessing!" During one Sunday sermon the minister quoted a verse listing animals, and Rob piped up, "You left out the donkey!" Without missing a beat, Yates said, "Thank you, Rob. 'And the donkey.'"

When Rob was admitted to formal membership at St. Andrew, he answered appropriately, saying, "I love Jesus, and I want to work for the church." At other churches Rob had made the same request to help and participate in some way, to no avail. This time, he was asked to help maintain the landscaping at the children's play area, which he did during the week, with great enthusiasm.

Rob had other jobs at the church. On Sunday mornings he handed out bulletins, standing when he could, sitting in his wheelchair when he couldn't. "He had a beautiful smile," Fran Jarratt recalled, "and with every bulletin he gave a big smile." The first

Christmas Eve after Rob and Fran joined the church, they were asked to light an Advent candle. "His eyes just shone," Jarrett recalled. "He was so happy."

Being at St. Andrew added incredibly to the quality of Rob's life, his sister said. "It was like taking a plant that was barely alive, but not flourishing. It was as if he was revived by living waters, because he flourished. He made friends. During fellowship, I would go to get him coffee, and he would always be engaged in conversation with someone in the congregation. Rob had a great sense of humor. Sometimes his speech was hard to understand, but people made an effort to understand him."

Rob died in 2008, just two years after joining the church. More than one hundred congregation members and friends attended a memorial service for him in St. Andrew's sanctuary. "It would be difficult to describe the overwhelming grief our congregation shared with Fran and her family when Rob died," Reverend Yates recalled. "As the worship leader at the memorial service, I could barely get through the sermon. I try very hard to keep my composure during memorial services. It was very, very hard to do so given that it was Rob who had won our hearts and touched us at a very deep point in our spirits. To come from the back, beyond the glass, to the front row and the depths of our hearts—what a journey for Rob, and what a blessed journey for us.

"One can hardly describe the deep and lasting impression Rob made upon our congregation. We absolutely loved him. He was full of smiles and fun and genuine joy. He loved coming to church and we loved having him. What we never envisioned was the impact Rob would make on us as a congregation." As one member of the congregation told Fran, "Whenever Rob came on with his bright smile, we were reminded that in God's love, *everybody* is *somebody*."

53

Completing the Community

Karen Jackson

Karen Jackson's daughter, Samantha, was diagnosed with autism at the age of three, and despite Karen's initial grief, she fiercely embraced her daughter. "God had a plan," she wrote a few years later. "He has turned my grief into joy." Still, it took a while to find the right faith home for the whole family.

When Samantha was ten, mother and daughter embarked on religious education at Blessed Sacrament Catholic Church in Norfolk, Virginia. Although Samantha, like her two brothers, had already been baptized, regular religious education classes and other activities in the parish community were difficult for her, because of her challenging, autism-associated behavior. Karen and her husband took turns going to Mass and caring for Samantha, so their attendance became inconsistent, and the family found it impossible to worship together.

Over time, however, Karen's involvement with Samantha at Blessed Sacrament—which Karen came to see as a new adventure—grew beyond providing an inclusive setting in which Samantha could participate in classes with her peers. It also increased the mother's awareness of issues of disability at the church. She began community outreach in the form of a prayer and support group for people with disabilities, one small step toward addressing the larger issue that faces all faith communities.

Karen, now director of the Faith Inclusion Network of Hampton Roads, Virginia, defines that issue by asking, "How do we not only make people with disabilities welcome in our faith communities but also encourage them to be active participants in the life of the parish? How do we recognize that we are not a whole, complete community of faithful Christians without including and accepting everyone?"

Awareness of what is unseen can be critical, Karen believes. For example, there may be reasons why no people with disabilities are visible in a congregation: Without welcoming signs or invitations, families may keep members with disabilities at home. It took the Jackson family nearly eight years to find a church that fully accepted all of them, including Samantha.

"The barriers that exist for people with disabilities, especially developmental disabilities like autism, can be insurmountable without help and support," said Karen. "Lack of child care, disapproving looks, and uneducated parishioners are just some of the barriers that hinder participation."

One spring morning when Samantha was twelve, she and Karen were attending Mass together. As was their custom, the pair sat in the area just outside the sanctuary doors, mostly because Samantha has difficulty staying still for very long, and she makes vocalizations that might be disturbing to others inside the quiet sanctuary. Around Karen and Samantha were many young parents with babies or toddlers. Although Samantha can be unsettled by crying babies, she did her best to ignore them that morning and follow along with the service.

Then it came time to go into the sanctuary to receive Communion. In many larger Catholic churches like Blessed Sacrament, ushers organize Communion with near-military precision. Samantha, however, wanted to get into the sanctuary immediately and "see Father Joe," the priest. She kept jumping up out of her seat, wanting to hurry things along. Finally, without waiting for everyone already in the sanctuary to get through the lines, mother and daughter sneaked in as the ushers were just halfway through the worshipers. Samantha kept trying to jump ahead in line, too, but Karen held her back, keeping her in her place.

When the pair finally navigated to the Communion rail at the front of the church, Samantha reached out for the Eucharist and put it in her mouth. Then she reached out again. Father Joe and Karen smiled as Karen gently restrained her from taking one or two more pieces of the Eucharist.

As mother and daughter walked quietly out of the sanctuary, back to their seats, Karen reflected on what she had just experienced with Samantha. With few learned social filters in place, Samantha had demonstrated an eagerness to receive Jesus. For her part, Karen had to admit that this eagerness was often missing in her own experience at church. Some might say that Samantha just doesn't like to wait in lines—which she doesn't—and that explains why she was eager to get through the Communion line. But Karen believes it was more than that. Her daughter was not trying to hurry and be done with church, nor was she trying to leave the building. Samantha was in a hurry to receive the body of Christ. She had an "I can't wait" attitude, an impatience to receive the Bread of Life.

"It's often thought that people with autism have difficulty understanding the abstract, like God and religion, but I believe otherwise," said Karen. "Despite having to overcome the many sensory-related difficulties of attending Mass, my daughter comes to God's table in eagerness, anxious to receive Jesus. Her excitement to receive the Sacrament of Holy Communion reveals a level of spirituality that inspires and humbles me. She can't wait to take Communion. Shouldn't all of us who call ourselves Catholic feel the same?"

Samantha often surprises her parents and brothers. For about ten years, the family has recited a simple blessing around the dinner table: "God is great, God is good, let us thank him for our food. Amen." The idea was that as the children grew, each could independently lead the grace. After a while, Samantha started to say individual words of the prayer, but rarely more than one or two at a time, and rarely in a conversational context.

Like many children along the autism spectrum, Samantha, if she hears something enough, will begin to repeat it. So when she began to clearly pronounce "A . . . men," her family was thrilled. Other words followed, until she could pronounce most of the prayer and sometimes lead it at the table. Still, Karen wasn't certain her daughter understood what she was saying. It seemed that after years of repetition, she had learned the simple mealtime blessing by rote.

Then, on a Saturday morning, Karen looked in on Samantha, who had been suffering from a severe cold for a week. As she often did, Karen leaned down next to her daughter's bed to say good morning and give her a hug. Out of nowhere, Samantha returned a huge smile and said simply, "God is great." Karen waited a moment, expecting to hear the rest of the prayer by rote. Even though she had never heard Samantha say the dinner blessing anywhere but at the table, Karen would normally have expected her daughter to finish the prayer once she started.

"What did you say?" Karen asked, just to make sure she had heard her correctly. Once more Samantha stated emphatically, "God is great," adding another winning smile. Amazed, Karen hugged her again and left the room to get on with the morning chores. But her thoughts kept returning to Samantha's statement. Karen had been feeling a little sorry for herself the previous week—a child with special needs, sleepless nights because of the child's cold, and the never-ending work of taking care of all the kids at home for the holiday break were wearing her down. She wondered, as she had many times before, how a mom with a child with autism kept going.

And then, Karen said, she got that wonderful little moment from God, a few well-chosen words from her daughter, who spoke so seldom. She had to agree: God *is* great. And Karen realized once again that she was blessed to be a part of her daughter's world, and blessed to be reminded of some of the simplest lessons.

"God is great and God is good," Karen said. "And I thank God for the many blessings in my life—especially for the one wrapped up in the special package of my beautiful daughter, Samantha."

Ultimately, Karen's experience with Samantha at Blessed Sacrament inspired her to found the Faith Inclusion Network, a coalition of faith communities and service providers working toward the inclusion in faith communities of people with disabilities.

On Samantha's thirteenth birthday, Karen wrote her daughter a letter, thanking her for the ways she had enriched her mother's life: "You have taught me to accept people with differences, to see past their physical or developmental challenges and get to know them.

"You have taught me to truly rely on my faith because in your challenges, as well as mine, I have learned to rely on God, giving him the glory and praise always.

"You have taught me how to trust, even when a situation is scary, because God will always be there for us, and he will not let us suffer needlessly.

"You have taught me to be grateful, not taking the 'normal' things of life for granted but appreciating the little miracles; the accomplishment of small but significant goals, your sense of humor, your hugs and kisses."

That same year, Karen and Samantha attended Ash Wednesday Vigil Mass, where they would receive the ashes in the Catholic tradition. As Karen recounted in a newsletter article, Samantha hadn't done this before, and Karen was unsure of how the girl—who, like many other people with autism, is slightly averse to being touched—would handle having the ashes applied to her forehead. Karen whispered her anxiety about this to a friend, a faithful volunteer to the disability ministry at the church, who happened to be sitting near her. In an act of community and support, the woman assured her that they should give it a try, offering to accompany them down the aisle and demonstrating to Samantha how the rite was performed.

After Samantha and her mother successfully made it through the "ashes" part of the Mass, they returned to their seats. But Karen's relief was short lived as she realized that Samantha, having already been down the Communion aisle, thought it was time to leave. Karen reassured her that although the predictable schedule of Mass had been changed, they still hadn't received Communion. Samantha happily sat back down and seemed to be enjoying herself—at a comfort level her nearly nonverbal daughter rarely feels anywhere except at home.

After the Ash Wednesday Mass, Jackson wrote, the two went to the social hall to participate in the church's traditional Mardi

Gras celebration, complete with a live Dixieland band. Karen had hoped but not expected that Samantha would want to stay. Nonetheless, the girl settled right in to listen to the music, and her mother slowly started to relax. As Samantha began rocking excitedly back and forth to the beat of the music, Karen looked around to see how others perceived her. In another concrete example of acceptance, what she saw were the understanding eyes of people sharing her daughter's enjoyment of the music.

The following day, Jackson had the rare opportunity of a quiet, overnight retreat and reflected on the whole experience. As she shared with the retreat directors her joy in Samantha's ability to participate in the activities of her faith community, Jackson realized how important and precious the opportunity of community really is to everyone.

"Being involved and accepted as part of a chosen faith community should not be a privilege of those who fit the norm of society," she wrote. "It should be a priority of every faith community, small or large, young or old, Christian, Jewish, Muslim, or any other faith, to make a way for all people, including those with disabilities and their families, to be involved and accepted.

"I believe that my daughter and I are not just the recipients of the many blessings a faith community can provide, but also contribute to the life of our diverse parish. Samantha provides not only a ministry of presence that often affects all those around her, but also a pureness of faith and love with her participation in the activities of our faith community. As I begin to understand the important role a faith community can play in a family's life, I hope you will embrace the mission of the Faith Inclusion Network. Reach out and include those who have experienced physical barriers or barriers of communication and attitude because of their perceived "dis-Abilities.""

54

The Right to Kindness and Charity

Laila

As a woman, an African American, and a Muslim, Laila knows about the dimensions of discrimination. She also knows about disability. She is the mother of a young boy with low-functioning autism, the daughter of a woman with crippling multiple sclerosis, and the sister and niece of two men with schizophrenia.

Laila is also a social scientist who studies social stratification, and she has an academic and professional background in social research, teaching, and direct services. But all the professionalism and all the degrees in the world, she said, never prepared her for the experience of navigating her faith within her religious tradition. Her Muslim faith has been a source of strength for her as a mother, daughter, and caregiver, but it has also raised some trying and frustrating challenges.

"I've always been aware of differentiation, and as an African American Muslim woman reared in working poor and underclass neighborhoods, it's never been lost on me that these differences are not simply about diversity," she said, "but also about social status, access to resources, and the experience of discrimination. Along with social stratification, culture informs the response to a diagnosis. Also, culture directs approaches to treatment and the relationship that the disabled and their loved ones have to society."

For example, doctors treating Laila's mother when she was in her early fifties were first convinced that she had arthritis, despite her symptoms: She fell repeatedly, without explanation, and she had three-day spells of debilitating immobility. She was finally diagnosed with rapid-onset multiple sclerosis, which progressed from an irritating limp to the full-fledged use of a walker. Laila's mother joined a support group, but her deteriorating condition kept Laila, who lived several states away, up at night. Members of her mother's Baptist congregation became a vital part of her support system, offering rides and running errands.

Still, Laila's Muslim faith spoke to her, especially when the MS forced her mother to give up her job as a department store sales associate and go on disability support. Although Laila was then a newly married graduate student, she recalled the verses from the Koran mandating that children should look after their aged parents. "I wanted to be the one she could count on to care for her," Laila said. So for a year, that is what she did. She moved her mother into her home and assumed the care of daily living, with the help of a home aide while she was at work. But eventually, her mother's rapidly deteriorating physical ability made placing her in a nursing home a medical and safety necessity.

The decision was difficult, for both cultural and religious reasons. In African American culture, Laila pointed out, it has traditionally been taboo to place relatives in nursing homes, and research demonstrates that historically, African Americans have done so at lower rates than whites. Although every religion shares scriptural admonitions to support parents, Laila said that "among Muslims, there has not been a contemporary movement to examine these texts in modern context." Few scholars of the faith are able to justify anyone but family members acting as caregivers.

"As a Muslim, I was convinced I would go to hell!" she said. "We cannot abandon our parents. Allah would not forgive me if I did not take care of my mother. There is nothing nobler than this. Caring for my mother is my path to heaven. As the only family member taking care of my mother, I had to wonder, and still do, Does God take the circumstances into consideration, or are these mere excuses for avoiding God's command?"

Yet when Laila's mother became completely dependent on her wheelchair and developed mild mental health issues, requiring therapy and more constant nursing care than could be provided in their home, Laila felt she had no other choice. She couldn't manage. "I resolved that I could not care for Mama at home, but I could still honor my mother by being present and attending to her needs while she resided in the nursing home. I knew that if I did my best to care for her, Allah would give me guidance toward a better way. And then the baby came."

At the age of two, Laila's son, Ahmed, was diagnosed with severe autism, and again, she said, "my faith compelled me to accept that this was part of God's plan. That part for me was easy. The daily act of living in his will has been my challenge." Ahmed had low cognitive ability, lack of verbal language and toileting skills, and extreme hyperactivity owing to a combination of sensory deregulation and chronic gastrointestinal problems. For Laila and her husband, it was difficult enough to endure the frustration of being unable to make their sick child well, but on top of that, the response from their religious community was mixed. "While most of our Muslim family, friends, and fellow congregants are supportive of us and accepting of our son," she said, "there are plenty of family and community members there to remind us that we had to have been 'bad,' or someone 'cursed' us, for this great misfortune to be visited upon us. . . . Belief in the evil eye is prevalent among the various cultures that make up Muslims."

Once, Laila's Muslim mother-in-law asked if she had prayed for her son. "I could feel my face turning red hot, my hands shaking, and my voice trembling," Laila recalled. "After my defensive 'Yes!' my mother-in-law interjected, 'Every night, you cannot miss one night!' The powerlessness I felt from my mother-in-law's allegation and interrogation was suddenly overcome by my response: 'He does not have autism because you think I'm a bad Muslim.'"

Laila continued: "I now understand that my mother-in-law's visceral response was due to her profound love for her grandson. Her devastation over his condition required that there be an explanation for his autism. If this misfortune could be explained by the belief that I did not pray correctly or that Allah did not answer my prayers because my Arabic was shabby, then she could take comfort in his disease being my fault—an anomaly that could be corrected."

"Many religious interpretations, cultures, and personal beliefs," Laila explained, "hold onto the hope that everything would be perfect if people would just become perfect. No one wants to believe that it's really out of our control. Trials are for spiritual purification, and the Koran states that no one can attest that they are believers without that faith being tried. But God does not curse people with diseases because they or their loved ones are 'bad.' Islamic liturgy doesn't refer to disabilities in this way."

On the other hand, Laila pointed out, the Koran "doesn't say very much about people with disabilities, either. What Islam does teach is that all people, Muslim or not, the high of status and the least among us, have the right to kindness and charity. The Muslim is obligated to care for others, whether that is physical assistance or a smile. Allah will make us account for each deed and the way we treated others. Muslims of all abilities worship and participate in the community; it is cultural beliefs, and not the religion, that excludes them. God will judge each of us according to our intentions and character."

"There's an arrogant folly," Laila said, "that leads us to believe that people with disabilities are the misfortunate or cursed. Perhaps we are misfortunate, obsessed about that which we have no control over and ignoring the blessings in those differently abled individuals in our lives. I know that my son and daughter are tremendous blessings. Islam teaches that there are countless blessings in the care of others, especially for children, parents, and those in need.

"But my son is also making me better in ways I never expected. This experience teaches me not to worry about how others perceive me, but God alone. I'm learning that the best-made plans may have to wait for another day or be put away altogether, and that's okay, because God is running the show anyway. I am learning humility, and how to let others help even when foolish pride gets in the way, because after all, why should I keep all the blessing to myself? I have learned that life is happening now, and everything counts, so get in the game. And with his amazing smile and infectious sense of humor, considered untypical of people with autism, my son has taught me that life is full of miracles. You just have to pay attention."

55

Links of Love

Courtney Smith

Even with her training as a registered nurse, Courtney Smith recalls that she felt overwhelmed when two of her sons were diagnosed with autism, while another of her four biological children (she and her husband have adopted two more) was found to have a learning and attention deficit disorder. Like many other parents of children with disabilities, Smith soon made herself an expert on the subject, and she focused how her faith could help. She founded the Links of Love Disability Ministry in Lansdale, Pennsylvania, and became a frequent conference speaker on topics such as "The Divine Power of Friendship."

"If I hadn't been affected by the disability, through my boys, I probably would have gone on in the same routine that many Christians do," Smith acknowledged. When her sons were diagnosed with forms of autism, it was almost too much for her. "I cried countless nights," she recalled. "Cried out of frustration, cried out of mourning for the son I originally envisioned, cried to God because I was sure he had left me." The family's finances took such a hit that their home was on the brink of foreclosure.

As he grew older, Smith's son Andrew was subject to behavior meltdowns, some lasting three hours or more. When these episodes took place in public, they would draw disapproving stares from onlookers, who saw only an otherwise normal-looking boy who appeared to be acting out. The Smiths' family situation took a toll on the couple, as such circumstances often do. "I was sure God had left me, and my already shaky marriage was dragged over rocks," Smith wrote in the *Journal of Religion, Disability, and Health*. Together with her husband, Paul, she now runs a marital support group through Links of Love, mentoring other couples affected by disability.

"My husband and I had tough times," Smith told Brian Bingaman, of the *Journal Register News* of Norristown, Pennsylvania. "It's not just the person with the disability; there's a whole family behind them." Faith is essential, she told the reporter. "In the Bible, it talks about how God will use struggles and suffering for good. It's all about how he takes those trials in life, and how it refines us. . . . We will get through this, bear each other's burdens and come together, like Christ asked us to do. I always say to people: 'We don't know everything, but if you come to us, and you have a need, we will try our best.'"

"God had me on my knees," Smith wrote in the *Journal of Religion, Disability, and Health.* "For quite some time I struggled with feeling like God owed me a break, owed me an answer. But gradually, there was a transition. God would poke tiny holes of light here and there and soon enough those little glimpses of light became my focus."

That focus grew out of a life-changing event that happened in 2007, when Smith and her family attended a summer camp sponsored by the group Joni and Friends, founded by the inspirational author Joni Eareckson Tada, which serves as an outreach resource to evangelical and nondenominational congregations. It was the first time someone had truly reached out to Smith's family—and it came not a moment too soon.

"We were in a time of major crisis with Andrew," Smith recalled. "Joni and Friends reached out to us, welcomed us, and loved us, and it changed our lives forever."

From the time the Smiths' car pulled into Spruce Lake Retreat in eastern Pennsylvania, "it felt like we entered heaven's gate and finally fell into the arms of acceptance. Acceptance for our outcast family, acceptance to call what looks like a curse to the rest of the world a blessing. I learned what God's arms feel like when the body of Christ embraces you as you are."

Smith almost wept when a member of the staff asked through the car window whether the family wanted a loud or a quiet greeting. "We answered, 'Quiet greeting please, for Andrew's sake.'" The family was accustomed to dirty looks, Smith said, but the volunteers welcomed them gently, waving bright and colorful signs.

Even more rewarding experiences unfolded as the week wore on. A camp volunteer noticed that Andrew was a gifted artist. On the Wednesday night designated for a talent show, Andrew was encouraged to share his art, and to his family's disbelief, he did. He talked about the characters in his sketches as his notebook was passed around. After the show, campers and volunteers came over to praise him.

Later that year Andrew was asked to share his work again, this time at a local Christian school's talent show affiliated with Joni and Friends. Once more he did, this time drawing some pictures of his favorite characters. Back at his own school, he was twice named his grade's artist of the year. Since then his artwork has been auctioned to raise money and awareness for autism groups in the Philadelphia area, as well as for Andrew's favorite Joni and Friends program, to show his appreciation for their support. But more than anything, Smith said, recognition of his talent has given her son a sense of worth and accomplishment.

Buoyed by the camp experience and what followed, Smith spent the next two years praying, reading books, and making contacts. She surveyed the needs of people with disabilities in her area and the services available at nearby churches. She was shocked to discover how great the need was and how few resources were available. Combining her personal experiences as a parent, her medical expertise, and her faith—and with the support of her pastor—in 2008 Smith founded Links of Love Disability Ministry, a local ministry for people with a spectrum of physical, psychiatric, and intellectual disabilities, including dementia, blindness, and hearing impairment, as well as for their families, friends, and caregivers.

Smith chose the word *links* for the organization's name to emphasize interdependence and mutuality. It refers only in part to the way a member of the congregation provides a one-on-one connection for someone with a disability, from behavioral coaching to driving the person to church. Service and altruism are fine, she told a reporter, but at the same time, people with disabilities "might want to serve us or have a gift. They might need someone to bridge the gap so that they can. We want them to be a participating member as much as anyone in the congregation." Each link has two sides, and Smith insists that "the families we work with bless us far more than we bless them."

One of the first people involved when Links of Love Disability Ministry was launched was Sara Hansen. Hansen had worked as a nurse and a public policy specialist until advancing multiple sclerosis brought her medical career to a halt. Instead of being a caregiver, she became a patient and a client. The financial hardship of trying to maintain her health and raise her child on disability income added to her stress. Survival was her primary concern, and she felt uncertain about how God meant to use her now. At times she felt useless.

When she joined Links of Love, Hansen became engaged on both sides of the link, receiving help from the programs and also helping to advocate for others. On others' behalf, she put to good use her considerable knowledge of how to navigate insurance, Social Security, and other services available to people with disabilities.

Later, at a Links of Love meeting that included Hansen's pastor, the Reverend J. R. Damiani, Hansen shared her feelings about her MS-related loss of mobility, fatigue, and partial deafness, as well as her loss of financial independence. The pastor suggested that the congregation's women's ministry needed a new leader, and Hansen might be the person for the job. Damiani had been praying for a while about this, and at the meeting, he said, he felt the Lord tell him that Sara was that person.

At first, Hansen was reluctant, uncertain whether she was up to it. "I still walk, but not real well," she told a reporter for the *Montgomery Advertiser.* "Obviously with my disability, I felt people wouldn't see me as someone who could contribute in a church setting." But she was accepted, and she found the ministry fulfilling, becoming a spokesperson in the congregation's Special Needs/Special Gifts ministry, a component of Links of Love's ministry in which the gifts of those with disabilities are shared and celebrated.

Because of Hansen's lack of mobility, other women in the congregation gathered around her, sometimes becoming her ears. Together with Marjorie Terry, another volunteer with MS, she performed a skit called "What's Your Problem?" when Courtney Smith preached a message called "Breaking Barriers Together."

When Hansen ministers, Smith said, "there is really something that speaks to others when they are doubting what God can do. Then they see someone whose body barely functions, yet who has gone from surviving to thriving."

Another example of the way Links of Love brings people together began when Smith, in her capacity as a nurse, was caring for a woman being treated in the hospital for cardiac arrhythmia. During the assessment interview, Smith asked about the patient's stress level. The woman told her that her teenage daughter had Asperger syndrome, and she, the mother, was feeling extremely frustrated.

"My heart went out to this single mom," Smith recalled, "a Christian woman who dedicated a majority of her time to home-schooling and working with her daughter. From the sound of it, she just needed someone to come alongside her, to help bear her burden and provide some direction. Although we're often taught as nurses not to share too much personal information with our patients, the look on her face reminded me of the time when I was in a very similar place."

Their long conversation that night bonded the two women, and Smith was not surprised when the woman called her several months later to see if Links of Love could help her daughter, who was experiencing difficulty in social situations, fit in as part of a congregation. The woman wanted her daughter to try to come to church again and to become involved in an inclusive youth program.

"Creating a relationship is the number one factor in making this work," Smith told her, "so let's start by getting to know each other. That way when she comes to church she will recognize at least a few faces with whom she is comfortable. It won't feel like a sea of strangers in a land of sensory overload."

Smith invited the mother and daughter to her home for a meal. To make the young woman feel comfortable, Smith prepared some of the teenager's favorite foods and laid out open books on subjects she was interested in. Through Links of Love, the young woman's mother learned much more about Asperger syndrome, and communication between mother and daughter improved dramatically.

Before long the teenager began attending Wednesday evening youth group. "She works through her social anxiety and discomfort because of her dedication and love for God," Smith said. Several months later she was sitting in the front pew as Smith preached her trademark sermon, "Breaking Barriers Together." Six months later the young woman was heavily involved as a volunteer in Links of Love's art show, "What God Does with Broken Things."

The young woman has begun writing stories and sharing them with Smith. "Her writings give me a glimpse into her mind that she cannot express through conversation," Smith said. "The detail and depth of her biblical understanding found in her stories ministers to me. We are working up to her sharing her stories with the world."

In the summer of 2010 Smith also began assisting Peaceful Living, in Harleysville, Pennsylvania. Links of Love helped that organization with its congregational coaching and community education related to disability and ministry. Today, Smith's ministry includes a prayer team, a marital support group, and a resource center that helps direct people to disability-related resources in the community. These include materials and devices such as large-print Bibles and audio amplifiers; the matching of one-to-one companions for Sunday school; the identification of roles, including teaching and leadership, for persons with disabilities in worship and Sunday school; and gifts designed to recognize and celebrate those with disabilities.

56

Experiencing a L'Arche Community

Caroline McGraw

Some faith communities, such as L'Arche, are designed from the beginning to enable people with and without intellectual and developmental disabilities to share their lives. Founded in France in 1964 by Jean Vanier, son of Canada's governor general, L'Arche has grown into an international organization present in forty countries. L'Arche homes are faith communities in which people with and without intellectual disabilities choose to live together and serve one another.

In some ways, L'Arche homes operate like many other group homes, using Medicaid moneys to fund care of adults with disabilities. L'Arche's mission, however, goes beyond direct care work. As its charter states, "In a divided world, L'Arche wants to be a sign of hope." The community is committed to developing each member's spirituality, regardless of religious affiliation. Its best-known advocate was Henri Nouwen, a Dutch-born Catholic priest who joined the L'Arche community of Daybreak, outside Toronto, in 1986 and wrote extensively about the experience.

After graduating from Vassar College in 2007, Caroline McGraw joined L'Arche Washington, D.C., as a live-in, direct-care assistant, accompanying residents to church and facilitating their participation in events such as community prayer night. Later she became program director for the L'Arche community in Arlington, Virginia. For her, the experience opened "an entirely new world, one I felt compelled to write about."

In the memoir McGraw is writing, she says that growing up, she felt slightly jealous of her friends who seemed to have passions that motivated their lives, whether it was ending world hunger, saving the whales, or teaching children. All these causes mattered to her, but none resonated with the core of her being, either breaking her heart or driving her forward to act. And then she realized that the heartbreaking injustice that would shape her life involved her own family. Her brother, who had a mild developmental disability, was at times treated insensitively—though not unkindly—at their local high school.

"My brother's exclusion riles me," she wrote. "It strikes me, hard, and I want to fight back. And my deepest need? I need to believe that my brother belongs with our family. I need to love my brother instead of fearing him. I'm still waiting for this to be true. And my deepest joy comes when my family is together in the truest sense of the word."

At a youth conference, McGraw heard a speaker quote Frederick Buechner, a theologian unfamiliar to her, who defined vocation as "where your deep gladness meets the world's deep need." Thinking about that propelled her to interview with L'Arche in Washington. Working there as an assistant, her task was to accompany the core members—those with disabilities—in the house during their regular routines. This accompaniment involved a good deal of one-on-one time and a great deal of responsibility. Among the stories McGraw shared with me from her work-in-progress memoir were some that illustrate what a transformational experience working at L'Arche could be for a well-meaning but initially inexperienced caregiver.

One Sunday morning, McGraw planned to take one of the residents, a man of Cuban heritage named Walton, who had severe physical and intellectual disabilities, to Mass at Sacred Heart Catholic Church in Washington. Although late for the service, Walton was having a hard time deciding what shirt to wear. The first one McGraw suggested, a navy blue cotton polo shirt, left him tugging the collar away from his neck as if it were choking him. She began pulling other shirts from the closet, but each time Walton replied, in Spanish, "Otro, otro!"—another, another.

At last she found a shirt acceptable to him, a pale blue one with a button-down collar and sailboats embroidered on it. "It wouldn't have been maddening if we'd not been running late," McGraw recalled. "I extricated myself from Walton's closet and said, 'Walton, sometimes you are such a diva!' This was the first time I'd said anything critical to him. He looked back at me with sweet bewilderment, as if to say, 'What? I only want to wear my sailboat shirt,' and suddenly I heard how ridiculous I sounded, how silly it all was. Walton giggled. We arrived at Mass ten minutes late, missing the prelude but arriving just in time for the Gloria.

"Walton loves to go to Mass. I love taking him, so perhaps my perspective is prejudiced. But he does seem to 'purr' a lot, shaking as many hands as possible when we pass the peace. He doesn't stand up, sing, or receive—he just sits in the worn, dark-wood pew, his hands rifling through pen after pen. He touches the pens over and over with the same sort of reverent concentration as an aged parishioner at prayer. The pens are like rosary beads in his hands. We're uncertain whether or not Walton prays. Yet he always anticipates the collection. He turns toward me, anxious as the baskets swish closer.

"Every week, I pull the bill from the ID wallet around his neck (I tuck it there each Sunday before we leave) and hand it to him. Walton takes it and stretches out his arm, distancing the dollar as far from his body as he can. He holds his right arm steady for as long as it takes the basket to arrive. He drops the bill slowly, not because he hates to let go but because he wants to be sure he puts the money in the right place."

In a similar vein, Walton's brother Johnny, who also has an intellectual disability, has a passionate commitment to the Catholic Church. Virginia, sister of the two men, wrote about Johnny's self-directed conversion to Catholicism after he moved from her house to L'Arche, and the motivation behind that conversion:

"Johnny started volunteering at Catholic Charities, where he met Sister Manuela from Spain and Father Sean O'Malley, who later became Cardinal O'Malley," Virginia said. "Johnny loved them because of the way they treated him, and soon he asked me if he could go to their church and worship with them. One day Father Sean called me and told me that Johnny had expressed an interest in becoming a Catholic. It was Johnny's decision as an adult, not mine. Father Sean confirmed Johnny, and Sister Manuela was his godmother. I think he wanted to go to the Catholic church because of the way the Mass is conducted, which does not make anyone feel left out, nor does it allow for impediments or handicaps to get in the way of participation. Plus the Masses were conducted in Spanish, and there were so many Latinos he could talk to in the congregation."

Evening meals are special at all L'Arche houses. Following dinner, assistants and core members pray together. Sometimes everyone simply prays as he or she feels led, and sometimes those present respond to a question, their thoughtful responses constituting a prayer. One night at the Washington L'Arche home, McGraw recounted, assistant Matt Rhodes took out a copy of *Seeds of Hope: A Henri Nouwen Reader*, a collection of writings by the man many consider to be the L'Arche movement's patron saint. Rhodes read a passage from the book with his customary, graceful deliberation. Then he asked, "What does it mean to be human?" The question hung over the table, McGraw said, "shimmering into my consciousness the way candlelight shines across glass." A fair question to ask anyone, she said, "but how is any of us equipped to answer? What would I hear, and what should I say?"

One core member, Debora, said, "I think to be human is to have a baby. To hold a baby in your arms and then help that child to grow up. To have a family." Later, an assistant named Mary expressed to McGraw her ovservation about how sad Debora's voice had sounded. "Indeed, Debora's words ached with the need to nurture," McGraw wrote. "I thought fleetingly of what a mother she would have made, if her life had been different."

When it was McGraw's turn to respond to Rhodes's question, she said that "to be truly human is to share in Christ's life; in particular, to share in his cross. The cross is both the symbol of greatest defeat and greatest victory, the greatest pain and the greatest hope. It's like L'Arche: We exist because of humanity's brokenness, but we also exist because of God's love. I mentioned how my family's cross takes the form of my brother's instability. That pain is what we would never have chosen to bear, but it is what God has transformed into grace."

Johnny responded to the question in the form of a prayer to the God "who created all of us," saying that to be human was to be created by God. "I liked that," McGraw recalled—"how for Johnny, the essence of humanity was our created-ness. We are God's handiwork—a fitting definition for a man who works so hard."

Rhodes repeated his question for a core member named Michael: "What does being human mean for you?" McGraw appreciated the way Rhodes posed the question, gently, "like a father tossing a slow underarm pitch to this usually sullen son." This night Michael wasn't sullen. Instead, he was composed, considering the question, furrowing his brow, deep in thought. "To be humble," he said. The phrase was spoken so softly, almost in a mumble, that others around the table almost missed it. McGraw could see the others considering it, translating it, turning it over in their minds. "Then we all got it," she said. "Everyone breathed in, out, amazed."

Rhodes probed further, asking Michael what humility looks like for him: "What does it mean for you to be humble?" McGraw wondered to herself whether humility might be just a word for Michael or if it had resonance in his life. When Rhodes repeated the question, Michael replied that although he wasn't certain, "I think it helps . . . to not be afraid of your faults."

Hearing this, McGraw had to sit back. "The force of Michael's truth pushed against me. No one had ever taken the veil from my mind to show me what it is to live outside of fear. To be humble and not to be afraid of your faults; rather, to be held by God's love. It was all I could do not to cry, not to jump up and hug Michael. Instead, I sat watching candlelight reflecting in his glasses. I counted seven candles on the table, seven small lights in his eyes."

57

Overcoming Awkwardness

Nancy Guthrie

The Guthrie family of Nashville, Tennessee, faced two great, heart-breaking trials at the turn of the twenty-first century and endured both with remarkable grace. Their daughter, Hope, and later their son, Gabriel, were both born with a rare metabolic disorder called Zellweger syndrome, which meant their lives were difficult and short—each lasting less than a year. Nancy Guthrie, a publicist and writer, and her husband, David, a music publisher, chronicled their experiences in a series of moving, knowing books: *Hearing Jesus Speak into Your Sorrow, The One Year Book of Hope,* and *Holding on to Hope.* Their story has also been told in publications from *USA Today* to *Time.* Most of this chapter is based on Nancy Guthrie's book *When Your Family's Lost a Loved One.*

"Some people tell us they can't imagine going through what we've been through," she wrote. "But when we look around at the losses others experience, ours often feel small and insignificant in comparison.

"We were blessed during Hope's life with people to talk to—including many from our church, who brought us meals. They were often surprised when we'd invite them to bring enough food to have dinner with us. We had incredibly precious visits during those days, with good friends as well as people we had not known well before. Meaningless conversations were rare. Instead, we talked about life and death and prayer and faith and eternity. It was a rich time, and we enjoyed engaging with people who cared enough to overcome the awkwardness to enter into our lives. Going through a life-altering experience gives us a unique opportunity to bond with those we may barely have known before. Conversations that go below the surface can become the foundation for new and deeper friendships."

But not all the Guthries' experiences were positive and uplifting, although they ultimately led to a deeper understanding of human nature—and the value of forgiveness. Nancy wrote:

"The reality is that when you go through something like this, while some people draw close, others disappear. They can't overcome the awkwardness or deal with the inconvenience. I think about a friend of mine who has a Down syndrome child. The truth is, it is harder for them to be at events, to participate in family activities, because her son has to be accommodated, and sometimes in congregations and social settings, those families slowly get left out. Moms who have a child who can't keep up and is not progressing feel great pain as they watch other children progress, and this can cause them to withdraw, become resentful, and create awkwardness with other families.

"People in a congregation are generally good to ask about what's going on in a medical situation that is working its way toward healing. But they hardly know what to say when it is a situation that is not going to get better. If you're getting medical reports that are at least sometimes positive, then you stay engaged and you keep asking. But when it is always the case that things are not getting better, and may be getting worse, it becomes easier to just stop asking.

"I realized along the way, however, that people do their best, and that if I focused only on their failure to say the right thing or do the right thing, I would become alienated from people and full of resentment. David and I have a theory about this. We've decided that when people hear about difficulty in your life, their brains search like computers for a connection. Because they don't know what else to say, and in an effort to fill the awkward silence, they tend to blurt out the first 'search result' that comes up: 'I knew a family who had this happen . . .'

"It makes people feel better to suggest a resource, a solution, a book—to tell you about someone who overcame the obstacle you face. But it doesn't always make us feel better, does it?

"While I seemed to keep tabs on who had reached out to us and who hadn't in our experience with our daughter, Hope, the second time we went through losing a child, in our experience with Gabe, I was free from the tyranny of expecting so much from so many. I was free from the tiresome task of keeping a scorecard on everyone around me, taking note of who'd made an effort in our direction.

"I've come to realize that much of what we label as uncaring is simply an inability to overcome the awkwardness and fear of doing or saying the wrong thing. The reason some people have never said anything to you about the death of the one you love or the diagnosis you've received is that they simply don't know how to overcome the awkwardness. It doesn't mean they don't hurt with you or that they don't care. They just don't know what to say, and they fear that bringing it up will only bring you pain. They don't know how much you long to hear some words of compassion—even if all they can say is, 'I don't know what to say.'

"You can choose to be angry and resentful about that, building up a barrier in your relationship. Or you can choose to give people grace, accepting their inability to know the right thing to say or do.

"During Hope's life and in the months after she died, I often found myself churning inside. It seemed some of the people we thought would be there beside us in the midst of this trial had disappeared. At the lowest point of our lives, they chose not to enter in. They seemed to diminish our loss by ignoring it. I was angry. But of course the anger was really a manifestation of hurt.

"After repeatedly waking up in the middle of the night and rehearsing my put-you-in-your-place, here's-how-you-hurt-me confrontations, I wanted things to change. I knew resentment was beginning to take root in me; I wanted to be free of it, to let it go. To do that, I knew I had to choose to release those who'd hurt me from the debt I felt they owed me. I knew I had to humbly ask the Lord to give me the spiritual strength to forgive them.

"Taking it one step farther, I had to start seeing my resentment as the real issue in my life—the sin I was responsible for. It was my resentment that was robbing me of joy, not what they had done or not done, said or not said.

"I know you may be saying, 'Don't even think about suggesting that I forgive the person who hurt me.' You're sure he or she doesn't deserve it. The person probably hasn't even acknowledged what he or she did to hurt you. To forgive seems like saying that what happened doesn't really matter.

"I understand. I've been there—or, I should say, I find myself there repeatedly, because no one goes through life without being hurt by other people. Sin takes its toll on all of us and our relationships. When we're already rubbed raw by the pain of loss, so many things and people rub us the wrong way, causing more pain.

"But forgiveness isn't minimizing what someone has done, or saying that it didn't matter. Real forgiveness is far more costly. It says, 'You hurt me deeply, but I'm not going to make you pay. You don't owe me anymore—not even an apology.' Forgiveness is choosing to absorb the pain and canceling the debt you are rightfully owed.

"It is a choice. You can choose not to forgive. You can continue to play the waiting game with the person who hurt you—waiting for him or her to apologize, to make things right. If you do, you'll be allowing that person to hold you hostage. By saying, 'If she apologizes . . .' 'When he finally acknowledges . . .' 'If they remember . . .' you depend on others to make the first move. And an unforgiving spirit weaves its way into the fabric of your entire life. Or, you can choose to forgive. You can choose to abandon the agonizing animosity."

58

Traveling Together

Monica and Mark Masiko

Siblings Mark and Monica Masiko have been on a long journey together, spiritually and geographically, a journey that has been both trying and rewarding. They grew up in a lower middle-class family in the suburbs of Camden, New Jersey. Mark was born with a cognitive disability, and their mother said that Mark did not walk until Monica came along, three years after her brother, and began to walk herself. As children, the two were as close as siblings could be, doing just about everything together. Monica often questioned why her brother was the way he was, but even as a child she understood that God had intentionally placed Mark with the family and that he was to be treasured as a gift.

"I don't always view him this way," she said. "We are siblings with a pretty normal sibling relationship. Sometimes he gets on my nerves, and sometimes I get on his. And I may call myself his caretaker, but he is also my caretaker. I have come to understand life differently as a result. My theology and vision for the church are shaped by the fact that Mark is my brother."

Monica left home in 1983 to attend college and later traveled around the country, working at various jobs, until 2001, when she moved from Texas to Idaho to become Mark's caregiver. Mark lived in the family home in New Jersey with their mother until he decided to follow his girlfriend, who was moving to Idaho with her mother. This decision was difficult for Mark's mother, but Mark was adamant. Monica helped allay her mother's fears, advocating for Mark's independence. Monica agreed to help get Mark back East if the "experiment" did not go well. Soon after Mark moved to Idaho, the family received reports from his day treatment providers that Mark was being abused by the girlfriend. Monica moved to Idaho, intending to move Mark back to New Jersey within a few months. Mark, however, was still adamant that he did not want to move back to his mother's home. He agreed to allow Monica to live with him and help care for him.

The move to Idaho turned out to be good for Monica, both professionally and spiritually. The two stayed there for ten years, attending several churches. "I absolutely gauge a church by its responsiveness and inclusiveness to Mark," she said. Her brother has "a very strong desire to know for himself what God has to say, through the Bible." Every morning he does independent study with a devotional Bible. With a little help, he can read most of the words on his own. Yet interestingly, said Monica, he is otherwise functionally illiterate—he can read nothing else, "not even instructions on a microwave meal."

For three years of their time in Idaho, the brother and sister attended a small, independent, Pentecostal church. "In close social settings, it is more obvious that Mark has a disability, or that he is different," said Monica. "He will talk at inappropriate times, doesn't clap with the beat, and makes confusing comments because he does not have the capacity to understand much of what is being taught. But the rewards of being patient and bearing with him have great dividends. I think he has much to add to any church, to any group. I just enjoy his presence and his positive outlook, and he is very friendly, loving, kind, and helpful." At this church, however, Monica caught the pastor speaking harshly to Mark, stifling his comments, and in general showing a lack of appreciation for him. After praying, she decided to try a different congregation.

The two next tried a Methodist church, where they were received with kindness and friendship. With Monica's encouragement and advocacy—although little was required—Mark helped the pastor's wife as a teacher's aide in Sunday school. After a year, Monica began to sense God's call to ministry and met with the pastor. But doctrinal differences with the Methodist pastor— having nothing to do with Mark—drew her to an Assemblies of God church. Monica gave Mark the choice of remaining at the

Methodist church, but several months later he decided to join his sister.

At the new church, too, Mark was made welcome, and he joined its Royal Rangers program, similar to Boy Scouts, as a junior commander. He was also active in the men's ministry program and attended weekly coffees and yearly retreats. Mark's welcome extended beyond the church and the pastor to the denomination's district superintendent, which was a source of joy to Monica. "It makes me happy when other people see how special Mark is, how much he has to give, and to see it lovingly received," she said.

In Idaho, Monica worked in the mental health field, often with people who were dually diagnosed with mental retardation and mental illness, and she volunteered with the Special Olympics. Her personal theology was shaped by her experience not only with Mark but also with many other people with intellectual disabilities. "I feel very strongly about inclusion of persons with disabilities in the church and the community," she said. "The church and the community are better places when we include all the people God has created. I believe that everyone has a voice, everyone has a gift."

Monica began taking online seminary courses through a distance education program and looking into Ph.D. programs. She came across a paper by Amos Yong, of Regent University in Virginia, on disabilities and the church. "I was amazed with the theology and how it resonated with my own thoughts," she said. Even though it required a move across the country, she applied to Regent's Master of Divinity program. Naturally, the move would include Mark, and it would bring the siblings much closer to "home" and their family in New Jersey. "We had some good conversations with our pastor that helped Mark understand God's call on my life and made sure he understood that this would require him to make some changes, some sacrifices. He agreed to go on this adventure with me. He saw this as reciprocal for the time I had spent in Idaho with him."

The trip across country was stressful, entailing a great deal of change for Mark to handle, but they made it. In Virginia, Mark got settled in with social and support services. The siblings visited several Assemblies of God churches and decided to join Glad Tidings Assembly of God in Norfolk. Their first time there, they sat behind a woman who introduced herself and, looking at Mark and understanding that he had a disability, declared, "We *need* him here!" Monica usually needs to advocate for inclusion of her brother. "I never expected to hear someone say they understand that the church needs people with disabilities," she said. Mark is a Royal Ranger commander again, and he volunteers, cleaning with the janitor one morning a week. He is excited that this church has asked him to be a full commander instead of a junior commander, which means a great deal to him.

As Monica works toward her Master of Divinity degree, her research for term papers revolves around a vision of the church as fully inclusive of all persons, especially persons with disabilities. She feels called to pursue a Ph.D. and to write and teach in academic settings, much like Professor Yong. It is her desire to teach this vision to others, especially future pastors, believing that it is a crucial element for the effective work of the church in the world.

59

Practicing What You Preach

Tom and Irene Powell

As a career academic and a conscientious "cradle Catholic," born and raised in the faith, Tom Powell believes there should be no difference between what you study and teach and the way you live your life—that is, between what you preach and what you practice. Powell was a pre-med student at a college in Fairbanks, Alaska, when he decided to switch to special education. "Why special ed?" he asks. "I always wanted to teach, and I began working with adults with significant disabilities when we lived in Alaska. It changed my perspective about how I could best serve others. It may sound strange, but I felt as if I was being called to spend my life working with and learning from people with disabilities."

So Tom and his wife, Irene, who met in Catholic school as teenagers on Long Island, where both their families were active in parish life, moved to Montana State University in Billings. Tom concentrated on teacher education, family intervention, and research into social interaction between children with disabilities and their siblings. While in Billings in the early 1970s, he helped start a community program to provide support and education for people with disabilities and their families.

Through this program, Tom and Irene met a six-year-old boy named Nick who had severe autism—the latest of three generations in his family with developmental disabilities. When it became apparent that Nick's court-ordered assignment to the program would not provide him with enough support, the couple took him into their home. "He needed us," Irene said. "We knew we could make a difference for this child. We started out as simply his foster parents, but when we needed to move from Montana, no way was the relationship going to end."

As Tom earned his Ph.D. at Vanderbilt University and began climbing the academic ladder at colleges around the country, first at the University of Connecticut, Nick became an integral part of the Powell family. Tom and Irene then legally adopted him, and over the years their family grew, with two biological children, Tom Henry and Cate. Later it grew again to include Stedman, a teenager with Down syndrome who lived with them for seven years. Family life, for Nick and all the children, included religious life.

"When Nick arrived in our lives, Irene and I insisted that he would always be a full member of our family, doing what families do," Tom said. "And for the most part, he did. Except when it came to church and our Catholic faith. Of course he was baptized and came with us to Mass. But when it came to religious instruction, we made few demands. He knew pictures of Jesus and Mary and something about the Christmas story, but nothing beyond that.

"It was never really about his salvation. My own faith in God and the teachings of the Catholic Church would never allow me to believe that God would not welcome Nick home when he died. No, I never needed to worry about his salvation. Nick's religious education and his participation in Mass were always more about family, acceptance, and community."

Tom found his thinking about Nick's aptitude for religious education challenged while the family was living in Storrs, Connecticut. One Sunday, Father Kevin Munn, associate pastor of St. Thomas Aquinas Parish, approached Tom after Mass to ask about preparing Nick for the Sacraments of Holy Communion and Reconciliation. Tom was shocked. "Father Kevin, you know Nick!" he said. "He'll never understand. He'll be too much trouble. He'll disturb the other kids." The priest just smiled and said he'd still like for Nick to participate. This was a new experience: Nick was being invited to be with the other children, and Munn wasn't concerned about his behavior, assuring Tom that his son would do just fine. "Father Kevin knew more than I about God's grace and the power of that grace present in the sacraments," Tom said.

So at the age of ten, Nick began to attend religious instruction. His parents were understandably nervous, expecting to be called about some behavioral crisis and believing that "special" arrangements would have to be made for him. But no call came. Like all the parents of children preparing for their first Communion, Irene and Tom were expected to participate in family sessions, which they found empowering. Being with young parents of typically developing children was both instructive and fun. Nick actually participated with the other children. Although he developed no friendships as a result, the other kids were kind and understanding of his disability, and the other parents were welcoming. Nick's teacher said she looked forward to seeing him every week. This was noticeably better than Tom and Irene's experience in special schools and special classrooms. This was the real thing.

Nick made his first confession to Munn, which Tom imagined was a memorable experience for both of them. The following Sunday, dressed in a new suit and a lovely stole that Irene made for him, Nick joined thirty other children and made his first Communion. He was happy; his parents smiled with pride and cried with joy. That memory has stayed vivid in Tom's mind. Maybe this was the way things should be for the rest of Nick's life. From that experience Tom began to question how he was parenting Nick and how he was working to build a world in which Nick was present and part of the community.

The day's memory remains vivid in Nick's mind as well. Typical of some people with autism, Nick can recall the exact date, what the weather was like, and the details of the day, especially the party that followed to celebrate this milestone in his life. For many of the ensuing years, Nick continued to attend Mass and receive Communion with his family, and there was joy in their pew. "We were a family going to church, and Nick was participating as best as he could," Tom said.

Unfortunately, as Nick's autism became more pronounced, his desire to attend Mass diminished. It was too much for him. The crowd, the noise, and the rituals were too painful. His temper tantrums in church were also too much for the Powell family and,

Tom and Irene imagined, for others in the congregation. The parents so wanted Nick just to tell them what bothered him, so that they could make adjustments, but he couldn't do so.

Tom and Irene accepted the situation as it was and stopped demanding that Nick come to Mass with them. Although their other children never said so, Tom believes they were somewhat relieved that they no longer had to endure another scene and screaming in church. Nick was happier on Sunday mornings, and, in a way, so were Tom and Irene.

Father Munn's invitation to Nick, Tom believes, was really an invitation to Tom and Irene to open themselves to the power of inclusion and grace. Because of the priest's example of acceptance, Tom said, he and Irene as parents "became more committed to giving Nick every opportunity to be with typically developing children and, later, teenagers. The last time I felt as moved as I did when Nick made his first Communion was when he graduated from high school as a part of his regular graduating class. His group senior photo still hangs in his home, and Nick can you tell you many of the names of the few hundred students who graduated with him. Thanks, Father Kevin. Your invitation was Nick's first and perhaps most significant venture in the world. Your invitation was a reminder that Jesus's message was about love and inclusion of all people."

When Nick was eighteen, the Powell family returned to Billings when Tom became a professor of education and dean at his alma mater. Five years later, when Tom was named dean at Winthrop University in Rock Hill, South Carolina, the family decided that Nick was ready to live on his own in Billings, rather than be uprooted again. Tom and Irene purchased a small house for him and arranged for a community-based nonprofit organization to provide a "supported life" program for him. Nick has been successfully living in his own house for the past eighteen years. Tom and Irene visit him a few times a year, and they find that although he still faces many challenges, he loves his life in his community.

In 2010, on the occasion of Nick's fortieth birthday, Tom—by then president of Mount St. Mary's University in Emmitsburg,

Maryland, and author of *Brothers and Sisters: A Special Part of Exceptional Families*—reflected on his parenting. "Have I done all I could to ensure that Nick has a full life?" he wondered. "Have I prepared him with the experiences to enrich his life and ensure his happiness? Have I spent enough time and energy nurturing all aspects of his life, including his spiritual life? I hope so, but others, most importantly Nick in his own way, will be the judge of my efforts."

"If you ask Nick today, he'll still tell you he is a Catholic," Tom says. "But I don't know. Frankly, I do not care. I do know that God loves him and that he'll be in heaven someday, when his disability will not be a factor in his full communion with God's love."

Today, Tom prays for Nick, for his happiness, and for God to watch over him and keep him in a state of grace. He also prays in thanksgiving for Nick, knowing that because of him, he has a better understanding of his faith and of God's wonder. "There is no doubt that Nick is here for a purpose," Tom said. "Maybe Nick's work on earth is to teach us about human difference and to help open our hearts to greater acceptance and love of others who are a bit different."

60

The Worth of an Individual Soul

Christopher Phillips

Christopher Phillips, the oldest of eight children, cannot remember a time when disability and his Mormon faith were not a central part of his life. Less than a year after Christopher's birth, his brother Patrick was born with Down syndrome. Growing up, Christopher and Patrick were almost inseparable, attending school, church classes, and Boy Scouts together. After Christopher's parents had five more children, they adopted Dallin Paul, also born with Down syndrome, when he was only three months old and named him after Christopher's father.

Christopher's parents felt they were uniquely prepared to care for Patrick and Dallin. While in his last quarter of university, Dallin Sr. had driven a bus for schoolchildren with disabilities, often with his wife, Rhonda. The couple spent three hours a day getting to know the passengers and learning to understand their feelings. After Patrick's premature birth, the family doctor told the parents he felt they had not dealt with their son's disability and were denying the "problem." The physician told his staff that he expected the parents to be utterly overwhelmed at some point.

What the doctor did not recognize, Dallin Sr. later wrote in a column in *Ensign* magazine, were the effects of everything the couple had learned through their bus-driving experience. Eventually, the doctor was so impressed by their attitude that he asked the Phillipses to visit other parents of children with Down syndrome.

"Some might call it chance that I spent the summer with a group of mentally disabled people who became my friends," Dallin Sr. wrote. "My wife and I feel, however, that through this episode the Lord prepared our hearts so that we did not experience fear or sorrow when we had a special child of our own. We have maintained our relationship with these bus friends for more than twenty years through Special Olympics and other events. My wife and I are grateful for the preparation we were given to have this son. Ours has been a journey of appreciation and joy."

For their first few years of life, Patrick and Dallin both had significant health problems. Patrick had multiple surgeries, and Dallin had surgeries, kidney stones, and a tracheotomy. At different times, each became so seriously ill that the family was unsure he would survive. Both now enjoy excellent health.

Although Patrick and Dallin have similar disabilities and family backgrounds, their experiences in their local congregation of the Church of Jesus Christ of Latter-day Saints in southeastern Idaho have been very different. Christopher Phillips has noticed the disparate experiences his two brothers have had in their faith community and how it has affected their lives.

Patrick, according to his brother Christopher, has been fully included in the church throughout his life, and his faith experience is very important to him. He has attended weekly Sabbath meetings, served bread and water for the Mormons' version of the sacrament of Communion, and even been an assistant teacher in a Sunday school class. At the age-appropriate times, he assumed priesthood offices and served in a mission, in which he helped at a local religious education center for young adults. "Watching Patrick, I've seen how his faith experience is an invaluable part of his life," said Christopher. "I've seen how it has been a strength and help to him in times of difficulty."

By contrast, Dallin has always had a difficult time conforming to authority, and he had some difficult experiences in Sunday school classes as a child. For one thing, his teachers held expectations about children's behavior that he was unable to meet, which resulted in power struggles that caused him to feel less welcome at church. With few positive social or spiritual experiences, he simply felt neither welcome nor motivated to attend church. In addition, his social phobias make him feel uncomfortable in large crowds. Watching Dallin, said Christopher, "I've seen how quickly and easily a person can feel unwelcome in and disconnected from a faith community."

Christopher learned other lessons from observing his parents advocate on behalf of both brothers. "Watching my mother fight so many battles for my brothers to be included, I knew fairly early on that my life's work would be in the area of disability," he recalled. Finding that many challenges existed even within his church, Christopher knew by the time he graduated from high school that his eventual vocation would be in the area of religion.

After high school, like many young Mormon men, Christopher served a mission, in his case in Albania, where he volunteered at a school for youths with disabilities. Later, working as a special educator and for a nonprofit disability organization, he was hired to teach religion classes at a school for students with disabilities. Recently, he became the manager of Disability Services for the LDS Church in Salt Lake City, where he works with individuals with disabilities, caregivers, church leaders, and members in general. He also provides accessible materials and helps departments of the LDS Church to be aware of members with disabilities.

"Not everybody can have the good fortune of having two brothers with Down syndrome," Christopher said, without irony. "Because of Patrick and Dallin Paul, I am a better person and have found an incredible job and sense of purpose in what I do. My brothers have also influenced my mother, a brother, and two sisters to get an education or work in the area of disability as well."

Even the highest leaders of the LDS Church have taken a strong stand on inclusion. On April 29, 1989, then President Ezra Taft Benson and his counselors issued a statement on disabilities. It read:

"The Church of Jesus Christ of Latter-day Saints is working to provide easier access to its buildings and facilities for people with disabilities. We also are seeking more creative ways of providing religious training for those with physical, mental, and emotional impairments. But there is an even greater need to reduce the barriers imposed by a lack of understanding and acceptance of those who have disabilities.

"We urge leaders, teachers, neighbors, friends, and families to:

"Help increase awareness and understanding of disabilities.

"Accept those with disabilities as children of God and help them to feel respected, loved, and understood.

"Provide opportunities for members with disabilities to learn about the Savior and pattern their lives after Him.

"Assist in the successful Church participation of people with disabilities and the appreciation of their unique gifts.

"Provide meaningful opportunities for members with disabilities to serve, teach, and lead others.

"It is our opportunity and our responsibility to follow the example of Jesus in loving our neighbors, and that includes those with disabilities."

More recently, the LDS Church included short, affirming videos about members with disabilities, including muscular dystrophy and Down syndrome, on its website. One video, *Dayton's Legs*, shows how a thirteen-year-old boy named Spencer Zimmerman, president of his congregation's Deacons youth group, competed in a triathlon, pushing and towing his friend and fellow church member Dayton Hayward, who has severe cerebral palsy.

The LDS Church is engaged in ongoing efforts to increase awareness and understanding of its members with disabilities, through training, online resources, and policy. "Working in the area of religion and disability is an incredible opportunity," said Christopher Phillips. "Instead of worrying about legal requirements and cost-per-user, we're able to make decisions based on something being the right thing to do and the worth of an individual soul. While many of the people I work with aren't disability experts, they generally want to help people. If something needs to be done to make a building, program, or curriculum more accessible, my work is simply helping people to understand the need, and the solution is usually forthcoming."

61

A Bitter Cup

Sue and Fred Odena

Sue Odena's spiritual journey has been ecumenical in the extreme—but no less sincere and heartfelt for its circuitousness. A Catholic convert living in central Florida, she has been a part of many different congregations during the course of her life.

In his native Northern Ireland, Odena's grandfather attended an Anglican church, as his family had done for hundreds of years. Odena was baptized a Methodist as a child in the United States but afterward attended an Evangelical Lutheran church and a Congregational church and was confirmed in the Presbyterian Church. She joined a Southern Baptist church, where she was again baptized; she was reconfirmed in the Lutheran Church; and finally, as an older teenager, she was baptized and confirmed once more in the Roman Catholic Church. Other members of her family are active members of Lutheran, Methodist, and Catholic churches. Wherever Odena and her family worshiped, she said, "the church has been an integral part of our lives."

Odena, who has worked as a commercial real estate broker, and her husband, Fred, an aeronautical engineer, have been married for more than fifty years and have five children and eleven grandchildren. "We have had a good life and are truly blessed," Sue said. As the couple neared the age of retirement, they began planning an active and exciting phase of their lives.

"I prayed for guidance and asked God, 'Is this what we are supposed to be doing?'" said Odena. "Is a scaled-down career and a bit of traveling what God wants for this 'empty nest' portion of our lives? Each moment you have is a gift from God, and the love that surrounds you is a precious blessing to be shared."

Before Sue could even reach an answer, the couple's plans were cut short when, after a series of confusion episodes, Fred was diagnosed with mild cognitive impairment and later, as his condition deteriorated, with Alzheimer's disease, which his doctor attributed to a head injury sustained decades earlier while Fred was serving in the U.S. Marines.

"'God will provide all that we need, here at the table of plenty,'" Sue said. "The hymn runs over and over through my mind like a mantra. I honestly don't know how I would cope if it weren't for my deep faith that there is a God who has a plan and who hears my prayers. A priest once told me that sometimes you are the comforter and sometimes you are the example and someone else's opportunity to provide comfort. Obviously, I would rather not need comforting, but right now we are going through an adventure that we never imagined for our 'golden years.' Quite frankly, it is a struggle."

Understandably, the struggle has been especially challenging for Fred. "My husband is a scientist, and over the years he says he has lost his faith," Sue said. "He does not believe that there is a God who answers prayers. He does not believe that a loving God would allow so much hate in the world or so much pain. He says the Church is mostly about power and money, and yet he goes to Mass with me and participates in Holy Communion. I pray that God will comfort both of us and that my husband will find God's love in his heart before his cognition is completely gone."

Ever the scientist, Fred enthusiastically joined the Florida Brain Bank Program, which he and Sue believe is important for research into Alzheimer's. They encourage others to enroll in the program, too, and they meet with elected officials to try to persuade them of the importance of Alzheimer's research and the need to direct more resource dollars toward finding a cure.

Sue and Fred were disappointed to find that neither their parish nor the diocese had significant programs for people with Alzheimer's, and they continue to push them to do more to educate and provide services to people with dementia inside the Catholic Church. But through the Alzheimer's Association website, she found the Early Alzheimer's Support and Education program (EASE), which offered a seven-week course spelling out what the couple faced and what preparations they could make for the disruptions in store for them. The EASE program led the Odenas to Reeves United Methodist Church in Orlando and to the support group it offers for both caregivers and the diagnosed. Other support groups, Sue found, were for caregivers of people who were institutionalized or close to it. She found them depressing, and Fred felt left out.

"How distressing it is to be very intelligent and realize the downward spiral into disconnect with all you love," Sue said, referring to a reaction typical in those affected by Alzheimer's. But through the Reeves support group, she and Fred found two other organizations, the Alzheimer's Resource Center and Share the Care Adult Day Care. The Alzheimer's Resource Center coordinates the Florida Brain Bank for thirty-one counties in the state. Share the Care Adult Day Care is a service of the nonprofit agency Share the Care™. It provides services and support to family caregivers, enabling them to keep their family member at home and delay or eliminate the need for institutional care.

"God puts people in your life for a reason," Sue said. "How very fortunate we are. At Share the Care, Fred has regained a bit of his dignity and feels useful in helping patients who come for care when they are unhappy or need assistance." The couples in the Reeves group share information and laughter and tears, secure in the knowledge that their conversations are confidential and enjoying the camaraderie of enduring a difficult path together.

"The Methodist church in Orlando has a leg up on all the other churches in the area," said Beverly Engel, program coordinator of the Central and North Florida Chapter of the Alzheimer's Association. "Reeves United provides space for at least two support groups. The United Methodist Church of Winter Park provides space and support for the Brain Fitness Club. The Methodist church in College Park has a Share the Care.

"Most of the programs I am aware of in faith-based settings are not necessarily religious in nature. However, what is religious is the willingness of these communities to embrace programs that are outside their usual menu of offerings, particularly when the

individuals benefiting from the programs can be of a different religion from the hosting church. Moreover, faith communities that
assist persons with disabilities often do so out of a service mission
and do not assume the help they give will result in new and active
members of the faith community."

Sue Odena feels she is now part of a divine plan. "God puts us
where we are needed. I tend to be good at organization, I know
people of influence, and I'm fairly articulate and outspoken about
issues I am passionate about. I am a bit resentful about picking up
this particular cross and following Him. At times, like the season
of Lent, that sounds almost heretical. Our lives could be so much
worse. We are so fortunate. How can I argue with God? And yet
this is a bitter cup we have been given. We hold hands and make
the effort to make our time together pleasant and productive.
This is our mission of the moment."

62

A Right to Faith

Safiyyah Amina Muhammad

Safiyyah Amina Muhammad has played many roles in her life: jazz vocalist, movie actress, poet, spoken word artist, radio host, classroom paraprofessional, and political lobbyist. But it is as a Muslim wife and African American mother of five, two of whom have developmental disabilities, that she may have had the greatest effect, together with her husband, Eric Smith. The two have made a place for their children to worship in the mosque, which required some groundbreaking but has opened the doors for many others.

Safiyyah's adolescent son Sufyaan has autism, and his younger brother, Isa, has attention deficit/hyperactivity disorder (ADHD) and a learning disability. When the children were younger, the family worshiped at a mosque where most members came from the Middle East, and they felt comfortable. "The reason Sufyaan fit in there was that a certain kind of culture existed that you should let the children run. He didn't stand out as a youngster, even with his repetitive actions and hand flapping."

But when the family moved to a predominately African American mosque, Masjid Waarith Ud Deen in Irvington, New Jersey, where Safiyyah's parents worshiped, a more traditional, Western concept of decorum prevailed. Children were expected to behave quietly during worship. Because Sufyaan did not have a visible disability, people in the congregation assumed the boy was not being disciplined by his parents. The whispers of some adults embarrassed Sufyaan's siblings. Sufyaan, however, was largely oblivious to the atmosphere of disapproval.

When Sufyaan was growing up, his mother played recordings of Islamic religious music, readings from the Koran, children's programs, and computer games for all her children. She soon found that Arabic recitations had a soothing effect on Sufyaan, especially while he rode in the family minivan. When Sufyaan heard the imam quoting the Scriptures in Arabic during the weekly, Friday afternoon Jumuah service, it stimulated him. "He got happy, excited," his mother said. "He wanted to repeat it out loud."

One of Safiyyah's male cousins often visited for Friday Jumuah services. Because males and females worshiped separately, his accompaniment was a huge help in keeping Sufyaan and Isa calm during the congregational sermon and prayer services. On the Friday of one Memorial Day weekend, however, school was out, the mosque was full to capacity, and neither the boys' father nor their cousin was able to attend. Sufyaan was in rare "autistic" form at the service, highly stimulated by the bright environment, by seeing more children than usual in attendance, and by having no male chaperone to distract him.

Safiyyah sat in the first row of the women's section and instructed the boys to sit directly in front of her, in the back row of the men's section. During the sermon, she did her best to contain Sufyaan and Isa's anxiety, but while she prayed, the boys ran around the mosque, interrupting prayer. When the service ended, Safiyyah's family members had to help restrain Sufyaan and his brother. Unfortunately, Safiyyah and two of her other children overheard some harsh comments and were upset.

Rather than leaving upset, Safiyyah decided to approach the imam and his wife about her disappointment with the way some members of the congregation were viewing the family. The imam listened, and the comforting conversation that followed proved to be a lesson for everyone, including Safiyyah. It sparked a continuing dialogue about how to help the Muslim community understand children with developmental disabilities.

A few weeks later, the imam, mentioning no names, preached a sermon on compassion, which touched obliquely on Sufyaan. He asked others in the congregation to reflect on their actions and said his sermon was a reminder to himself.

"What the imam said," Safiyyah recalled, "struck a chord, that everyone has a right to worship and that one person's behavior should not impede another's right to worship. 'Want for your brother what you would want for yourself.'" How, the imam asked, do we find a middle ground? That place, he suggested, was simple awareness—education and reminding one another to be compassionate. Things are not always as they appear.

Privately, the imam asked Safiyyah to share information about autism with the congregation by doing things such as posting flyers, providing literature about autism, and speaking to small groups. Several weeks later, a film crew preparing a documentary on faith and disabilities was given permission to videotape the Muhammad-Smith family at worship. The video crew's two appearances spread the story of Sufyaan more fully, and on the second visit the imam took the occasion to talk more about the family with the congregation. Several months later the film aired as a segment on Public Broadcasting's *Religion & Ethics Newsweekly*.

"The first time Sufyaan attended the mosque," Safiyyah said on the show, "not only was he talking out loud and using his hand motions, but he was running in and out of the rows. It wasn't received well. There were whispers, there was talk: 'He's a bad kid. He obviously wasn't raised right. That's bad parenting.'

"When I think back to when I was a child, I don't remember seeing anyone like Sufyaan at the mosque, no one. I don't remember any children or adults like Sufyaan attending the mosque, and I don't think that was by mistake. I think that we parents look at it as not just a distraction but an embarrassment. But he deserves to pray. He has a right to faith, too."

The congregation's spiritual leader, Imam W. Deen Shareef, agrees. "I think the primary challenge is a lack of knowledge, because sometimes families conceal the information that they have family members that have disabilities," he told PBS. "Sister Safiyyah Muhammad made us aware of her son's disability in terms of autism, and she's made it almost like a quest for our community to become more knowledgeable about it."

These days, when Safiyyah and Sufyaan come to the mosque for Jumuah and her husband, Eric, cannot join them because of his job, older male members jump up and take Sufyaan under their wing in the section where adult males worship. That caring, inclusive attitude has had an effect on Sufyaan, his mother believes. "I'm certain he absorbs what is going on around him and is less disruptive." There have been other changes as well.

"People are talking to me more openly about family members, and I've been asked to do some workshops. The community is more patient and cognizant. They don't think that every child who can't sit still is a bad child, but there's still a stigma."

Sufyaan attends a small, private school called New Beginnings, where he loves to learn and spend time on the computer. His mother reaches out well beyond the Muslim community, participating in a YMCA program aimed at creating an after-school program for children with disabilities. She also serves as a member of the Consumer Advisory Council of the Elizabeth M. Boggs Center on Developmental Disabilities. On August 13, 2009, she delivered an address about an autism health care funding bill to New Jersey state legislators and to then governor Jon Corzine.

63

Take a Break

Tim and Marie Kuck

As the families arrived at Calvary Assembly of God in Winter Park, Florida, on a sunny Saturday morning several years ago, anticipation showed on the faces of both parents and children—but for vastly different reasons. The kids, from tots to teens, had a variety of disabilities, including cerebral palsy, Down syndrome, and autism. Some could walk; others used wheelchairs. During the week, they were in special programs, mainstreamed in the public school system, or homeschooled.

Disabilities notwithstanding, these young people knew that they would soon be among friends for a good time on the campus of the gleaming glass megachurch. Their companions would be other kids with disabilities whom they had come to know, as well as handholding volunteers called "buddies." For the next three hours they would be VIPs as they went from room to room, singing, doing crafts, listening to stories, eating lunch, and playing games. Outdoors, they could enjoy a mobile petting zoo. Meanwhile, their parents dashed off to visit Home Depot, ride bikes, clean their houses, spend quiet time together, or just sleep.

Both parents and children benefited from a program called Buddy Break, founded and developed at Calvary by Tim and Marie Kuck. The couple know firsthand how physically exhausting and emotionally draining it can be to care for a child with severe disabilities. Their son, Nathaniel, was born prematurely with multiple birth defects and died in 2001, before his fifth birthday, without ever speaking or eating on his own. In 2002 the Kucks established Nathaniel's Hope as a living memorial to their son, to help families like theirs. Their programs, designed to make children with disabilities feel special, include Christmas visits to hospitals and a "VIP Birthday Club," which remembers each child with a card, a "Bearing Hope" plush bear toy, and other surprises.

That program, in turn, grew to include Buddy Break, which provides respite care for children with disabilities at central Florida churches, without regard to denomination. With Buddy Break, parents can bring their children with disabilities—and their siblings who may not have disabilities—for a few hours on a Friday night or Saturday morning. Trained volunteers care for the children with the support of volunteer medical personnel while the parents take a break. In explaining the need for Buddy Break, the Kucks cite the high rate of divorce among parents who have a child with a disability. Their goal is to help such families, whose children they dub "VIPs," and to train volunteers, called "buddies."

The organization has an intensive, twenty-four-hour, weekend training program called Buddy Break Basic Leadership Training (BLT), which teaches church leaders how to run a safe and enjoyable respite program. This includes performing a national background check on each volunteer. The program has to be covered by each church's liability insurance, and Buddy Break has its own coverage for its role in training. The parents of all prospective participants are required to fill out detailed, online applications to assist Buddy Break volunteers.

One of those buddies at Calvary is Brenda Whidden, a respiratory therapist who had helped take care of Nathaniel at the hospital. "Every once in a while you bond with a child," she recalled. "I fell in love with Nathaniel." So Whidden decided to volunteer. "I'm here if anyone needs me" in a medical capacity, she said, "but I just like playing with the kids. By doing this, I feel like Nathaniel's still alive, that his life has purpose."

Karen Jones, a radiographer and single mother who drove to Winter Park from her home in Apopka, ten miles away, said these hours of respite were "priceless," enabling her to do errands and clean her house while her eleven-year-old son, David, a quadriplegic, was being cared for. "When I take the time to relax and reenergize myself, I feel like I'm a better mom," Jones said. "I'm able to be more patient, more attentive, more playful, and less stressed out, and to appreciate David for the blessing he is."

Buddy Break has grown to a dozen central Florida congregations and one in Tampa. The Kucks' dream is to take the program nationwide, providing training materials for churches around the country. And there is more. "It's our dream to have a permanent respite facility in central Florida to provide overnight care or extended care when families need it," Marie said.

Calvary Assembly's pastor, the Reverend George Cope, has known Marie Kuck for decades. "I was always impressed with her passion and compassion," he said. "It's not a surprise that her tragedy became other people's triumph." Experts in the field also laud the program. "Parents rarely are able to get an actual break," said Robert A. Naseef, a Philadelphia psychologist and author of *Special Children, Challenged Parents: The Struggles and Rewards of Raising a Child with a Disability*. "What's great about [Buddy Break] is that there are professional people there," said Naseef, who co-authored a recent article on respite care.

Each year, Nathaniel's Hope holds a support festival, "Make 'm Smile," at Orlando's Lake Eola Park, which in 2011 drew ten thousand people. Rather than a fund-raiser, it is an event held to honor and celebrate the VIPs—such as the three daughters of Matt and Diane Hayes. The couple moved from St. Louis to Orlando so that their children, ages ten, twelve, and fifteen, could attend Princeton House Charter School, a public program that focuses on children with disabilities. For the Hayeses, Buddy Break has been a godsend. They also attend programs at three other area churches each month. "We'll go anywhere," Diane said, knowing that her girls were "safe and loved and cared for." Her daughters, like many other children, look forward to the breaks, where they meet other kids, who often become their friends. The break works both ways, said Matt: "It's a respite from their parents."

Chip Tolman, of Orange County, said his two young children felt the same way. "They enjoy it too—probably more than us," he said. "When they get to the door, they let us know they're glad to be here."

64

Standing Some Disorder

Stanley Hauerwas

As he recounts in his moving autobiography, *Hannah's Child: A Theologian's Memoir,* Stanley Hauerwas was a working-class kid from central Texas, the son of a bricklayer. He grew up in a family that was centered on its small Methodist church, and he more or less stumbled into a career as a distinguished religion professor—most prominently at Duke University Divinity School, where he was teaching when *Time* magazine named him "the best theologian in America" in 2001.

Hauerwas's first wife, Anne, was mentally ill for the twenty-four years they were together, increasingly plagued by bipolar personality and psychotic breaks, a condition he believes she inherited from her mother. When you live with someone who is seriously mentally ill, he writes in *Hannah's Child,* "you cannot live without hope, but you certainly need to learn without expectation. . . . The world comes crashing in on you. . . . I know the feelings of abandonment, loneliness that accompany this discovery."

This was not Hauerwas's only personal experience with the world of disability. Early in his academic career, as a young faculty member at the University of Notre Dame, he became involved with the Logan Center for people with physical, emotional, and intellectual disabilities, situated across from the campus. The first time he visited the center, he recalled in his memoir, he was terrified when he was clutched tightly by a seven-year-old with Down syndrome.

"I soon began to think that learning to live with the mentally disabled might be paradigmatic for learning what it might mean to face God," he later reflected. "The world that mental illness creates is lonely enough, but not to be able to share what you are going through with friends makes that world almost unbearable."

So Hauerwas has given this issue of faith and disability a good deal of thought. He is the author of three books that consider faith and disabilities: *Living Gently in a Violent World: The Prophetic Witness of Weakness* (with Jean Vanier); *God, Medicine, and Suffering*; and *Suffering Presence: Theological Reflections on Medicine, the Mentally Handicapped, and the Church*.

Hauerwas's influence in what has become known as the field of "disability studies" is considerable, as John Swinton, of Scotland's University of Aberdeen, has written. "Hauerwas emphasizes that the lives of people with disabilities do not constitute an 'unusual case' or an 'ethical dilemma.' Their lives simply remind us of what we all are."

One sunny autumn afternoon, the notoriously crusty and plainspoken theologian reflected on people with disabilities and congregations. In his book-lined garret office, looking out at the soaring Duke Chapel, he reluctantly agreed to offer some general principles for congregational inclusion, although he said he has never had much use for such strictures. "As a rule, you have the obligation of hospitality. You want to make your space as hospitable as possible for people with difference. You want and hope that people with disabilities will be able to share in everything you do to the extent they're able."

What is to be gained when they—we—are successful, said Hauerwas, is "a sense of community." People with disabilities "are able in these decisive acts to share their life with other people and not feel like an exception is being made for them. Those of us who are not disabled have got to be very careful about these matters, because there's always a temptation to think, 'Aren't we great that we're so tolerant of these disabled people.' Of course that's just an invitation to self-righteousness that has to be resisted. What benefits us who are not disabled is the sheer joy that we see in those who are disabled sharing what we share, just the sheer joy of it."

There is, he says, a continuum or spectrum of congregational involvement, but "that's true of us all, whether we're disabled or not disabled. Most of the time I'm sitting there and participating with a lack, I'm sure, of soul awareness. So I depend on my brothers and sisters around me to believe for me. And I think that's true for people with disabilities. Often they depend on others to do what makes their life possible, just as I depend on them to make my life possible." At the same time, the sometimes profane professor offers a caveat that will set many at ease (and some on edge) about working with people with disabilities. "You've got to be careful about turning them into holy innocents. They can be manipulative just like anyone and that kind of thing, which means they're human beings. They have to learn to love us, and we have to learn to love them.

"I think one of the most important things about people with disabilities is people in the pews' willingness to stand some disorder. After all, the God they're worshiping is a God that is going to disorder your life, and you ought to be ready to house people who may shout out at times that you hadn't anticipated. And you ought to be ready to house people ready to charge to the altar to stand beside the priest while the priest celebrates the Eucharist. And you ought to celebrate that they want to be that close to the celebration. So I think that having the disabled among us as we worship is a lovely way for us to recognize what we're really doing when we worship a God that is as surprising as the God of Jesus Christ.

"That means if a guide dog is present, you're happy that the guide dog is present. At the Church of the Holy Family we have two blind people with guide dogs, and I think the church as a whole thinks this is wonderful that animals are part of our worship life. And that may mean you have to change some things.

"I think it's very hard for Christians to be vulnerable and to ask for help. And we need to do that. We need to learn to ask for help.

"Kids who are autistic, who can be an absolute pain in the ass in worship, are also capable of feeling and being shaped by habits that are helpful to us all. And I think it is very important not to leave families who have disabled people as part of their lives alone. Knowing how to share those lives with one another outside worship is really crucial."

Respite care, while not explicitly part of the Christian tradition, Hauerwas said, "is a way of showing that we understand we're all part of the same body of Christ and that those with disabled family members just wear out. They just become tired, and from time to time it's extremely important to have a vacation. And so a respite care, I think, in terms of the mentally handicapped institutions that I've been associated with, has always been very important, and I see no reason that the church shouldn't copy that."

Conclusion

The Power of Stories

Preachers like to say that people listen to sermons but remember stories. Stories have power—they linger and do not flee the way facts do, and they move us to action.

As I hope the stories told in these pages have demonstrated, the "amazing gifts" of the book's title embody a duality. People with disabilities and their families, friends, and caregivers benefit greatly when those with disabilities are embraced by faith communities, and congregations are enriched at least as much by the inclusion. Still, for those of us who have no intimate relationship or connection with disability, it is easy to fall into what is known as the "we-they" trap, separating or distancing ourselves from people with physical and intellectual disabilities. Even perceptive and caring pastors and lay members can fall into the snare of unconsciously distancing themselves from people with disabilities, in the process turning them into "objects" rather than seeing them as unique individuals.

Including children and adults with disabilities in the day-to-day life of a congregation is an unfamiliar project for many, if not most, religious leaders. This unfamiliarity can and certainly has produced unexpected, awkward, and embarrassing situations. Still, any first steps, stumbles and all, are worthy and can succeed. In the words of the Catholic theologian Henri Nouwen, "The

299

question is not 'How can we help people with disabilities?' The more important question is how can people with disabilities give their spiritual gifts to us and call us to love?" Learning how to recognize the gifts and talents of children and adults with disabilities can transform congregations and their leaders. The question "What are we going to do about Mrs. Jones?" as if she were a project, changes to "How can we make it possible for Mrs. Jones's gifts and abilities to lead all of us into a deeper spirituality?"

"Who is the God we worship?" asks John Swinton, a disability theologian at the University of Aberdeen in Scotland. The type of God we assume God to be determines, to a greater or lesser extent, how we understand what it means to be human, which in turn determines how we respond to disability. It is therefore a deeply theological and practical question.

"Being deaf is only disabling if the people around you haven't bothered to learn sign language," according to Swinton. "Being blind is only disabling if the environment around you is built around the assumption that everyone can see. In other words, impairments (blindness, deafness, lack of mobility) are not the things that produce disability. In a different environment these impairments would not cause a person to be disabled."

A growing number of faith communities are trying to change the environment to accommodate people with all sorts of abilities. One example is Al-Rahman Mosque at the Islamic Society of Central Florida. Most mosques have no chairs; everyone worships in rows on the carpeted floor, signifying the equality of all worshipers. But staff at Al-Rahman have placed chairs in the front row and in the back of the hall for the use of seniors and people with disabilities. At least three men and one woman navigate to the mosque from their designated parking places by scooter. When the primary caretaker of one of the men was severely injured by a drunk driver, members of the community rallied to support the couple, jamming the hospital's corridors and waiting rooms.

"People with disabilities are loved by all, and they bring everyone together, including people who never spoke to each other before," said Imam Muhammad Musri, the Islamic Society's president. "Their presence reminds us all that each of us is disabled in some way, and only God is perfect. In the Koran, God told us he was going to test each of us with something, and disability is a sign of God's love."

As Rabbi Steven Engel, of the Congregation of Reform Judaism—where my family worships in Orlando, Florida—observed, "When a person with a disability does something that we don't expect from them, we are reminded of the most fundamental religious idea, that each and every person is created *b'tzelem Elohim*, in God's image. It is amazing that in the disability itself we see the beauty and wonder of God's creation and we realize that 'imperfection' is not a divine creation but a human one."

Engel was reminded about this, he said, "when a young man with a serious brain injury became bar mitzvah in our sanctuary. As he chanted the prayers, read from the Torah, and spoke about what his religion and community meant to him, there was not a dry eye in the entire room. In his accomplishment, in his wisdom, in his smile, God was surely present for each and every person there. Out of the supposed imperfection came one of the most sacred moments for our congregation."

At Northland Church in suburban Orlando, the Reverend Joel Hunter says that his megachurch "is learning much from those with disabilities. I have watched our congregation be drawn closer to God because their definition of 'normal,' even preferable, now includes those with obvious imperfections. We are learning lessons like the more you love someone, the less apparent their imperfections become, leaving just the person-to-person relationship to be enjoyed. Those thinking they are the givers (by including those with disabilities) become surprised that they receive so much in the relationship. We have a better perspective on our own challenges."

The Reverend Samuel Wells, dean of the Duke University Chapel and author of numerous books, including *Speaking the Truth: Preaching in a Pluralistic Culture*, has thought about the issue of disability a good deal, partly on the basis of his experience as a congregational minister for more than twenty years in his native England.

"Questions surrounding disability bring us close to the heart of theology and ethics," said Wells. He tells the story of a middle-aged woman he calls Jill, who had both small mobility issues and a more substantial developmental disability and whose life was dominated by her elderly parents. The woman's mother and then her father died shortly after Wells met the family. During the announcements at the end of the Sunday service following the father's death, Wells mentioned from the pulpit the man's passing and the fact that Jill now had no surviving relatives. He said, "Sometimes God asks a congregation what it's made of. I think that may be happening now."

To the congregation's credit, he said, members responded according to their gifts. Those who had advocacy experience came forward; those who were already active in programming found ways Jill could join in; and those who just cared made arrangements to take Jill out to lunch every Sunday and have a serious conversation with her. These efforts were coordinated by the pastoral care group.

Jill taught through questions, sometimes challenging ones, such as asking those she loved, "Why can't you adopt me?" In doing so, Wells said, "she made the congregation think deeply about the difference between being family, being a friend, and being a fellow member of the body of Christ. In such a way she was a blessing. She said, 'I like to be with people. I like their company. I'm not too fussy what they're talking about. I need you.' By being so open about her needs, she pushed congregation members to look at themselves and the heart of their own neediness, which, in a culture of understated intellectualism, many were adept at hiding. The things Jill wanted and loved about them were not their achievements or the status they had acquired but the humanity they showed—not their thoughts but their gentle touch; not their speed of reflection but their patient presence. In such a way she was a blessing."

But make no mistake: Interactions between people with and without disabilities, between individuals and congregations, between clergy and laity can be difficult. Sometimes they can disappoint, resulting in hurt feelings or worse, as the disabilities advocate and scholar Bill Gaventa notes:

"The signs are not all good. Neither are the stories. Some continue to haunt me. A parent responded to one of my 'Spiritual Journeys' columns in the national Arc newsletter, *Insight*. She had worked hard to involve her son with autism in the worship life of the congregation, practicing at home and then taking him to church. His noises became problematic, and she moved with him to the rear of the church, then into the lobby. There, she noticed that while his speech and sounds were not intelligible, they were mimicking the pattern and cadence of the litany and liturgy. It was then that a deacon came up and asked them to leave because of the ongoing disturbance. The irony was that the Scripture reading for the morning was about welcoming the stranger and those who are different.

"Many congregations have not yet begun to address the possibilities of inclusive ministries and faith supports. Nor have professionals and service organizations. That inertia or reluctance is shaped by a number of issues and barriers." The barriers, Gaventa explained, include a lack of awareness of disability and of the importance of faith and spirituality in the lives of people with disabilities; stereotypes and misconceptions about disability and about religious organizations; false assumptions about church-state relationships; and simple inaction on the part of congregations and agencies who think, "We never did it that way before."

Although congregations and individuals have taken varied approaches to the subject of faith and disability, made creative adaptations, and developed many innovations—especially technological and architectural ones—few genuinely new ideas are needed or perhaps even possible. Goodwill, respect, empathy, and compassion are constant sources of innovation. Family support is invaluable. Allies, determination, and thick skin are often necessary, and as in much of the rest of life, it must be acknowledged that it helps to have education and money. The more of all such assets a person with a disability and his or her advocates are endowed with, accumulate, or develop, the better their outcome is likely to be.

There may be less in these pages about spiritual surcease than some readers might have expected. A number of the storytellers talk about questioning God and faith in the face of disability. That is a matter I have left to the theologians. I have tried to focus on the concrete—on what members of faith communities can *do* to become more inclusive and to assist people with disabilities.

Jacob Artson, a young Southern California man with autism, has written articulately about the effect faith can have on people with disabilities. "I think that people vastly underestimate the importance of spirituality for people with special needs," he wrote in a March 2011 online essay. "Of course I have some friends who are confirmed atheists, but many more for whom Judaism is a lifeline. My body and emotions are very disorganized, but the one time that my mind, body, and emotions feel totally connected and in harmony is when I pray. I have also learned many important lessons from listening to my rabbis' sermons, because we all need to live with meaning and know that we are not alone in our struggles.

"For many years I had been praying for God to cure my autism and wondering why God didn't answer my prayer. I realized at that point that I had been praying for the wrong reason. I started to pray for the strength to accept autism and live with joy, laughter, and connection. My prayers were answered more richly than I ever imagined! Sometimes I still hate autism, but now I love life more than I hate autism.

"The best peers and aides I have had didn't have any special background. It doesn't actually take any training to be a leader who models inclusion. It just takes an attitude that all people are made in God's image and it is our job to find the part of God hidden in each person."

It is difficult to match Jacob's eloquence, and his words can serve as a call to action based on the power of his and the other stories in this book. These are real stories by and about real people. Their power is to move readers and congregations to do something, to start, to embrace the person who has been avoided. Start with just one person, the person in front of you. Befriend that person and ask at the appropriate time, "What is it we can do to make it easier for you and your family to worship with us?"

As someone outside the disability community, I thought myself an unlikely choice to be asked to write a book about faith and disability, both physical and intellectual. In the course of more than two decades as a religion writer, I had written just a handful of stories about faith and disability. But Richard Bass, director of publishing at the Alban Institute, explained to me that in many ways I represented exactly the intended readership of this book—people of religious faith who may have no expertise or personal experience with disability but who, as congregation members and clergy, make the congregational decisions about accessibility and inclusion. The Alban Institute didn't want a book that would read like homework or another resource manual—as valuable as some of those are—much less like a book of theology.

Writing the book changed me in a profound way. I came to the issue of faith and disability with much of the ignorance and unconscious prejudice that characterize almost anyone who has never personally experienced a serious disability or been closely connected to someone who has. Listening to these storytellers enabled me to overcome my discomfort and anxiety. Despite their repeated disclaimers, I found the people with disabilities whom I met and their family members, friends, caregivers, and clergy to be inspiring—often in the most matter-of-fact ways. Like me, you may find it difficult, as you read their stories, not to ask yourself whether you could do what they have done. As I was repeatedly cautioned, this is not the question to dwell on. Our only job is to understand and to help in any way we can.

Resources

There are many excellent sources of resources on disabilities and faith communites. The following organizations, from different faith traditions, maintain helpful online resource lists and are available to assist those seeking more information:

Congregational Accessibility Network, http://www.
accessibilitynetwork.net/
Congregational Resource Guide, www.congregationalresources.
org
Faith Based Supports, Elizabeth M. Boggs Center on
Developmental Disabilities, rwjms.umdnj.edu/boggscenter/
projects/faith_based.html
ISNA Leadership Development Center, Islamic Society of North
America, www.isna.net/Leadership/pages/WHERE-DO-WE-
GO-FROM-HERE.aspx
Jewish Community Inclusion Program for People with
Disabilities, www.jfcsmpls.org/inclusionresources.html
Joni and Friends International Disability Center,
www.joniandfriends.org
National Catholic Partnership on Disability, www.ncpd.org
National Council of Churches Committee on Disabilities, www.
ncccusa.org/nmu/mce/dis/
Religion and Spirituality Resources for Congregations/Faith
Communities, Tennessee Disability Pathfinder, kc.vanderbilt.
edu/pathfinder/resources/page.aspx?id=1140

The following are resources that appear in the text of this book. They were created by the subjects of the stories, used by them, or proved important in inspiring them develop their ministries by, with, and for people with disabilities:

Alban Institute and National Organization on Disabilities, *Money and Ideas: Creative Approaches to Congregational Access* (Herndon, VA: Alban Institute, 2001). Available at congregationalresources.org.

American Association of People with Disabilities Interfaith Initiative, www.aapd.com/what-we-do/interfaith/.

Anabaptist Disabilities Network (ADNet), *Connections* newsletter, www.adnetonline.org.

Becker, Amy Julia, *A Good and Perfect Gift: Faith, Expectations, and a Little Girl Named Penny* (Grand Rapids: Bethany House, 2011).

Bolduc, Kathleen Deyer, *Autism and Alleluias* (Valley Forge, PA: Judson Press, 2010).

——, *His Name Is Joel: Searching for God in a Son's Disability* (Louisville, KY: Bridge Resources, 1999).

——, *A Place Called Acceptance: Ministry with Families of Children with Disabilities* (Louisville, KY: Bridge Resources, 2001).

Bridges to Healing, a division of Campus Crusade for Christ's Military Ministry, http.militaryministry.org/families/bthm-2/.

Buddy Break, http.nathanielshope.org/events-programs/buddy-break/.

Christensen, Shelly, *The Jewish Community Guide to Inclusion of People with Disabilities, 4th ed.* (Minneapolis: Jewish Family and Children's Service of Minneapolis, 2010).

Chryssavgis, John, *The Body of Christ: A Place of Welcome for People with Disabilities* (Minneapolis MN: Light and Life, 2002).

Copen, Lisa, *Beyond Casseroles: 505 Ways to Encourage a Chronically Ill Friend* (San Diego: Rest Ministries Publishers, 2002).

——, *When Chronic Illness Enters Your Life: 5 Lessons for Individuals and Groups* (San Diego: Rest Ministries Publishers, 2002).

D'Archangelis, Jo (ed.), *Wings: A faithletter for United Methodists with disabilities and those who care about them.* Available at www.umdisabledministers.org.

Davie, Ann Rose, and Ginny Thornburgh, *That All May Worship: An Interfaith Welcome to People with Disabilities* (Washington, DC: National Organization on Disability, 1994). Available from the American Association of People with Disabilities Interfaith Initiative.

Douglass Developmental Disability Center, Rutgers University, dddc.rutgers.edu.

Early Alzheimer's Support and Education program (EASE), www.alz.org/seva/in_my_community_16027.asp.

Eiesland, Nancy. *The Disabled God: Toward a Liberatory Theology of Disability* (Nashville: Abingdon Press, 1994).

Ephphatha Ministry, journeyroad.org/ministries/ephphatha/.

Friendship Ministries, www.friendship.org.

Gillum, William, *Awakening Spiritual Dimensions: Prayer Services with Persons with Severe Disabilities* (AuthorHouse, 2006).

Gould, Toby, *We Don't Have Any Here: Planning for Ministries with People with Disabilities in Our Communities* (Nashville: Discipleship Resources, 1986).

Guthrie, Nancy, *Hearing Jesus Speak into Your Sorrow* (Carol Stream, IL: Tyndale House Publishers, 2009).

———, *Holding On to Hope: A Pathway through Suffering to the Heart of God* (Carol Stream, IL: Tyndale House Publishers, 2006).

———, *The One Year Book of Hope* (Carol Stream, IL: Tyndale House Publishers, 2005).

———, *When Your Family's Lost a Loved One: Finding Hope Together* (Carol Stream, IL: Tyndale House Publishers, 2008).

Hauerwas, Stanley, *God, Medicine and Suffering* (Grand Rapids: Eerdmans, 1994).

———, *Hannah's Child: A Theologian's Memoir* (Grand Rapids: Eerdmans, 2010).

———, *Suffering Presence: Theological Reflections on Medicine, the Mentally Handicapped, and the Church* (Notre Dame, IN: University of Notre Dame Press, 1986).

Hauerwas, Stanley, and Jean Vanier, *Living Gently in a Violent World: The Prophetic Witness of Weakness* (Downers Grove, IL: InterVarsity Press, 2008).

Holmes, David, *Autism through the Lifespan: The Eden Model* (Bethesda, MD: Woodbine House, 1998).

HopeKeepers, restministries.com/hopekeepers-groups/

Hubach, Stephanie, *Same Lake, Different Boat: Coming Alongside People Touched by Disability* (Phillipsburg, NJ: P & R Publishing, 2006).

Jewish Deaf Resource Center, www.jdrc.org.

Joni and Friends International Disability Center, www.joniandfriends.org.

Journal of Religion, Disability & Health, www.tandfonline.com/loi/wrdh20.

Kacie's Kloset, www.kacieskloset.org.

Kramer-Mills, Hartmut. "Walter's Ingress: How a Young Man Transformed a Church," *Journal of Religion, Disability & Health* (Vol. 14, Iss. 3, 2010).

Kutz-Mellem, Sharon. *Different Members, One Body: Welcoming the Diversity of Abilities in God's House* (Louisville, KY: Witherspoon Press, 1998).

Lift Disability Network, www.liftdisability.net.

Links of Love Disability Ministry, Lansdale, PA, www.familyworshipcenter.org/ministries/disabilities/index.shtml.

Lundy, Angela Victoria. *Uphill Journey* (Kent, DE: Ecnerret Publishing Company, 1996).

Maxwell, Chris. *Changing My Mind: A Journey of Disability and Joy* (Franklin Springs, GA: LifeSprings, 2005).

"Mental Health Matters." Monthly public access television program. Available at www.mpuuc.org/mentalhealth/mentalTVshow.html.

Mental Health Ministries, www.mentalhealthministries.net.

Meyers, Barbara. *The Caring Congregation Program* (Fremont, CA: Mission Peak Unitarian Universalist Congregation, 2006). See www.mpuuc.org/mentalhealth/caringcongcurr.html.

Naseef, Robert A. *Special Children, Challenged Parents: The Struggles and Rewards of Raising a Child with a Disability* (Baltimore, MD: Brookes Publishing Co., 2001).

National Alliance on Mental Illness, www.nami.org.

National Invisible Chronic Illness Awareness Week. Online annual conference.

National Multiple Sclerosis Society, www.nationalmssociety.org.

Nouwen, Henri, *Seeds of Hope: A Henri Nouwen Reader* (New York: Image Books, 1997).

Parents' Place/Club de Padres, a program of Catholic Family and Community Services, Diocese of Paterson, New Jersey, www.spannj.org/support/parents_place.htm.

Pinsky, Mark I., "Churches Mustn't Neglect the Disabled," *USA Today* (January 11, 2011).

———, "Making God More Accessible," *Wall Street Journal* (September 3, 2009).

Point Man International Ministries, www.pmim.org.

Powell, Thomas H., *Brothers and Sisters: A Special Part of Exceptional Families* (Baltimore, MD: Brookes Publishing Co., 1985).

Preheim-Bartel, Dean A., et al., *Supportive Care in the Congregation* (Harrisonburg, VA: Herald Press, 2011).

Rejoicing Spirits Ministry, www.rejoicingspirits.org.

Rejoicing Spirits Ministry, *How to Start a Rejoicing Spirits Ministry* (Exton, PA: Rejoicing Spirits Ministry, 2004).

Religion & Ethics Newsweekly, "Faith Communities and Disability," www.pbs.org/wnet/religionandethics/episodes/july-3-2009/faith-communities-and-disability/3440/.

Religious Action Center of Reform Judaism, www.rac.org.

Rest Ministries, restministries.com.

Richard, Mark, *House of Prayer No. 2: A Writer's Journey Home* (New York: Nan A. Talese, 2011).

Ruby Pictures, *Praying with Lior.* The DVD includes the bonus feature, *Creating Room in God's House,* www.prayingwith lior.com.

Share the Care, helpforcaregivers.org.

Sippola, John, *Welcome Them Home, Help Them Heal: Pastoral Care and Ministry with Service Members Return from War* (Duluth, MN: Whole Person Associates, 2009).

Smith, Courtney. "Bitter Water Sweet," *Journal of Religion, Disability & Health* (Vol. 15, Iss. 1, 2011).

Tada, Joni Eareckson. *Joni: An Unforgettable Story* (Grand Rapids: Zondervan, 2001).

Talking Photo Album, www.attainmentcompany.com/product. php?productid=16163.

Temple Beth Solomon of the Deaf, Northridge, California, www.tbsdeafjewish.org.

Thompson, David A., and Darlene Wetterstrom, *Beyond the Yellow Ribbon: Ministering to Returning Combat Veterans* (Nashville: Abingdon, 2009).

United States Conference of Catholic Bishops, *Built of Living Stones: Art, Architecture, and Worship* (Washington, DC: United States Conference of Catholic Bishops, 2000).

Wilke, Harold, *Creating the Caring Congregation* (Nashville: Abingdon, 1980).

Yochelson, Michael R., and Penny Wolfe, eds., *Managing Brain Injury: A Guide to Living Well with Brain Injury* (Washington, DC: National Rehabilitation Hospital, 2010).

A version of this list with clickable links is available at www.alban.org/amazinggifts/.